APPLIED ANTHROPOLOGY

This collectiᴏ ... ᴉecent innovative work in applied and practicing anthropology around the central theme of unexpectedness, the volume gives consideᴉ ᴏ some of the novel spaces, topics, and methods that anthropologists are ıɴvolved with today. There is an emphasis on non-traditional fields and areas where the relevance and importance of anthropology has received little attention. A range of 'real life' examples offer insight into the authors' research and work, as well as providing practical professional advice. The detailed ethnographic case studies cover a variety of contemporary settings, mainly in the United States, from law and finance to education and health care. The contributors give simultaneous consideration to practical applications, theoretical reflections, and professional experiences. Students will gain a valuable understanding of the diverse areas and industries where anthropologists operate, as well as how anthropology is being used to address some of the pressing issues facing society today.

Sheena Nahm is an Adjunct Professor (Anthropology and Sociology) at The New School for Public Engagement, USA. She is also Director of Senderos, a parent and community engagement program.

Cortney Hughes Rinker is Assistant Professor in the Department of Sociology and Anthropology at George Mason University, USA.

APPLIED ANTHROPOLOGY

Unexpected Spaces, Topics, and Methods

Edited by
Sheena Nahm and Cortney Hughes Rinker

Routledge
Taylor & Francis Group

LONDON AND NEW YORK

First published 2016
by Routledge
2 Park Square, Milton Park, Abingdon, Oxon OX14 4RN

and by Routledge
711 Third Avenue, New York, NY 10017

Routledge is an imprint of the Taylor & Francis Group, an informa business

© 2016 S. Nahm and C. Hughes Rinker, editorial and selection matter;
individual chapters, the contributors

British Library Cataloguing in Publication Data
A catalogue record for this book is available from the British Library

Library of Congress Cataloging in Publication Data
Applied anthropology : unexpected spaces, topics, and methods / edited by
Sheena Nahm and Cortney Hughes Rinker.
pages cm
Includes index.
1. Applied anthropology--Case studies. I. Nahm, Sheena, 1979- editor of
compilation. II. Hughes Rinker, Cortney, editor of compilation.
GN397.5.A665 2016
301--dc23
2015020516

ISBN: 978-1-138-91453-7 (hbk)
ISBN: 978-1-138-91452-0 (pbk)
ISBN: 978-1-315-69074-2 (ebk)

Typeset in Bembo
by Taylor & Francis Books

To our colleagues who inhabit both the academic and applied worlds

CONTENTS

ACKNOWLEDGMENTS

This volume first came into being in late 2011 as we started to reflect on our career trajectories. We finally had a moment to take a breath after graduation and the job search and to think about our lives and careers as anthropologists. We found ourselves in the same boat and struggling with some of the same issues – Who are we? What are we doing? What is the anthropology that we practice? Where do we belong? We embarked on co-authoring an article for *Practicing Anthropology* that allowed us to address many of these issues and to offer some of the lessons we learned to those anthropologists who are just starting out. Through the writing process and the feedback we received upon publication, we realized how our own quandaries and reflections resonated with our colleagues out in the field. It was from this vantage point that we began envisioning an edited volume that would present seemingly unexpected case studies in contemporary anthropology. We thank interlocutors that we met along the way, propelling forth deeper reflections on the unexpected and applied in anthropology.

We are forever grateful to the contributors to this volume. The book could not have been possible without their dedication and passion for the topic and their willingness to share their experiences with a broad audience. We put out a call for abstracts through several different venues and we were excited by the response. We were ecstatic to find that there are other anthropologists like us who consider themselves to engage with hybrid anthropology. We truly have enjoyed reading their work and getting to know them professionally and personally and are hopeful that this volume has helped develop collaborations that will last for many years to come. To the authors, please know that your work has inspired us and encouraged us to expand our horizons as anthropologists. It has been a pleasure putting together this volume.

Jesse Roof and Emily Harvey, two undergraduate research assistants at George Mason University, helped put the finishing touches to this manuscript. We are grateful for their hard work and long hours in helping prepare this volume for publication. We thank Susan Trencher for writing the conclusion to the volume. We are also grateful for the continuous support of our counterparts at Routledge, in particular Katherine Ong, Lola Harre, Andrew Watts, and Andy Baxter, who have made the editing and publication process a seamless experience.

Awards from the College of Humanities and Social Sciences and the Office of Research and Economic Development at George Mason University have supported Cortney's research on Islam and end-of-life care in the United States. She thanks Dr H and Dr S for their sincere interest and commitment to her ethnographic project. Cortney presented a draft of her chapter at the 113th Annual Meeting of the American Anthropological Association in Washington, D.C. in December 2014. She would like to thank her co-organizer Amanda Andrei and the panel's discussant Allison Fish for a careful read of her paper and for their constructive feedback. Additionally, she would like to thank her colleagues in the Department of Sociology and Anthropology at George Mason University, particularly those who took part in her pre-tenure review in 2014. They pushed her to think more about how her work in medical anthropology has real-world implications. She is incredibly grateful to be in a department where public sociology and public anthropology are a focus of faculty and students and is thankful for the encouragement she has received to figure out ways her work can speak to the wider community.

Cortney thanks her husband Justin and her daughter Sophie for their unending support of her anthropological endeavors, no matter where it takes them. She also thanks Sheena Nahm for not only being an amazing co-editor, but for being a great friend. She truly has enjoyed all the laughs and funny moments that have come out of emails, text messages, and coast-to-coast FaceTime calls while putting this volume together. She is so thankful that not only a professional collaboration developed out of their time in graduate school together at UC Irvine, but also a friendship that she values.

Sheena thanks her family and friends for their constant encouragement. In particular, she thanks SHSK for their support and constant encouragement in this endeavor. She is also grateful for the chance to work with her dear friend and colleague, Cortney Hughes Rinker. For a long time, she has been floored by the energy and commitment Cortney brings to her research and teaching and could only dream of collaborating with someone as thoughtful – in every sense of the word – as her. She cannot think of anyone better to have worked with on this project. Through long days of work and life, she saw Cortney set aside more hours than in a day to make this project happen and was inspired to rise to the occasion as well.

Chapter 10 is reprinted by permission of *Practicing Anthropology*, volume 35, issue 1. New material has been added to the original article for this volume.

CONTRIBUTORS

Jo Aiken, PhD Candidate, University College London

Chelsey Dyer, PhD Student, Vanderbilt University

Allison Fish, Assistant Professor, School of Informatics and Computing, Indiana University

Cortney Hughes Rinker, Assistant Professor, Department of Sociology and Anthropology, George Mason University

Lauren Miller Griffith, Assistant Professor of Anthropology, Hanover College

Deborah Murphy, Contractor to Cherokee Nation Technology Solutions (CNTS); Senior Program Manager, the National Intrepid Center of Excellence (NICoE) Network Research Program

Sheena Nahm, Adjunct Professor, The New School for Public Engagement

Michael Scroggins, PhD Candidate, Teachers College, Columbia University

Susan Trencher, Associate Professor, Department of Sociology and Anthropology, George Mason University

Jonathan Zilberg, Visiting Research Scholar, Universitas Islam Negeri Syarif Hidayatullah

INTRODUCTION

What Is Unexpected Anthropology?

Sheena Nahm and Cortney Hughes Rinker

Although it feels like a lifetime ago, it was not so long ago that we were graduate students huddling together at coffee shops near campus to discuss the week's reading assignments. Along with our peers, we discussed the role of anthropology and anthropologists in the public sphere. We wondered aloud what it meant to advance research within the academy while also engaging the public. We identified some concrete examples of scholars effectively engaging the public while living simultaneously inside and outside of the academy. But the examples seemed somewhat few and far between in the United States (US), with most being squarely situated in one and having brief excursions into the other. If anything, more examples of hybrid forms of scholarship seemed to have emerged from outside of the US. We recognized that this was due in part to the structural pressures and supports that made dual "citizenship" in applied/academic worlds a necessity.

Not long after we completed our graduate work, we both managed to find employment in roles that required one foot inside and one foot outside of academia. As colleagues graduating during an economic recession (Nahm in 2009; Hughes Rinker in 2010), any employment seemed like a notable feat, much less one that allowed us to think and do anthropology both inside and outside of the university setting. Still, we could not help but delve into a deeper round of our earlier conversations as students. What did it mean for us to live in both worlds? Would we eventually have to choose one or the other? And if so, which was the "better" choice? Why even conceive of professional development in such dichotomized terms? Ultimately, there was and is no one simple answer for any of these questions. But in asking these questions, we became keenly aware of the tensions in anthropological discourse around why anthropology has meaning and how it makes sense to an ever-changing discipline (and an ever-changing world around that discipline).

We realized that the job market as we knew it needed to be understood in a historical context that includes the trajectories of both education and employment.

If we turn back the dial just a few decades we see that in 1950, a total of twenty-two anthropology PhDs were awarded in the US. As the discipline developed and grew, more and more scholars emerged in the field. In 1974, 409 doctorates in the discipline were awarded. In the last two decades, the number of PhDs in anthropology has held at around 400 per year (Givens and Jablonski 2000). When we include masters' degrees, the overall enrollment in anthropology remained constant from the mid-1970s to the late 1980s. It has increased in more recent decades, with a 7% increase from 1993 to 1995, and of 27% since 1989.

In the early 1970s, the vast majority (74%) of anthropologists in the US who completed their doctoral degrees took academic jobs. The remainder took jobs in research centers and departments other than anthropology within academia (13%) or in non-academic jobs (13%). By 1990, the percentage of graduates taking academic jobs in anthropology dropped from 74% to 38% (with 21% of the remaining graduates in research or non-anthropology academic appointments and 41% in nonacademic jobs). This point begs repeating. In the course of two decades, the post-graduate career trajectory of anthropologists has taken on a dramatically different look and feel. The number fluctuated again by the mid-1990s when 42% took academic jobs in anthropology, 29% took jobs in research or other non-anthropology departments, and 28% took nonacademic jobs (Givens and Jablonski 2000).

Looking at even more recent trends, we see that this shift continues to shape our discipline. The drop in academic positions for anthropologists may seem troubling, but in broader terms there are also new opportunities developing elsewhere in applied social science fields. According to the US Department of Labor, there were 7,200 jobs for anthropologists and archeologists in 2012. By 2022, it is projected that the field for anthropologists will increase by 19%, which is faster than the average projection for all occupations. However, a major caveat is that "because it is a small occupation, the fast growth will result in only about 1,400 new jobs over the ten-year period. Jobseekers will likely face very strong competition" (US Department of Labor 2012). These numbers are promising in one sense because they show how the job market is growing for anthropologists, with their employment rate after graduation rising from just under 20% in 2006 to about 50% in 2012. And yet, because of the way we think about anthropology and the places we expect to find it, any amount of job growth will always be measured through a narrow net of search terms and key words. It is with this in mind that we propose an examination and exploration of applied anthropology in unexpected spaces, topics, and methods.

In comparison to the 1970s, the number of graduates and the percentage of graduates that pursue nonacademic jobs has greatly increased. It is within this context that Louise Lamphere's words remind us that there is much work to be done in creating collaborative bridges between academic and nonacademic settings. Lamphere, former President of the American Anthropological Association stated:

> At a time when some of our colleagues are still decrying the disunity of our
> discipline, there are signs of increased unity and the potential for increased

communication across subfields as we look for better strategies for collaboration, outreach, and advocacy. There is still much work to be done, particularly
in institutionalizing techniques for collaboration, outreach and policy research
as part of our ... training. Nevertheless, the current sea change within the
discipline suggests that anthropology is and will continue to become a more
respected, better known, and unified discipline.

(cited in Briller and Goldmacher 2009, 16)

A decade later, Lamphere's words still ring true. There are still concerns about the
disunity of the discipline of anthropology in the US, and perhaps even more reflection
around what seems to be an ever-deepening divide between theory and practice, but
there are also new spaces opening up. The re-articulation of academic projects with
consideration of new audiences – audiences open to anthropological perspectives
but not deeply entrenched or formally trained in disciplinary culture(s) – allows us
to think about why anthropology matters and is key to addressing pressing societal
issues. By audiences open to anthropological perspectives but not deeply entrenched,
we mean to include professionals who have interests in including anthropological
perspectives or who have questions and insights that integrate well with anthropology but lack formal training. Such audiences are important interlocutors because
they are both receptive to anthropological inquiry, but not so familiar with it that
we are able to default to theoretical jargon or presumptions of understanding and
utilizing the same categorical definitions.

Certainly, within the academic or the nonacademic context, one could argue
that there are those "decrying" and perhaps even contributing to the disunity of the
discipline. And yet, in our own work and in our conversations with colleagues across
contexts, we find that there are a great many signs of increased unity and possibility for
collaboration. We, the editors, ourselves live in applied and theoretical worlds and
find that "unexpectedly" theoretical conversations happen in the applied world – just
as "unexpectedly" practical conversations happen in our ivory-tower-like academic
worlds. In no way do we intend for the word "unexpectedly" to mean that
anthropology is done haphazardly, but rather, we want to show that anthropology
has found itself in new niches and spaces which one may not always expect. From
these meta-reflections that challenge the theory–applied divide, and from the seeds
of conversations with colleagues – many of whom have contributed chapters in this
volume – we found the need to create a new type of forum for thinking and doing
anthropology. This is a space where theory and application merge together, and do
so in unexpected spaces, on unexpected topics, and with unexpected methods.

Applied Anthropological Research in the United States

By its very definition, "unexpected" calls for us to be surprised. It challenges our
notions of where we expect to find anthropology, what we expect to find, and
how we expect to see it in action. These assumptions create a kind of unspoken
backdrop from which our research questions emerge. In order to properly delve

into that which is unexpected, we must first examine why we expect things in the places they are or in shapes familiar to us. In other words, what, where, and how we expect something to be is deeply situated in how we first, and perhaps most often, encounter it.

We expect to see anthropology in certain places because we have configured our expectations into categories, and then mark data points that fit into the buckets that exist. We expect to find anthropology alive and well in the academy and we expect to find anthropology in practice in certain social science (or humanities) friendly sectors. Where we find applied anthropology, then, is where we look for it. Where we look for practices is part of a broader discourse in which we have decoupled our expectations. That which we seek to problematize – the applied–theory divide – itself only exists in a deeply situated world of Stateside anthropology where theory and practice have been decoupled.

In reality, this divide or decoupling is not a major issue in many other parts of the world where the theory–practice or applied–academic distinction is irrelevant because the two have merged. For example, in Canada and the United Kingdom (UK), a good proportion of anthropologists either work outside of academia or combine applied and academic careers. In the UK for instance, 30–35% of anthropologists with PhDs are employed outside of academia (Spencer, Jepson, and Mills n.d., 4), meaning that students are exposed to texts written from the perspective of applied and practicing anthropologists early on in their professional development.

A wide variety of socio-economic issues created contingent factors that influenced this very different history of intellectual thought (and its pragmatic politicization of disciplinary divides). But in the limited space of this volume, let us begin to examine the contingent factors that led us to see the divide that we find ourselves writing, speaking, and practicing against.

The history of anthropology in the US often focuses on the purely academic, leaving out its application in the real world. We note that we focus primarily on examples from scholars anchored in the US, but the approaches, methods, and theoretical orientations of the authors will be of interest to those working globally. Certain anthropologists claim "application has been more at the forefront both in the earliest visions and through subsequent activities" (Ervin 2005, 14). In the US, some of the first organizations to employ anthropologists focused on policy research (Van Willigen 2002, 23) and one of the first Codes of Ethics in the discipline was developed by the Society for Applied Anthropology (SfAA) in 1949, nearly twenty years before the American Anthropological Association (AAA) adopted its first ethics code in 1967 (Reed 1998). In addition, one of the most well-known anthropologists and student of Franz Boas, Margaret Mead, was recruited by the Department of Defense during World War II to study food habits of Americans prior to the introduction of rationing (her research team included Ruth Benedict). Domestic meat was being shipped overseas to feed American soldiers and allies and there was a general shortage of protein-rich foods, meaning that dietary change needed to be accomplished, and she aided in studying how this could be done (Wansink 2002).

These examples show "a fundamentally important fact that is often not acknowledged in the literature on the history of anthropology is that applied anthropology serves as the foundation for the development of much disciplinary infrastructure" (Van Willigen 2002, 23). Mead's research often appears in the study of cultural anthropology's theoretical canon in the US, but those very studies have always been engaged in both theory and practice.

Because it can be argued that application – or method – came before theory, the very beginnings of the discipline were inherently shaped by its ability to address real-world issues. Anthropological scholarship in the US was always-already applied. Boas, considered the father of American anthropology, paved the way for many applied anthropologists as he showed how anthropology could be used to effectively change and implement policy, even though he did not consider himself an applied anthropologist per se. He was staunchly anti-racist and submitted two studies to the US Commissioner of Education showing that the physical development of children and adults is heavily influenced by social context rather than genetics. His research demonstrated that within just a few generations, the characteristics of immigrants were similar to those of North Americans of British descent. These results were counter to policies in the 19th century which limited immigration to the US to British and Northwest Europeans based on the fear that including other groups would lead to a lower-quality population (Ervin 2005).

By the early 1900s, "changes to Native American and disruptions on North American Indian reservations increasingly attracted the attention of American anthropologists. One breakthrough was Margaret Mead's (1932) study of the deteriorating condition among the 'Antlers,' a pseudonym for a Plains tribe" (Ervin 2005, 16). Anthropologists were involved in applied work with the Bureau of Indian Affairs (BIA) during the Indian Reorganization Act of the New Deal. The BIA Commissioner, John Collier, reached out to the Bureau of American Ethnology to study the organization of tribes and to offer information on how best to address land acquisition given that the "1934 Act provided the means to recover land by drawing from the public domain and consolidating holdings under the control of elected tribal council" (Ervin 2005, 16). It is argued that anthropologists who took part in the New Deal were not servants of imperialism, but rather, "wished to mitigate its more heavy-handed approaches" (Ervin 2005, 17). Collier believed that "the specialized skills of anthropologists should be utilized in public sector programs" (Reed 1998) in order to adequately address issues at both the local and policy levels.

John Van Willigen (2002) notes, "With the coming of the Great Depression and the New Deal, the number of anthropologists employed in application grew dramatically in the United States. This related to an apparent increased need for information on the part of the government, as well as a need to provide jobs for anthropologists" (25). Anthropologists' involvement in government affairs continued into World War II. Besides heading the Committee on Food Habits and advising on rationing, Mead also studied the impact of having thousands of US soldiers in Britain and how their presence affected American–British relations (Ervin 2005). Another student of Boas, Ruth Benedict, also became involved with the war effort and wrote about Japanese and European cultures for the State Department and the Office of War Information. Her well-known book *The Chrysanthemum and the Sword* (Benedict 1946) was based on her studies of Japanese culture and began as a working paper for the military. Benedict was unable to conduct fieldwork for her research in Japan due to the war, but researched Japanese militarism and patriotism using materials available in the US. She writes on the first page, "Conventions of war which Western nations had come to accept as facts of human nature did not exist for the Japanese. It made a major problem in the nature of the enemy. We had to understand their behavior in order to cope with it" (Benedict 1946, 1). In 1941, just as World War II began for the US and Mead and Benedict were conducting studies as part of the war effort, the Society for Applied Anthropology, an organization that continues to thrive in the 21st century, was established. Shortly thereafter, the inaugural issue of the journal *Human Organization* (previously called *Applied Anthropology*) was published.

After World War II, anthropologists returned to universities and due to the expansion of higher education in the 1950s and 1960s, they found many opportunities for employment in addition to research grants for scholarly work (Ervin 2005, 21). Academic anthropology flourished through the 1970s. However, "There was also growing disillusionment about associating with policy makers and the possible corrupted use of scientific information" (Ervin 2005, 25). International and domestic development, particularly after World War II, became a major focus of academic anthropologists and also offered job opportunities for those working outside of the academy; at the same time, it became evident that anthropologists could no longer study societies and untouched cultural practices. What Michael Angrosino (1976) refers to as the "new" applied anthropology has:

> its foundation … laid in the 1960s, which saw a rising public consciousness of social issues. This was an era of anti-imperialistic struggles, manifested in the emergence of nationalism, the establishment of new African states, the Cold War, and the outbreak of nationalist wars such as Vietnam. Domestically, it was expressed through movements focusing on civil rights, feminism, gay rights, environmentalism, and Native self-determination, as well as a growing awareness of the negative consequences of development, consumerism, enforced dependencies, and ravages of the environment.
>
> *(Ervin 2005, 23–24)*

Several academic anthropologists took on part-time applied activities in the post-war period or consulted for the government or organizations focused on international development. Their expertise was sought because of the "cultural and linguistic knowledge that anthropologists had about specific groups affected by policy proposals" (Ervin 2005, 24). Although anthropologists' participation in applied activities has continued since the 1990s, there also

> has been increasing awareness within anthropology in general about the need for a more engaged role in both academic and the public arena, as well as calls

for greater relevance with regard to addressing social problems and the structures that produce and maintain them.

(Rylko-Bauer, Singer, and Van Willigen 2006, 178)

There has been a push in the discipline for anthropologists to better connect their work with a wider audience both inside and outside of the academy. We suggest that part of this is due to the focus on securing an academic position and producing academic publications. Many of these normative practices begin early on in the mentorship of graduate students.

In reality, this divide between anthropologists is not a major problem in other parts of the world where the theory–practice or applied–academic distinction is not as relevant because the two have merged, or developed in tandem. As mentioned earlier, in Canada and the UK, many anthropologists either work outside of academia or combine applied and academic careers. And though the preceding history of the development of anthropology focuses on milestones within the US, broader insights might help anthropologists across the world reflect on how their own discourse and practice have developed within the context of socio-historical movements. While it may seem largely insular to look at our own discourse or struggles with employment, especially when answering the question of how to integrate public engagement into scholarship, we argue that many of the tensions within anthropological circles shape how research questions are constructed, funded, and published. They shape the prioritization of efforts, and without understanding this backdrop, it is difficult to imagine reframing our own theory and practice to reach beyond the expected.

For some students graduating from anthropology PhD programs in the US, finding work outside of the academy is sometimes done begrudgingly as a kind of second place to their desired academic goals. But for us, graduating in the midst of a recession and beginning our careers in hybrid positions created a new understanding of how theory-driven projects are indeed meaningful in praxis and how practice-driven projects produce theory. The re-articulation of academic projects with consideration of new audiences – audiences open to anthropological perspectives but not deeply entrenched in disciplinary culture(s) – often allows us to think about why anthropology matters and is key to addressing pressing societal issues. Anthropology is not just about abstract theory, but rather about developing and testing theories that can help advance humankind. In moments of deepest reflection, the conversion process has become reframed as a question of why theory ought to be practical and why practice should be theoretical. Anthropologists, particularly those employed outside of academia, grapple with whether or not applied anthropology is a separate field or if all anthropological work should be applied in some way, given present funding constraints for the humanities and social sciences in general.

Within the academic or nonacademic contexts, one could argue that there are those who divide the discipline between applied and theoretical work, with applied anthropology taking place outside of the academy. Van Willigen (2002) writes of the father of academic anthropology in the US, "Franz Boas, although not usually thought of as an applied anthropologist, completed some important policy research. Most noteworthy is his research sponsored by the United States Immigration Commission" (24). However, *The Nation* published a letter by Boas in 1919 entitled "Scientists as Spies" charging that four anthropologists

> had abused their professional research conducting espionage in Central America during the First World War. Boas strongly condemned their actions writing that they had "prostituted science by using it to cover their activities as spies." Anthropologists spying for their country severely betrayed their science and damaged the credibility of all anthropological research.
>
> *(Price 2000)*

While the AAA Code of Ethics does not condone using deception or not gaining informed consent of research participants – a large reason why the AAA does not endorse the Human Terrain System – working for the government in general is not and should not be wholly dismissed.

But, as demonstrated by several contributors in this volume, many applied anthropologists have hybrid positions and live in both worlds. For instance, as a postdoctoral fellow, Hughes Rinker had one foot firmly situated in the university, publishing in academic journals and participating in academic conferences; at the same time, she was doing applied work with a large health care organization to improve their processes and patient outcomes and also publishing in journals intended for the medical community. Many anthropologists do not locate themselves in one place or another. Satish Kedia (2008) notes that a 1999 survey by the AAA of US anthropology departments showed that

> only half of all faculty were in full-time, tenure-track positions, and a US Department of Education study reported that only slightly more than one third were tenured, further evidence that anthropologists are increasingly pursuing practicing opportunities outside academia rather than teaching positions.
>
> *(18–19)*

We find that skills we have gained from being in academia are beneficial to our work in applied research. While continuing to teach and conduct research, Nahm also used lessons from her academic work as an anthropologist in her applied work. For example,

> In her various roles at nonprofit organizations, Nahm has facilitated meetings and given presentations alongside professionals who represent the tops of their fields ... When colleagues ask whether she took special training classes for communication and public speaking, she often reminds them that expensive

workshops or private lessons could never compare with teaching college students who demand engagement at all times and will make it evident when articulation falls short of clear command of the content.

(Hughes Rinker and Nahm 2013, 42).

Similar to Kedia's observation, in our own work and conversations with colleagues across contexts, we find that there are many signs of increased unity and possibility for collaboration.

Emerging Trends

Ideally, we would have the space to add anthropological discourses around the world. But we recognize that there are other volumes that cover cases in applied anthropology for the UK or for other regions in depth and fine grain detail. What we desire to do in the remaining introductory pages of this volume is to focus on some of the emerging trends within anthropology in the US. With its unique four-field history in the Boasian tradition, anthropology in the US has always had some desire to be engaged with the broader public. In comparison with anthropology in other countries where structure and context have always-already made anthropology part of the applied world, anthropology in the US manages to dwell in a yet to be resolved angst around whether "applied" should be a separate field within the discipline. But this angst is a constructed one because the integration between applied and academic are actually core to the history of the "always-already applied" nature of anthropological scholarship in the US. It is in this vexed and yet also productive context that we find a unique space to re-examine how the academy can be built "for" the applied and vice versa. We keep in mind Lamphere's call to support the building of more collaborative bridges and to narrow the gap between what many consider to be the academic–applied divide.

We are not alone in this discussion. If we look at professional conversations within American anthropology since the early 2000s, using the annual AAA meetings of anthropologists (academic and applied, across the four fields) as a barometer, we can see several key themes emerge. In 2009, the conference theme was "The End/s of Anthropology" and posed questions around "examining the relevance and goals of our field today" (Jackson and Thomas 2009, 2). The following year, the theme was "Circulation" and explored "what triggers, facilitates, constrains, disrupts or stops flows" (Heller 2009, 16). The theme of circulation also called for participants to think across boundaries – including those that separate fields or disciplines. In 2011, the annual meeting theme of "Traces, Tidemarks and Legacies" called for papers and presentations hinging on the shifting character of things that still carry with them remnants of the past. As the character of things and how they are understood shifts, definitions of differences and distinctions emerge. This productive tension around the exploration of differences and distinctions then evolved further in the following year's theme of "Borders and Crossings." In 2013, the conference made more explicit this tension between the things that make anthropology relevant to the world with its theme of "Future Publics, Current Engagements." In promoting meeting registration, the theme was described as follows:

> Anthropologists have long been engaged with diverse publics and with other social sciences. The influence of anthropological methods, concepts and research is growing, as witnessed by the fact that over half of us are now employed outside the academy. Our journals are experimenting with new formats to link research to contemporary concerns … By locating the human at the center of its inquiry, anthropology through all of its fields provide crucial methodological and political insights for other disciplines.
>
> *(AAA 2013)*

Finally, in their call for proposals in 2014, meeting organizers described "Producing Anthropology" as a convening that "offers a provocation to examine the trust we encounter, produce and communicate through anthropological theories and methods. As a discipline built on blending archives of narratives, actions, sediment and bone, anthropology has well-established methods for grappling with complex, multidimensional artifacts" (AAA 2014).

Since 2009, we see a consistent and constant preoccupation with what anthropology is, who it speaks of and to, and how it produces and is produced. Within these more philosophical reflections lies the simple question of how something so essential and all-encompassing as "the study of humans" can indeed be applicable to the world around us. This question of applicability, though incredibly simplistic, is important for many reasons. How applicable our research is impacts support in spirit as well as in terms of concrete support via public and private funding. Support is a relevant factor for anthropology both inside and outside of the academy. Anthropology itself as a discipline – whether embodied as professors who teach courses to students or as practitioners in nonacademic spheres – was being challenged to articulate and demonstrate its relevance in society. The challenge to the discipline as a whole rather than to any group within a so-called "theory versus applied" spectrum itself creates a unifying space for anthropologists to gather and reflect.

These concerns may seem overly reflective and perhaps even insular. Why even focus on conference themes and proceedings of gatherings that are geared toward attracting those within the discipline versus those accessible to a broader public? We are, after all, speaking about anthropology at the intersection of public engagement. But anxieties within the discipline are a breeding ground for how we think, do, and speak anthropology. How do we conceptualize our work and how do we formulate our research questions? How do we practice anthropology and what are the ways in which our methods adapt to "work" better in answering these questions? Finally, how do we describe our work to colleagues as well as to a broader public that exists outside of the academy?

When debates and concerns about the applicability of the discipline in today's world emerge, anthropologists can quickly point to examples of practitioners impacting the world. But these examples are often expected. Public health, education, law, and public policy are domains within which applied anthropology has long been situated. These fields need to be promoted more, so that people less familiar with the discipline can recognize it as such in action, particularly when the title of someone using anthropology in a public health project is not necessarily "anthropologist." We argue that something more profound needs to happen in how we as practitioners think about ourselves and consequentially, how others think about our work and its applicability. We need to think about what and where we expect anthropology to be. We desire to create a space to ponder on all of the unexpected places and spaces where anthropology is already in action. In thinking about the unexpected, we may be able to broaden what others might one day expect.

Anthropologists on the Job Market

Before we reflect on the unexpected spaces that anthropology occupies today, we need to wind back the clock to just a few years before these tenuous discussions around applicability emerged. While we were filing our MAs en route to our PhDs in anthropology in 2006, just over 20% of surveyed PhDs in anthropology were reporting that they had a tenure-track job in academia upon graduating (Nerad, Rudd, Morrison, and Picciano 2007). Those low numbers were not a deterrent to us as we continued on to pursue our doctoral degrees, believing in part that the market would grow bit by bit. Another helpful indicator was that Nerad et al.'s study showed that the majority of respondents to their survey were employed in academia: 52.3% self-reported as ladder faculty, 13.5% as non-tenure-track faculty, 11.9% in other kinds of academic employment, and 22.4% in business, government, or the nonprofit sector. While the numbers for tenure-track employment were discouraging, employment didn't seem so grim if we included the job market outside of the academy.

Another survey conducted around the same time by the AAA showed that while academia was still the most cited place to find an anthropologist, there were many alternatives. Other common places included museums, nonprofit organizations, government (federal, state, local, and tribal), museums, and research organizations. Federal government was arguably the largest employer of anthropologists outside of academia (Fisk 2008). Specific examples included the US Census Bureau, National Park Service, National Marine Fisheries, Centers for Disease Control and Prevention, USAID, and Cabinet-level agencies such as the Department of Defense, Department of Agriculture, Department of Homeland Security, and Department of the Interior. Other examples included the Department of Justice, Department of Veterans Affairs, and Department of Health and Human Services. A small number reported working in the private sector for corporations or smaller firms or as independent contractors/consultants. The remaining few reported working in K-12 education or for international nongovernmental organizations.

There were certainly a variety of places that anthropologists could work. The existence of job market alternatives to academic positions was reassuring. We were not, however, fully prepared to deal with writing cover letters and applying to positions in the wake of an economic recession. In fact, around the time we were writing our dissertations in 2008, it was reported that of the anthropology graduates completing their undergraduate studies, just over half were employed within six months; furthermore, employment ranged from sales (8%), business and finance (6%) and public or private sector management (12%) to catering (15%) or clerical jobs (20%). It is probably not surprising that a good portion of these graduates (21%) chose to go on to graduate school either in anthropology or in other related fields such as law, journalism, teaching, or business (Scott 2010).

At the graduate level, peers who were trained with an eye toward critical theory found themselves expanding their job search from specifically academic tenure-track faculty positions to "applied" work. Simple things like converting a curriculum vitae to a meaningful resume for employers became a necessary process. "When new anthropology PhDs read a job ad that states, 'Please send a one page resume and cover letter,' their blood pressure rises and their heart beats a little faster" (Hughes Rinker and Nahm 2013, 41). This is what happened to us as we began the job hunt during our last year of graduate school. We thought, "Is it even possible to cut down a multi-page curriculum vitae … to a one page document that is comprehensible? Our fear came from the fact that we felt the interviewers would not get a sense of our accomplishments and what we could bring as anthropologists to their organization" (Hughes Rinker and Nahm 2013, 41). We knew we could not depend on the degree alone as most employers wanted to see that we could do, be, and think beyond the academic setting. We began to articulate what we had learned and experienced through fieldwork in terms that the nonacademic world was more familiar with, including policy analysis, community outreach, public speaking, data collection and analysis, and grant writing.

If we look at the very title of this volume, we note that there is a focus on the term "applied anthropology" which is different from "public anthropology" in that our work may not be explicitly advocacy related but is still being used for some purpose by an organization or group outside of the academy. It is, however, not simply a mere matter of putting anthropology to use or applying it without reflection; our definition of applied anthropology includes deep engagement with theory as much as practice.

An Unexpected Collection

While many volumes provide important perspectives for applied anthropologists, this book differs in two critical ways. The first is that there is a strong emphasis on fields and topics where anthropology has been less centrally identified as a key discipline. The second is that our volume addresses innovations in content and in practice, dissecting the spaces, topics, and manner in which anthropology is encountered in contemporary contexts. In doing so, it challenges the applied–theoretical divide as contributors examine both practical applications and theoretical reflections simultaneously. In addition, this volume's chapters are organized around two key themes. The first being the hybrid nature of anthropology, which refers to the fact that anthropology is often interdisciplinary with anthropologists drawing on concepts and methods from multiple disciplines to address a research question or problem. The second theme is the inherently applied nature of some academic research, and this is particularly true for many anthropologists who straddle the academic and applied worlds. Given they have one foot in each of these, their academic work is often useful for both broader scholarly inquiries and to policy makers, governments, and organizations outside of academia who are interested in similar pressing societal issues – this may or may not be intended by the anthropologist.

The contributions in this volume are clustered into three ways of thinking about "unexpected" anthropology: spaces, topics, and methods. The first cluster of ethnographic case studies explores spaces where anthropologists and non-anthropologists alike may not expect to find their work. Jo Aiken's work with NASA asks how space exploration pushes the limits of humanity's innovation. Aiken writes,

> Organizational culture, collaboration, and technology design are other subjects which anthropologists and like-minded ethnographers have engaged with in regards to space exploration ... Anthropologists are uniquely suited to take part in these complex, interrelated areas of research because of their holistic training in culture and *in situ* approaches to studying human behavior.

The space of Aiken's work challenges expectations of where anthropology lives for many reasons. The communities of practice at the center of this research are based in future-oriented questions, relevant to a human survival and livelihood beyond the Earth. Aiken's chapter reviews the history of anthropologists engaged in space exploration research and highlights the contributions of ethnographic research in furthering humankind's efforts to travel among the stars. A case study, from research conducted for the NASA Johnson Space Center, is presented in which populations from various space analogs were explored in order to identify privacy considerations for a Mars habitat design.

Aiken's community of practice is both future-oriented and grounded in present-day collaborations among scientists. And though governmental agencies are not a new space for anthropology to be found, Aiken's work provides new insight into how anthropologists might gain access and relevance in less-expected areas. Similarly, Deborah Murphy's work with military service members in medical centers administered by the Department of Defense is grounded in the governmental sector. Although medical anthropology is one of the most well-known subfields in which scholars are identified as relevant to real-world applications, Murphy's study is unique specifically because of the spaces in which she has been able to collect data – spaces that are traditionally difficult if not nearly impossible for outsiders to gain access to and trust. Beyond functioning as hospitals and rehabilitation centers, Military Treatment Facilities are charged with maintaining the health of personnel from all branches of the services so that they can carry out their military missions. Murphy conducted ethnographic research at Walter Reed National

Military Medical Center in Bethesda, Maryland to probe whether perceptions of disability and perceptions of deservedness are linked in the lived experience of patients, family members, and caregivers there. She examines the language of stories and materials that fill up the space of this medical site. From this textual analysis, Murphy explores how people interpret illness and injury whether they be service members or others. Just as specific wings within a traditionally expected sector (government) can provide spaces to glean new and unexpected insights, specific spaces within the traditionally expected world of nonprofits can also produce unexpected spaces. Chelsey Dyer's work situates her analysis in the personal struggle to navigate the boundaries of an anthropological education and various nonprofit employers in Australia. She recalls her journey through nonprofits from academia and back again and focuses on how her identity as an anthropologist emerges in each context, defining what she does rather than being defined by title or organization. Her chapter is a personal and professional exploration of a recent graduate discovering what anthropology can be in today's world.

The second cluster of ways in which anthropology can be unexpected is an exploration of topics that interlocutors might respond to with supportive but quizzical "I didn't know that was even anthropology"-like statements. Michael Scroggins provides a brief history of the FAIR Money collective and explores its research on predatory lending. FAIR Money is a research collective composed of designers, design researchers, and anthropologists devoted to producing research and tools to understand and alleviate predatory lending. Scroggins argues that the participation of amateur anthropologists is something that ought to be encouraged and valued.

The topic of finance is an arena in which cultural anthropologists like Bill Maurer and Hiro Miyazaki have made notable contributions and continues to be an unexpected space of anthropology, making deeper ripples into broader social discussions. Scroggins reflects on the productive space of a collaborative like FAIR Money and also provides insight into parallel reflections anthropologists might have on how the university and industry can overcome decoupled assumptions about theory–applied work in the contemporary world.

Jonathan Zilberg also takes a look into anthropology in action outside of the academy through an examination of unexpected non-traditional research projects. In particular, Zilberg argues that living abroad and working in Indonesia long term aided in his ability to contribute to the discipline "from the margins." His work in documenting crisis in religious and cultural freedom in Indonesia (2005–2014) includes: the conflict over the Aceh Tsunami Museum (2006–2009); the problems at the Museum Istiqlal (National Islamic Museum) (2009–2011); and the Jambi Melayu Cultural Revitalization Project (2011–2013) which culminated in the First International Conference on Jambi Studies. His chapter links the genesis of each of the projects, his affiliations at the time, and the goals and outcomes. In exploring the topics addressed in each of his unexpected projects, Zilberg also brings us into a deeper reflection on how anthropologists can learn from the concept of serendipity. Location on the margins can be thought of as a productive space from which an anthropologist can contribute to hybrid worlds and as a hybrid interlocutor.

This question of location and perspective is further expounded by Lauren Miller Griffith's chapter on faculty development as itself a topic of applied educational anthropology. Rather than seeing ethnographic methods and projects that simply contribute to one's development as faculty, Miller Griffith demonstrates how her training in ethnographic methods and anthropological theory helped solve problems that faculty were facing in their courses. While her methods were traditional – the heart and soul of ethnographic projects conducted "in the field" – her impact was felt in the classroom and in the office. The academic anthropologist usually occupies three roles: college instructor (and undergraduate/graduate mentor/advisor), researcher (including anthropologist in the field and writer), and university employee who needs to keep up with administrative duties. Miller Griffith applied practices honed while "in the field" to her new roles as mentor, instructor, and administrative personnel. She conducted interviews among students when faculty members stated that they needed assistance in better understanding classroom sub-cultures. By developing strategies to bridge the divide between faculty and administrative cultures, Miller Griffith brought her own anthropological perspective and practice into the university setting. Rather than separating out the academic role of the anthropologist as doing research off campus and teaching on campus, she found opportunities to make anthropology applicable in studying faculty–student interactions. Her chapter challenges us to think of the anthropologist's traditional and expected role of being a "cultural translator" as one that can also be found in the unexpected topic of faculty development.

Rounding out our discussion of unexpected topics is the research of Cortney Hughes Rinker who explores important issues in end-of-life care. Although medical anthropology and the anthropology of Islam are not new to anthropological queries, Hughes Rinker's study positions her research at the intersection of discussions around end-of-life care and cultural competency in Muslim communities in the metropolitan Washington, D.C. area. Her chapter examines the relationship between Islam and end-of-life care and how Islamic beliefs intersect with the US model for the end-of-life, which champions technology and views death as failure. Hughes Rinker suggests anthropological research on the experiential nature of end-of-life care and on how individuals view medicine as interfacing with their religious beliefs has a critical place in discussions of cultural competency in the US.

We then examine the unexpected methods that can be used by anthropologists. Sheena Nahm explores the role of time in ethnographic methods, as seen in both academically situated research as well as in her work in the nonprofit sector. She asks how the notion of time as both compressed and elongated can help us to better understand applied anthropology in its hybrid forms. In her chapter on the Access to Knowledge (A2K) movement, Allison Fish also looks at unexpected ways in which anthropology can be applied while contributing to theoretical discussions. Through the examination of specific cases in intellectual property law, Fish explores the multiple stakeholders that work to redefine the cultural commons. She explores this space that is ever-changing in its technologies and legal practices, teasing apart how culture and access to it are defined and redefined.

We also turn to some practical reflections for students on the cusp of entering the job market (or for those advising those about to enter the job market). Hughes Rinker and Nahm reflect on lessons learned from their own transitions to hybrid positions after graduate school. In their reflections on converting academic work and preparation into intelligible terms for the "applied" market, the authors discuss practical strategies and tips as well as reflecting on the new nature of academic–applied hybrids.

Finally, Susan Trencher, Associate Professor of Anthropology at George Mason University and a scholar of "the anthropology of anthropology" brings together some of the vital learnings around examining the unexpected spaces, topics, and methods that have emerged in applied anthropology in the Conclusion of the book.

In assembling this diverse collection of case studies and queries, it is our hope that by creating this space for thinking anew about what we expect anthropology to be, where we expect to find it, and how we expect it to be used, we might reframe the lively debate around its applicability and relevance in the world. The world not as academic or nonacademic but as the world – full stop.

References

AAA (American Anthropological Association). 2013. "Annual Meeting Theme: 112th Annual Meeting Call for Papers." Accessed March 20, 2014, www.aaanet.org/meetings/Annual-Meeting-Theme.cfm.

AAA (American Anthropological Association). 2014. "Event Information: 113th Annual Meeting." Accessed July 14, 2015, https://avectra.aaanet.org/eWeb/DynamicPage.aspx?webcode=EventInfo&RegPath=EventRegFees&REg_evt_key=9cff7640-9949-4438-b055-32ef417f576c.

Angrosino, Michael. 1976. "The Evolution of the New Applied Anthropology." In *Do Applied Anthropologists Apply Anthropology?*, edited by Michael V. Angrosino, 1–9. Athens: University of Georgia Press.

Benedict, Ruth. 1946. *The Chrysanthemum and the Sword: Patterns of Japanese Culture*. Boston: Houghton Mifflin.

Briller, Sherylyn H., and Amy Goldmacher. 2009. *Designing an Anthropology Career: Professional Development Exercises*. Lanham, MD: AltaMira Press.

Ervin, Alexander. 2005. *Applied Anthropology: Tools and Perspectives for Contemporary Practice*. New York: Pearson.

Fisk, Shirley. 2008. "Working for the Federal Government: Anthropology Careers." *NAPA Bulletin* 29(1):110–130.

Givens, David B., and Timothy Jablonski. 2000. "1996 Survey." Accessed March 24, 2015. www.aaanet.org/resources/departments/96Survey.cfm.

Heller, Monica. 2009. "Call for Papers, 109th Annual Meeting, American Anthropological Association: Circulation." *Anthropology News* 50(9):16–18.

Hughes Rinker, Cortney, and Sheena Nahm. 2013. "Stress, Survival, and Success in Academia 2.0: Lessons from Working Inside and Outside of the Academy." *Practicing Anthropology* 35(1):40–43.

Jackson, Jr., John L., and Deborah Thomas. 2009. "The End/s of Anthropology." 2009 Preliminary Program. Accessed March 24, 2015. www.aaanet.org/meetings/upload/2009_prelim_program.pdf.

Kedia, Satish. 2008. "Recent Changes and Trends in the Practice of Applied Anthropology." *NAPA Bulletin* 29(1):14–28.

Nerad, Maresi, Elizabeth Rudd, Emory Morrison, and Joseph Picciano. 2007. "Social Science PhDs – Five+ Years Out. A National Survey of PhDs in Six Fields." Highlights Report. Accessed March 24, 2015. http://depts.washington.edu/cirgeweb/wordpress/wp-content/uploads/2008/02/ss5-methods-paper.pdf.

Price, David. 2000. "Anthropologists as Spies." *The Nation*. Accessed March 24, 2015. www.thenation.com/article/anthropologists-spies#.

Reed, Ann M. 1998. "Subdisciplines: Applied Anthropology." Accessed October 13, 2013. www.indiana.edu/~wanthro/theory_pages/Applied.htm.

Rylko-Bauer, Barbara, Merrill Singer, and John Van Willigen. 2006. "Reclaiming Applied Anthropology: Its Past, Present, and Future." *American Anthropologist* 108(1): 178–190.

Scott, Craig. 2010. "What to do with a degree in anthropology." *The Guardian*. Accessed March 24, 2015. www.theguardian.com/money/2010/aug/21/anthropology-degree-career-options.

Spencer, J., A. Jepson, and D. Mills. n.d. "Where Do All the Anthropologists Go? Research Training and 'Careers' in Social Anthropology." Accessed October 8, 2012, www.theasa.org/downloads/networks/apply/news.doc.

US Department of Labor. 2012. "Anthropologists and Archaeologists." *Occupational Outlook Handbook*. Accessed March 24, 2015. www.bls.gov/ooh/life-physical-and-social-science/anthropologists-and-archeologists.htm.

Van Willigen, John. 2002. *Applied Anthropology: An Introduction*. Third Edition. Westport, Connecticut: Bergin & Garvey.

Wansink, Brian. 2002. "Changing Eating Habits on the Home Front: Lost Lessons from World War II Research." *Journal of Public Policy & Marketing* 21(1):90–99.

1

OTHERWORLDLY ANTHROPOLOGY

Past, Present, and Future Contributions of Ethnographers to Space Exploration

Jo Aiken

Space exploration is a uniquely human activity. As we continue to push the limits of exploring the unknown, our knowledge of what it means to be human and our capacity for supporting human life beyond the comforts of our Earthly home continues to evolve. Scientists and engineers develop new technologies and advancements in medicine in order to support life among the stars. Likewise, social scientists aid space agencies in understanding human behavior so that astronauts and cosmonauts are selected and trained for mission success. Social science, particularly through ethnography, also aids space explorers who must learn to utilize the new technologies and medical advances in the extreme environment of space while becoming accustomed to life as a space community. It is important that researchers address these challenges so that human survival beyond Earth is not only achievable but so that life among the stars is worth living and sustaining. Ethnography is a useful tool for obtaining an insider's perspective and holistic viewpoint on the life of the space explorer. Through the application of ethnography and cultural knowledge, anthropologists are uniquely suited to address such topics and help extend the trajectory of space exploration as well as our understanding of humanity to new horizons.

"An anthropologist who studies outer space?" I wish I had a nickel for every puzzled look I receive when telling people, even fellow anthropologists, about my chosen occupation as a researcher in space systems and habitat design. The physical sciences are in familiar territory when it comes to space exploration research. The opportunities for advancements in astronomy, physics, chemistry, geology, and even the life sciences made possible by the space industry are rarely debated. Social scientists, anthropologists in particular, have been slow to acknowledge outer space as a useful domain of research and have only recently participated in applied space-related research. However, space exploration is a phenomenon offering unique views of behavior, culture, and community, though it is a research domain that often receives little attention from anthropologists. When I conducted my first applied study concerning crew privacy needs in long-duration spaceflight, I was the only anthropologist at the space agency even though anthropologists' fascination with this aspect of humanity began shortly after men first traveled to outer space. The following sections of this chapter provide an overview of areas in which anthropology has engaged with and continues to be involved in space exploration research and introduce a domain of anthropological research with a value that is truly out of this world, though often unexpected.

Anthropology and the Domain of Outer Space

The onset of engagement between anthropology and the domain of outer space centered on the subject of extraterrestrial life. In 1961, the National Aeronautics and Space Administration (NASA) commissioned a study to assess the impact contact with alien life would have on the public. The investigators referenced anthropological studies of societies negatively affected by the introduction of a new group possessing a different set of attitudes, values, and technologies (Dick 2006). Even though this report highlighted the benefits of applying anthropological knowledge to the task, it was not until the 1970s that anthropologists were formally involved in the discussions. In 1971, the Soviet Union invited two anthropologists to attend an international meeting on communication with extraterrestrial intelligence. NASA followed suit in 1972 by inviting anthropologist Ashley Montagu to a symposium in which Montagu made a case for the study of culture contacts. Extraterrestrial life continued to be in focus as the first substantial support of anthropology's involvement in space cultures came with the sponsorship of the popular science book *Cultures Beyond the Earth* (Maruyama and Harkins 1975) by the American Anthropological Association (AAA). The book, a result of a 1974 AAA symposium, not only covered extraterrestrial life of the alien variety, but it also classified human explorers as possible extraterrestrials.

Building on anthropological discourse on extraterrestrial life during the 1970s, anthropologist Ben Finney (Finney and Jones 1986) conducted the first fieldwork study with NASA's Search for Extraterrestrial Intelligence (SETI) project during the mid-1980s. His work with SETI in the mid-1980s was significant in that it was the first time a formal relationship between an anthropologist and a space agency was established (Dick 2006). Finney, referred to by many as the father of space anthropology (Harris 1995; Stuster 1996), was also the first to move beyond extra-terrestrial speculation and look at space exploration as a topic worthy of practical anthropological inquiry. Finney continued his work in space exploration through-out the 1980s and 1990s in a consultant role for NASA, where he was the first to formulate a case study as the basis for planning future space societies (Finney 1987). The construction of space societies and extraterrestrial encounters continue to be contemporary topics of interest among social scientists and space enthusiasts (Battaglia 2006; Harris 1995; Pass 2006; Riner 1987).

Future space societies represent only one area of anthropological inquiry posed by space exploration. In addition to futures studies, the domain of space exploration presents opportunities for research regarding other topics often explored by both academic and practicing anthropologists. Space-related research questions of anthropological interest are seen in projects focused on the physiological, psychological, and behavioral impacts of living and working in isolated and extreme environments. Historically, space agencies placed more importance on investigating the biological sciences, but funded projects have increasingly incorporated behavioral and communication perspectives. Although progress has been made in involving the social sciences in space research, agencies' objectives have remained fixed on improving productivity and mission success (Kanas 2005; Stuster 2010; Clancey 2003, 2012). For this reason, topics of research regarding the environmental, physical or biological, and psychosocial aspects of space travel have remained prevalent in this domain. Organizational culture, collaboration, and technology design are other subjects which anthropologists and like-minded ethnographers have engaged with in regards to space exploration. A closer examination of the five themes of research, (1) environmental, (2) physiological and psychological, (3) organizational and collaborative, (4) technological, and (5) anticipatory, provide a glimpse into the opportunities for present and future engagements between anthropology and space research. Anthropologists are uniquely suited to take part in these complex, interrelated areas of research because of their holistic training in culture and *in situ* approaches to studying human behavior.

Environmental

Space is an inhospitable environment. Few places, if any, on Earth require their inhabitants to be isolated from outside contact and remain confined to a small volume of space in order to survive the extreme environmental conditions that characterize space. Scientists and engineers tasked with designing both crewed and un-crewed spaceflight missions are rightly concerned about the extremity of space. The harsh temperatures and diminished gravity of outer space designate which materials are needed to construct satellites, robotics, and space vehicles that are functional and sustainable. The lack of a breathable atmosphere drives the need for providing an artificial, confined environment for living space explorers. The isolated, confined, and extreme (ICE) environment of outer space impacts the construction of space structures, as just noted, as well as influencing the social aspects of space exploration. Astronauts and cosmonauts are selected according to personal characteristics considered desirable and necessary for a successful mission living and working in this ICE environment – traits identified by social scientists.

Several anthropologists have embraced outer space as a source for exploring human perceptions and behaviors regarding their environment. Research in this area, including research from within academia and that applied in industry, brings into question spatial and temporal aspects of environmental adaptation and ecological evolution that result from living in the ICE environment of space (Olson 2010; Palinkas 1990). As crewed missions move beyond low Earth orbit, the impact of the unfamiliar environment that these works address becomes magnified. Combine the challenges of an ICE environment with the time required for a trip to Mars or a near-Earth asteroid, and the risks to human safety and well-being become intensified. It is unknown if feelings of isolation are magnified by the sensory awareness of being unable to see Earth. Likewise, questions remain unanswered as to the impact of being confined in a small volume for longer than a year without the ability to freely enter the surrounding environment. Indeed, the ICE environment, an acronym formalized in American space studies, is central to the challenges faced by space explorers.

Physiological and Psychological

The restrictions imposed on a spaceflight crew are arguably unique to the environment of space. As noted above, most empirical research studies have and continue to focus on the physiological and psychological impacts of space travel. Spaceflight is dangerous, and every aspect involved in traveling outside the safety of Earth's atmosphere poses a certain amount of risk to the health and well-being of humans. Weightlessness, exposure to radiation, and sensory deprivation living within an artificial habitable environment are all risks of spaceflight that affect the crew. The Human Research Program (HRP) at the NASA Johnson Space Center (JSC) investigates and works to mitigate the risks to human health and performance (NASA 2014). The HRP outlines activities aimed at identifying and addressing the undesirable effects of spaceflight on humans, and within each identified risk, they identify knowledge gaps in need of further research. The opportunities for research presented by the HRP that could benefit from anthropological insight are too numerous to list in this chapter, yet two topics deserve special mention: the development of individualized countermeasures and identifying potential interpersonal conflicts while living in space.

Even though humans have been traveling through space for over fifty years, mitigating the physiological and psychological effects of long-duration, long-distance spaceflight remains a challenge. Space agencies develop countermeasures as a means to mitigate or counteract the undesirable effects of spaceflight on humans (NASA 2011). Countermeasures include medical devices such as medication to counteract space-induced insomnia as well as formal procedures for allowing crewmembers to have free time in order to relieve work-related stress. NASA is currently investigating the potential use of countermeasures that are individualized to the needs of each crewmember. Since the permanent occupation of the International Space Station (ISS), space researchers have remarked on the inadequacy of a one-size-fits-all approach in developing countermeasures due to differences in body composition along with differing levels of compliance. Biological and applied cultural anthropologists with a focus on medicine could possibly add much to their efforts in exploring genetically and behaviorally individualized countermeasures. Lawrence Palinkas (1990, 2003, 2010) is one notable anthropologist conducting research aimed at cross-cultural medicine, but he also addresses the interpersonal dynamics among people living and working in space and how these psychosocial issues evolve over a long period of time.

Organizational and Collaborative

Space exploration affords the opportunity for a greater understanding of human society through the diversity of its explorers and the complexity of the organizations to which they belong. NASA is synonymous with space exploration and provides an excellent example of this complexity. Since the beginning of the Space Race, space exploration has been a highly politicized activity. Policy-driven mandates from Congress shaped the earliest days of the US space program and created an operational paradigm of international involvement that continues today. To this day, the US Congress and Administration remain the most prominent political influences on the planning and implementation of American spaceflight missions. NASA's strategic plans and goals are directed by American national policy, and in turn direct the design of spacecraft and the establishment of mission objectives. Throughout its history, individuals from the Legislative Branch, Congress, and the Administrative Branch of the US federal government have often played a direct role in conceptualizing the Agency's designs (Logsdon 2002). More frequently, Congress influences the design of spacecraft by appropriating funds for NASA's budget.

In addition to the direct political influence on the organization, NASA is a highly complex organization dependent on multi-sited collaboration between its various centers spread throughout the US as well as international cooperation from its partners. In this way, NASA is representative of many large, international organizations. Diane Vaughan's well-known book *The Challenger Launch Decision* (Vaughan 1996) provided the first substantial look into the organizational and work culture of NASA. Communication styles, skill sets, and problem-solving abilities differ among astronauts, scientists, and engineers due to the nature of their occupational norms and their regional culture (Clancey 2003; Kanas 2004, 2005; Stuster 2010). However, the complexity of culture, location, and performance as a virtual organization is taken further, in that NASA also works with people and technology located off-planet and in time zones that do not align with the Earth's rotation. Computer scientist and ethnographer William Clancey (2012) describes distributed teams of scientists working onsite at the Jet Propulsion Laboratory (JPL) and abroad in his book *Working on Mars* (2012). These scientists and engineers supported the Mars Exploration Rovers (MER) while living on Mars time.

As NASA historian John Logsdon reminds his readers, space exploration has long been the ultimate example of international collaboration (Logsdon 2002). Since the last days of the Apollo program, NASA has built its program around the aim of fostering international relationships, as evident in programs like Spacelab, Space-Shuttle–Mir, and the current ISS. The emphasis on international cooperation is apparent in that a greater number of NASA-sponsored studies focus on international crew relationships than on any other topic except biology. Studies including the frequently cited Shuttle–Mir and ISS research by Nick Kanas (Boyd et al. 2009; Kanas 2004, 2005) and polar and space expedition studies by Palinkas (Palinkas 1990, 2003) highlight the interactions and interpersonal conflicts among international crews. Anthropologist Jack Stuster's Astronaut Journal Flight Experiment (Stuster

2010) is notable in providing ethnographic insight on this topic and his continuing project will be essential in understanding how crew behavior evolves over time.

The people involved in carrying out future spaceflight missions, as crew or as ground support, are likely to remain multinational, interdisciplinary, and multi-sited for reasons other than political appeal. Scholars and agencies agree that space exploration is more successful when approached through international and inter-disciplinary collaboration due to the increased availability of financial resources and diversity in expertise (Boyd et al. 2009; Logsdon 2002; Olson 2010; Pass 2006). Space exploration is costly not just in terms of financial resources but also in respect to the diverse, expert skills and knowledge needed to travel to the stars. The crew composition aboard the ISS continues to be a multinational, multidisciplinary mix of men and women. Therefore, it is plausible that NASA will partner with other space agencies and seek diversity in the expertise of future spaceflight crews to meet the financial, technical, and social challenges of space exploration beyond near-Earth orbit. As crews move out from Earth for longer periods of time, anthro-pologists are provided with a domain rich in aspects of culture, intersubjectivity, and connectedness. Few, if any, territories of research offer such a complex milieu of sociality and identity coupled with techniques and environment as that which is characteristic of space exploration. Anthropology is the reasonable choice for exploring these issues because of the discipline's familiarity with addressing complex questions regarding the human condition through synthesizing cultural, material, and biological knowledge.

Technological

In line with the complexity of the organizations involved in space exploration, the development of space technology is a complicated and painstakingly involved process. Engineers and scientists are working towards missions to the Moon, Mars, and beyond. Over the years, NASA's approach to technology design has evolved from a purely machine-centered paradigm to a practice more accepting of con-temporary human-centered ideas. This shift opens the doors for design anthropologists and ethnographers with expertise in technology design and human–computer interaction to become engaged in space research. The growing opportunities in this area have the potential to increase our knowledge of how humans think about and interact with cutting-edge technologies but also provide engineers with the insight needed to design technologies that are easily adopted and function as desired.

Since the 1990s, design researchers have turned increasingly towards ethnography as a means to understand users (Cefkin 2013; Wasson 2000) and, essentially, cut the cost of development by seeking the user's perspective throughout the production cycle. Engineers' uncertainty about the future, as a result of budget cutbacks and ever-changing political mandates, continues a tradition of establishing standards "designed to the threshold of acceptability" established in the Skylab era (Compton and Benson 2011, 136). Engineers and program managers set design standards under this paradigm so as to establish what is the least amount of resources (e.g. spatial volume, industrial material, tools, etc.) necessary to sustain life and achieve mission success. Within the boundaries of what-is-affordable, NASA engineers attempt to engage in the design process to meet the demands of what-is-safe.

Anthropologists who apply ethnography to understanding and evaluating human–technology performances are extremely helpful in ensuring a successful space mission. Space travel is dangerous, and NASA has gone to great lengths over the years to create and sustain a culture of safety (Vaughan 1996). As part of these efforts, NASA continues to publish standards which engineers must follow as they endeavor to design spacecraft to effectively facilitate human space exploration. These standards are typically developed with a design reference mission, or a planned mission, in mind. However, since the end of the Space Shuttle Program in 2011, budget constraints and shifting directives from Congress have led managers to request standards be developed that could be applied to any long-duration spaceflight mission. Generalizing spacecraft design standards has proven to be a significant challenge, as definitions of long duration and habitability are often tied to the particulars of a mission (Whitmore et al. 1998, 2013). For example, perceptions of isolation during a one-year mission orbiting the Earth could be dramatically different from a one-year mission orbiting Mars. Similarly, design criteria that guide the development of a terrestrial habitat are different from those that guide the development of a vehicle used in a microgravity environment. Therefore, experts are continuously identifying user-centered risk factors associated with spaceflight and knowledge gaps that need to be overcome in order to achieve and sustain a successful long-duration mission. These risk factors and knowledge gaps benefit from anthropological insight focused on technology use and acceptance. Ethnographers evaluate human–technology interactions in situated conditions so that insight is obtained from a holistic viewpoint, taking into account the peripheral environment within which the interactions exist. Anthropological insight gives the analysis of such ethnographic data meaning and actionable understanding within the domain of space exploration.

Anticipatory

Predicting the known technological and social difficulties of an unplanned, future space mission presents a challenge to any discipline. For cultural anthropologists, the challenge cuts to the core of our field's emphasis on *in situ*, participant observation. Direct participant observation of the target population is arguably the most common approach to fieldwork in ethnographic, anthropological inquiry. Indeed, "being there" is the hallmark of cultural anthropologists' claim of gaining insight (Hannerz 2003). To study a space community, which does not yet exist, researchers seek fieldwork opportunities to study analogous populations from existing space-like settings. When space scientists and engineers need to test space systems and simulate space mission operations, they conduct tests at an analog site that meets the required physical aspects of the space environment they need to study. Space analogs are field sites or laboratory setups identified as having characteristics similar to the environment of space. Space analogs vary according to which aspects of spaceflight are represented in the environment and according to what fidelity, or level of accuracy, is needed for the study. For example, the effect of weightlessness is best experienced underwater while the effect of the relocation of fluids in the body can be simulated through bed-rest studies. Analogs, therefore, provide a contemporary mode for exploring research questions with pragmatic, future applications.

The nature of space-related research coupled with themes of pioneering, exploration, and discovery adds to the future-oriented, science fiction undertones of adventure in space exploration. Research activities allow for the future planning of relatively near-term projects such as missions to Mars and near-Earth asteroids, but also allows for speculation about projects to be carried out past this century. The ultimate example of futures rhetoric is found in sociologist Jim Pass's (2006) work on planning space societies. The uniqueness of space as a future field site for research and its assumed importance to the future of humanity have led many social scientists to propose a shift in disciplinary paradigms. Astrobiology was created as a biology sub-discipline for the study of life in the universe, effectively shifting the paradigm of Earth-based life to universe-based life. Similar, less successful attempts have been made within the social sciences. Finney (1992, 186) proposed "astro-anthropology" as a new subfield of anthropology to study the humanization of space while Pass (2006, 2) proposes the similarly named "astrosociology." In corresponding fashion, psychologist Philip Harris (1995) proposes a paradigm shift from conceptualizing mankind or humankind into the broader term spacekind. Regardless of the terminology, these researchers agree that a futures perspective is needed in applied space research. Furthermore, the future-oriented aspect of space research provides opportunities to develop anthropological theory and ethnographic methodologies useful in other areas of futures research, such as city planning and technology development.

Space in Space: A Case Study of Space Anthropology

The themes, or areas of inquiry, of space research often overlap. The best way to illustrate the interrelatedness of topics in space research and the richness of the ethnographic data is with an example of a study conducted for NASA regarding habitat design. In 2013, I conducted ethnographic research to explore perceptions of privacy and privacy needs among astronauts living and working in space as part of a long-distance, long-duration mission.[1] The study addressed the complexities involved in determining the privacy needs of a future spaceflight crew and offered practical insight regarding design considerations for providing privacy through an ethnographic study of space analog crews and designers. I triangulated evidence from in-depth interviews, photo and video narratives, archival research, guided walk-throughs of habitats, and direct participant observation to gain an understanding of privacy issues experienced by a space crew. As a case study, the research represents the often overlapping themes of space research outlined above as well as illustrating the benefits of applying anthropology within the domain of space exploration.

NASA, other national space agencies, and the commercial space partners of these agencies are working to develop vehicles and habitats capable of sending humans beyond low Earth orbit. The development of habitable environments suitable to long-duration spaceflight, informally defined as a mission lasting longer than one year, has become an agency priority for NASA. In recent years, the focus of their mission objectives has turned from missions in near-Earth orbit, such as the ISS to missions to asteroids, Mars, and beyond. The researchers in the Habitability and Human Factors organization and the Behavioral Health and Performance organization represent two groups at the NASA Johnson Space Center tasked with exploring the challenges anticipated for a long-duration space mission. One area of their investigations focuses on determining the minimum habitable volume requirements for habitats supporting the day-to-day life and work of a long-term crew. The need for privacy has been identified as particularly challenging to account for in defining the minimal habitable volume for optimal, long-duration crew performance. I joined these organizations as a research apprentice in 2013 to address this challenge.

The Problem of Privacy

From lessons learned during spaceflight missions lasting less than six months, the NASA Human Research Program (HRP) recognized habitat volume and layout as a contributing factor to human health and performance in space (NASA 2011; Simon et al. 2011). An incompatible vehicle or habitat design poses a risk that can affect crew safety and mission success (Whitmore et al. 2013). Future vehicle and habitat design strategies will need to address adequacies in the livable, or habitable, volume and acceptable architectural layouts in order to mitigate design-related stressors during a long-duration mission. Design-related stressors include sleep deprivation from high ambient noise levels and interpersonal conflict arising from issues of confinement and the inefficient designs of working and living spaces (NASA 2011; Whitmore et al. 2013). The effects of these design-related stressors are generally understood with regards to short-term missions, but it remains unknown how these stressors evolve over long periods of time.

Habitability design standards are established as a means of guidance for engineers responsible for creating the concepts, prototypes, and operational space systems supporting human life. These standards must meet the needs of crewmembers with regards to their physical and mental health and well-being in order to assure mission safety and success (NASA 2011). In 2011, NASA identified issues of privacy as a top-priority design-related stressor concerning habitability designs for long-duration, space exploration missions (Simon et al. 2011). The allocation of space, or habitable volume, becomes an increasingly complex issue in outer space due to the costs associated with maintaining an artificial, confined environment bounded by limitations of mass while located in an extreme environment. Given the challenges of sustaining life in such a limited environment, NASA deemed it necessary to determine the acceptable minimal amount of habitable volume for activities requiring at least some level of privacy so as to support optimal crew performance.

In addition to the environmental challenges associated with spaceflight, the number of crewmembers, objectives, and duration of a space mission drive the amount of habitable volume required. Evidence from American spaceflight shows that the larger the crew and the more cramped the volume, the more likely behavior and performance will be impaired, and feelings of being confined or cramped are noted to intensify over time (Perner and Langdoc 1994). Frequently cited work from the 1960s by Thomas Fraser (1966, 1968) suggested that a volume of 4.24 m^3 per person would be adequate for flights as long as thirty days. However, standards for the acceptable net habitable volume (NHV) of a spacecraft had yet to be determined for missions lasting longer than one year at the time this research was conducted. NHV, also referred to as functional volume, is defined as the total volume that is not occupied by other elements occupying space within a given environment and which is therefore accessible by crewmembers for performing tasks (NASA 2011).

Addressing the Problem

The need for an improved understanding of the relationship between habitat volume, social stressors, and privacy served as the foundation of the study. The goal of the applied project was to obtain a more thorough understanding of how privacy concerns related to habitat and vehicle design issues as well as to social issues affect crew performance and quality of life for long-duration spaceflight. Rather than determining a numerical value for the optimal, minimal habitable volume as called for by the NASA HRP, the research objectives of this project were to advance the knowledge of the space research community concerning the elements that constitute privacy that influence spatial volume and habitat design considerations.

The examination of "space in space" required an integrated investigation of the design of the astronauts' living environments, their work processes and relationships within NASA, as well as an understanding of the values and viewpoints of the NASA organization. An understanding of both privacy as a human condition and the effect of the space environment on the human condition was needed to design and carry out a successful study that would effectively address the research question. Moreover, knowledge of NASA as an organization would be key in producing actionable results to meet the needs of both the Habitability and Human Factors group and the Behavioral Health and Performance group.

At the beginning of the study, I was familiar with NASA as a highly complex, highly technological organization because I had worked within the agency for several years in the Mission Operations Directorate.[2] However, I was only somewhat familiar with the NASA HRP based on a brief, independent study I conducted in 2011 (Aiken 2012) during which I went through the HRP to gain access to potential participants. In order to reacquaint myself with the activities and culture of the NASA space agency, I spent five months conducting an in-depth review of literature and embedded myself in the everyday activities of the researchers onsite at JSC prior to conducting the fieldwork. During this period of discovery, I learned that the inability of experts to agree on a definition was central to the complexity of addressing privacy. The engineers I worked with at JSC and other American space researchers generally follow NASA's definition of privacy as documented in the Human Integration Design Handbook (NASA 2011), "an acceptable level of control over the extent of sharing oneself (physically, behaviorally, or intellectually) with others" (NASA 2011, 997), yet my colleagues struggled to accept this definition as universal and, more importantly, actionable in all aspects of designing for life in space. The need for me to address particular definitions of privacy in my study was guided in part by their reluctance to design for the individualistic nature of perceptions of privacy and also as a direct result of my training in anthropology and fondness for user-centered design research. Therefore, I made the decision early on in the project's design to allow my participants to define privacy, instead of examining perceptions of it based on a pre-determined definition. I chose this approach so that the voice of the unique study population, or the community of practice that characterizes space exploration, could best be heard.

The methods used in the study were selected so that the results would contextualize participants' behavior and their perceptions of privacy, and included interviews, photo and video narratives, the review of archival material in the form of mission debriefs, habitat walk-throughs, and direct participant observation. In-depth, semi-structured interviews were conducted one-on-one by myself with fifty participants and served as the primary method for this study. To supplement the interviews, I used photo and video narratives to examine observed behaviors and contextualize behaviors within the ICE environment. In each interview, I presented the participant with previously published photos and archival video footage, if available, to trigger past memories of a particular experience. When possible, the participants were asked to map out behaviors chronologically using a printout of the habitat floor plan. While onsite at JSC, I was allowed to attend and indirectly participate in the post-flight mission debriefs for the NASA astronauts who had recently returned from the ISS. I was also allowed to view transcripts from previous ISS post-flight mission debriefs and debrief data reports, which are archived by a team within the Habitability and Human Factors branch. As a method, guided walk-throughs of habitat mockups allowed for the collection of photographs and video that would otherwise have been unobtainable. High-fidelity mockups are currently used to prototype and test design strategies as well as train spaceflight crewmembers.

As noted previously, direct participant observation is perhaps the most challenging aspect of ethnographic research involving astronauts. Like many topics of interest in this domain, the future-oriented nature of the research question called for a uniquely defined population, which is uncommon in traditional ethnographic studies. Ethnographers typically study an existing population or community. Schensul et al. (1999, 7) define ethnographic research as that which is conducted "locally" within the particular community of study. However, the community of study for this research does not yet exist. Earth has yet to send humans beyond low Earth orbit (LEO) for a mission lasting longer than six months. Astronauts and cosmonauts have lived aboard space stations for long durations, but these space stations have remained in orbit around the Earth. The Apollo Program sent men to the Moon, beyond LEO, yet the longest mission time averaged only twelve days. To study a space community that does not yet exist, I elected to use crewmembers from existing space analogs. In addition to providing the parameters for the study's population, I utilized a space analog as a site for direct participant observation. In August 2013, I was selected as a member of the inaugural Human Exploration Research Analog (HERA) crew, HERA-1. The mission took place in September onsite at JSC with the goal of evaluating the newly reconfigured habitat used in previous Desert Research and Technology Studies (Desert RATS). The four crewmembers, including myself, another female and two males, spent three days and two nights in HERA, located inside a building onsite. Even though the mission was short and severely limited as a high-fidelity space simulation, I was able to observe how crewmembers interacted with each other and with their analog environment first-hand.

Research Outcomes

The study resulted in twenty-five key findings regarding perceptions and behaviors relating to privacy in a space habitat environment. The user-centered definition of privacy I sought for this study offered the opportunity to conceptualize privacy in terms of both practical, technical applications and social affordances in the situated voice of a space crew. Participants used the term "ability" most often when defining privacy. The term ability implies the capacity to do something that achieves a specified goal or that enables a specific function, and is therefore task-oriented. Related to the idea of privacy and successfully completing tasks is the suitability or the effect of the design of the physical environment for affording individuals living and working within it the needed level of privacy. Participants often referred to privacy within the context of a physical space or setting that either provides or impedes the desired level of privacy. The aspect of the participants' definition most surprising to my NASA colleagues and myself was the reported social or "shared" element of privacy. As evident in participant narratives, privacy is a social affordance as well as a group need. However, in relation to the social aspects of privacy, participants emphasized the need to control or have a "choice" about how they share and receive information.

The findings, grounded in a shared definition of privacy, offered insights and recommendations that were of practical use in the design of space vehicles and habitats. The individual as well as the social aspects of perceived needs illustrated the attributes of privacy that affect performance and the well-being of humans in an ICE environment. The study also contributed to the growing body of knowledge within anthropology on subjectivity, personhood and what it means to be human. The domain of space exploration, as evident in my work, offers unique insight into our understanding of how humans conceptualize self, space, and time, and their corresponding, permeable boundaries, and how the built and "natural" environments influence the formation of ideas. Through my applied work with space crews, I am also addressing theoretical notions of distributed cognition and sensemaking within anthropology and design research. My past and continuing work with NASA illustrates the inherent nature of anthropology as a discipline that is able to address both practical, applied problems while also contributing to theory development.

Conclusion

Space exploration is a domain of anthropological inquiry rich in opportunity. The uniqueness of space presents an ethnographic field site like none on Earth for understanding spatial, temporal, and material perceptions of self and community. The themes of research described in this chapter speak to the prospects for research that is beneficial for both the discipline of anthropology and the interdisciplinary space research community. The subject of space in space, as explained in the case study, proved to be a challenging and rewarding endeavor in which ethnographic methods were stretched to address a practical problem in an unreachable, future field site while staying true to anthropological principles. More importantly, what began as a study aimed at meeting the needs of the NASA stakeholders proved to be mutually beneficial to all disciplines of researchers involved in the task of habitat design. The study provides an illustration of the benefits of applying anthropology to a practical space exploration problem, and also demonstrates the benefits of space research to the discipline of anthropology. The anthropology *of* space exploration and anthropology *for* space exploration both provide new resources for obtaining knowledge that contributes to our understanding of what it means to be human.

Future space travel seems certain, at least for now. Although this chapter has focused on American, government-supported activities, other national space agencies continually incorporate the social sciences in their research and training endeavors. Commercial space corporations present another exciting avenue for engaging in space-related research. Often referred to as NewSpace (Valentine et al. 2009), entrepreneurial space companies maintain growth in their efforts to privatize space exploration. As long as nations and industry partners continue to develop our exploration capabilities, practicing anthropologists will have otherworldly opportunities to further our understanding of humanity and help push boundaries further beyond the confines of Earth.

Notes

1 This work was funded by the National Space Biomedical Research Institute via NASA Cooperative Agreement NCC 9-58.
2 The Mission Operations Directorate leads overall crewed spaceflight mission activities including mission planning, astronaut training, and flight support through the Mission Control Center at the NASA Johnson Space Center.

References

Aiken, Jo. 2012. "Integrating Organizational and Design Perspectives to Address Challenges of Renewal: A Case Study of NASA's Post-Shuttle Workforce Transition." Ethnographic Praxis in Industry Conference Proceedings.

Battaglia, Debbora, ed. 2006. *E.T. Culture: Anthropology in Outerspaces.* Durham, NC: Duke University Press.

Boyd, Jennifer E., Nick A. Kanas, Vyacheslav P. Salnitskiy, Vadim I. Gushin, Stephanie A. Saylor, Daniel S. Weiss, and Charles R. Marmar. 2009. "Cultural Differences in Crewmembers and Mission Control Personnel during Two Space Station Programs." *Aviation, Space, and Environmental Medicine* 80(6):532–540.

Cefkin, Melissa. 2013. *Introduction to Ethnography and the Corporate Encounter: Reflections on Research in and of Corporations.* Oxford: Berghahn Books.

Clancey, William J. 2003. "Principles for Integrating Mars Analog Science, Operations, and Technology Research." In *Workshop on Analog Sites and Facilities for the Human Exploration of the Moon and Mars.* Golden, Colorado: Colorado School of Mines.

Clancey, William J. 2012. *Working on Mars: Voyages of Scientific Discovery with the Mars Exploration Rovers.* Boston: MIT Press.

Compton, W. David, and Charles D. Benson. 2011. *Living and Working in Space: A History of Skylab.* New York: Dover Publications.

Dick, Steven J. 2006. "Anthropology and the Search for Extraterrestrial Intelligence: An Historical View." *Anthropology Today* 22(2):3–7.

Finney, Ben R. 1987. "Anthropology and the Humanization of Space." *Acta Astronautica* 15(3):189–194.

Finney, Ben R. 1992. "Space Migrations: Anthropology and the Humanization of Space." *Space Resources* 509:164–188.

Finney, Ben R., and Eric M. Jones. 1986. *Interstellar Migration and the Human Experience.* Berkeley: University of California Press.

Fraser, Thomas Morris. 1966. "The effects of confinement as a factor in manned space flight." NASA CR-511, NASA contractor report. Washington, D.C.

Fraser, Thomas Morris. 1968. *The Intangibles of Habitability during Long Duration Space Missions.* Houston: NASA Lyndon B. Johnson Space Center.

Hannerz, Ulf. 2003. "Being There … and There … and There! Reflections on Multi-site Ethnography." *Ethnography* 4(2):201–216.

Harris, Philip R. 1995. "The Impact of Culture on Human and Space Development – New Millennial Challenge." *Acta Astronautica* 36(7):399–408.

Kanas, Nick. 2004. "Group Interactions during Space Missions." *Aviation, Space, and Environmental Medicine* 75(1):C3–C5.

Kanas, Nick. 2005. "Interpersonal Issues in Space: Shuttle/Mir and Beyond." *Aviation, Space, and Environmental Medicine* 76(1):B126–B134.

Logsdon, John M. 2002. "The Development of International Space Cooperation." In *Exploring the Unknown: Selected Documents in the History of the U.S. Civil Space Program.* Chicago: The University of Chicago Press on behalf of The History of Science Society.

Maruyama, Magoroh, and Arthur Harkins, eds. 1975. *Cultures beyond the Earth: The Role of Anthropology in Outer Space.* New York: Vintage Books.

NASA (National Aeronautics and Space Administration). 2011. "Human Factors, Habitability, and Environmental Health." *NASA Space Flight Human-System Standard*, vol. 2. Washington, D.C.

NASA (National Aeronautics and Space Administration). 2014. Human Research Roadmap. *Human Research Program.* http://humanresearchroadmap.nasa.gov.

Olson, Valerie A. 2010. "American Extreme: An Ethnography of Astronautical Visions and Ecologies." Dissertation. Houston: Rice University.

Palinkas, Lawrence A. 1990. "Psychosocial Effects of Adjustment in Antarctica: Lessons for Long-Duration Spaceflight." *Journal of Spacecraft and Rockets* 27(5):471–477.

Palinkas, Lawrence A. 2003. "The Psychology of Isolated and Confined Environments: Understanding Human Behavior in Antarctica." *The American Psychologist* 58(5):353–363.

Palinkas, Lawrence A. 2010. "Coming out of the Cold and Stepping into the Light: Human Adaptation in High Latitude Environments." *International Journal of Circumpolar Health* 69(3):214–216.

Pass, Jim. 2006. "The Astrosociology of Space Colonies: Or the Social Construction of Societies in Space." *AIP Conference Proceedings* 813(1):1153–1161.

Perner, Chris, and William Langdoc. 1994. "Design of Interior Areas." In *Space Biology and Medicine*, eds F.M. Sulzman and A.M. Genin. American Institute of Aeronautics and Astronautics (AIAA), Joint US/Russian Publication, 139–165.

Riner, Reed D. 1987. "Doing Futures Research – Anthropologically." *Futures* 19(3):311–328.

Schensul, Stephen L., Jean J. Schensul, and Margaret D. LeCompte. 1999. *Essential Ethnographic Methods: Observations, Interviews, and Questionnaires*, vol. 2. Lanham, MD: AltaMira Press.

Simon, Matthew, Deborah Neubek, and Alexandra Whitmire. 2011. *Factors Impacting Habitable Volume Requirements: Results from the 2011 Habitable Volume Workshop*. Houston: NASA Lyndon B. Johnson Space Center.

Stuster, Jack W. 1996. *Bold Endeavors: Lessons from Polar and Space Exploration*. Annapolis, MD: Naval Institute Press.

Stuster, Jack W. 2010. *Behavioral Issues Associated with Long-Duration Space Expeditions: Review and Analysis of Astronaut Journals Experiment 01-E104 (Journals): Final Report*. Houston: NASA Lyndon B. Johnson Space Center.

Valentine, David, Valerie A. Olson, and Debbora Battaglia. 2009. "Encountering the Future: Anthropology and Outer Space." *Anthropology News* 50(9):11–15.

Vaughan, Diane. 1996. *The Challenger Launch Decision*. Chicago: University of Chicago Press.

Wasson, Christina. 2000. "Ethnography in the Field of Design." *Human Organization* 59(4):377–388.

Whitmore, Mihriban, Meredith L. McQuilkin, and Barbara J. Woolford. 1998. "Habitability and Performance Issues for Long Duration Space Flights." *Human Performance in Extreme Environments: The Journal of the Society for Human Performance in Extreme Environments* 3(1):64–74.

Whitmore, Mihriban, Kerry McGuire, Sarah Margerum, Shelby Thompson, Christopher Allen, Charles Bowen, Bernard Adelstein, Susan Schuh, Vicky Byrne, and Doug Wong. 2013. *Evidence Report: Risk of Incompatible Vehicle/Habitat Design, Human Factors and Human Research Program*. Houston: NASA Lyndon B. Johnson Space Center.

2

REMEMBERING AND RE-MEMBERING

Lived Experience of Military Service Members in Rehabilitation

Deborah A. Murphy

Disclaimer: The views expressed in this chapter are the author's and do not reflect the official policy of the Department of Army, Navy, Air Force, Marines, Department of Defense, or any agency of the US government.

As an applied linguistic anthropologist, I conduct ethnography to study and understand local semiotics. At my field site I observe, collect, and interpret signs and symbols – elements of communicative behavior including texts of all kinds. "Text" is situated language use (language in its broadest sense) that marks itself and its users' location within economic, social, cultural, and historical settings (Leap 2003). Texts include actual words in narratives and life stories, content in distributed media (Chandler 2007; Fairclough 2003; Johnstone 2008); and things we say, read, write, hear, see, smell, move through, and wear. Even space is a kind of text (Soja 2003). Texts also include objects, artifacts, and materials (Leone 2005). They are signified and apprehended within systems of meaning that are learned; and are covertly and overtly reproduced among people (Bourdieu 2003; Decena 2008; Pêcheux 1982).

Textual data offer entry points for understanding points of view and the prevailing ideological and socio-cultural constructs through which people recognize themselves and are being recognized. They offer ethnographers the opportunity to glimpse and attempt to understand the lived experience of people across terrains of experience and subjectivity that are always-in-formation (Leap 2004). Texts signify and are signified within systems of meaning, or interwoven "orders of discourse" that are learned and reproduced among people who can communicate intelligibly with each other, and who act on their inter-intelligibility (Fairclough 2003). Gathering texts provided by people in their own contexts enables ethnographers to understand peoples' senses of themselves within their lived experience (Dahlberg, Drew, and Nyström 2002).

My field site is a military treatment facility (MTF). With the consent of study participants there, I probe how perceptions of ability (and disability) and perceptions of deservedness are linked in the lived experience of patients, family members, non-medical attendants[1] (NMAs), and caregivers who are in rehabilitation – either being treated or providing or supporting treatment. With their help I study whether there is a felt link between disability and deservedness, how the linkage is sustained, and how it affects levels of recognition and access to resources. By "recognition" I mean being acknowledged, being addressed, being thanked, being saluted for example; and by deservedness I mean gaining access to such things as parking privileges, gifts, rewards, and privileged modes of communication including devices like tablets or smart phones. By collecting and analyzing textual data that both inscribe and circumscribe wounded, ill, and injured military Service Members' (SMs) and interrelated others' lived experience, I learn how research participants are actually interpreting, making sense of, and coping with their unforeseen experiences and conditions. For example, with permission, I listen to stories, study posters, announcements, and flyers, join in or observe activities, take notes, and examine material culture such as uniforms, medals, patches, and prosthetics.

My idea has been that studying the effects of adventitious alterations to "ability" in a structured and text-rich system like an MTF – a distilled space in which human socio-culture takes on an exaggerated and particular range of expression – will shed light on how it is that people decide on who deserves what, and how we subsequently confer or withhold recognition and access to resources. I hypothesize that while some material and immaterial results of being wounded, becoming ill, or being injured might be "obvious," some might be "unnoticed"; and that these differences in perception might account for differences in levels of recognition and access to resources, and their consequences (Althusser 1971; Lancaster 2003; McRuer 2006). In other words, in this space I can observe and hear about what happens when people are unexpectedly changed; how their subjectivities are affected; and in what ways and depending on whom, recognition and access to resources get re-calibrated. By gathering textual data and critically analyzing them, I get at the particular mechanisms governing practices and experiences at my site. My overall aim is to gain insights into aspects of lived experience that are significant to people's inclusion or exclusion at this site and beyond, how those aspects are constructed and reproduced, and the degrees of deservedness we accept or deny or negotiate when our own or others' subjectivities (and their embodiments) are unexpectedly altered.

By studying corporeal, cognitive, and conative changes and their consequences in a space and time devoted to managing adventitious change, i.e. at an MTF, my projects address large questions about the body, identity, and disability; while at the same time indexing – or pointing to – how ideas and ideology centered on "fitness" (and unfitness) are applied; i.e. their real effects in lived experience. The existentialities that I track, the mechanisms that construct and sustain them, and the evidence I find and document regarding the tacitness of these processes may be useful in theory and in practice – for social scientists, care providers, and researchers. By connecting theoretical questions and propositions regarding subjectivity with actual lived experience of alterations in self and others' perceptions of worth to recommendations for change(s) in practice and policy, my ethnography at an MTF provides an example of applied theoretical anthropology.

Context

In the United States of America (US), SMs who receive health care are treated under the auspices of two federal agencies: The Department of Defense (DOD), and the Veterans Administration (VA). The DOD is broadly responsible for the care, treatment, and transitioning of active duty and retired members of the Armed Forces and their families, or military beneficiaries; whereas the VA is a system-of-care that is largely responsible for "veterans," persons who are former and not career members of the Armed Forces, including those who have been designated as disabled, medically discharged, or separated from the Armed Forces; and not their families.

The DOD provides care, treatment, and rehabilitation at MTFs; the VA provides short-, medium- and long-term health care, hospice care, job assistance, educational support, home loans, and insurance at dedicated veterans' facilities including offices and hospitals (DODI 2009; VA 2011). Beyond functioning as hospitals and rehabilitation centers, MTFs are charged with maintaining the health of personnel from all branches of military service so that they can carry out their military missions; they are also charged with providing clinical settings for health care trainees across the uniformed services, which include the Public Health Service, as well as the Armed Forces (Army, Navy, Marines, Air Force, National Guard, Coast Guard, and Reserves).

Objectives for care and rehabilitation at MTFs include whether to return SMs to active duty in their respective forces, including being re-deployed; to place them within other federal agencies in internships or on a permanent basis; to direct them towards employment beyond the military; or to medically retire them. These factors influence the choice of treatment modalities that are assigned to and undertaken by wounded, ill, and injured SMs. By contrast, choice-of-care for veterans at VA facilities involves strategies for sustaining maximum long-term health and welfare in institutions or communities of care, within neighborhoods, and at home. The mandates, budgets, and administration of these two federal agencies are unique and separate – although they may sometimes overlap at patient or "client" scales; and they are frequently, confusingly, and sometimes disruptively conflated in public discourse.

While therapeutic services for wounded, ill, or injured SMs and veterans are also offered at hospitals, clinics, and rehabilitation facilities that are not part of the DOD or VA systems, there is a gap in the literature comparing SMs' lived experience inside MTFs and VA facilities with their experiences at outside facilities. And some wounded, ill, or injured SMs get no treatment at all or discontinue treatment, either because of assessments that do not acknowledge, sanction, or allow them; because of their own or their family's or advocate's inability to secure or support further treatment; because they are isolated and cannot attend treatment programs; or because the US health care system writ large simply fails them through oversight, denial, incompetence, undependability, or neglect (Benedict 2009; Woolhandler 2007).

Noting these distinctions may serve to bring into focus who is offering what to whom (and where), who is to be condemned or commended (or, indeed, "co-mended"), and what can or may need to be done in order to address inequities that may be expressed in lived experience among SMs and veterans at various health care sites. In turn, just as advances in military health care offer critical knowledge for care of civilians – locally, nationally, and globally – knowledge regarding uneven rehabilitation outcomes at an MTF may also offer insights with broader application.

My Field Site

Walter Reed National Military Medical Center is an MTF that was formed in 2011 when Naval National Medical Center in Bethesda, MD and Walter Reed Army Medical Center in Washington, D.C. merged in Bethesda. The restructuring that prompted their merger was part of a series of federally mandated military base closures and realignments (DOD 2005). While the scope of medico-therapeutic care offered at the merged location is broad, and its patient population diverse (including family members and beneficiaries), its focus and renown are in the care and treatment of active duty male and female SMs from four branches of the Armed Forces (Army, Navy, Air Force, and Marines) whose fitness for duty has been adventitiously, i.e. unexpectedly, altered by wounds, illnesses, or injuries.

At Walter Reed I collaborate in writing research grant proposals, securing funding, conducting ethnographic research to understand the lived experience of people whose abilities have been adventitiously altered, and applying knowledge to practice and policy. As in many kinds of work, administrative work takes up a third of my time, and training and security requirements for working at a military facility occupy a number of hours of every month; yet I am able to work with researchers, investigators, and participants at least half of each day. Co-investigators who collaborate in my research include military and civilian health care practitioners across a spectrum of specialties. Some of the studies we have collaborated in have probed the ethics of conducting research among people who have been harmed and are undergoing rehabilitation; the effect on wounded, ill, and injured SMs of practicing Qigong (a meditative movement practice); and the challenges of inculcating a culture of inquiry (seeking out and using evidence-based practices) in nursing units.

To gain entrée to my field site and the world of my research participants, I first became a research assistant in a DOD-sponsored mixed-methods (qualitative and quantitative) study being conducted at Walter Reed in D.C., working as a contractor for a military medical research foundation that was administering the study's granted funds. I disclosed to my colleagues that I was an applied linguistic anthropologist planning to submit my own research protocols to the Walter Reed Institutional Review Board (IRB). I consented potential participants, conducted interviews, administered surveys, and aggregated and managed data.

My role blossomed into being a research study coordinator in the Center for Nursing Science and Clinical Inquiry at Walter Reed in D.C., and after July 2011, in the Department of Research Programs in Bethesda. I wrote grant proposals, managed submissions in the local online tracking system, responded to administrative requirements, defended proposals to the IRB, and become certified as an onsite human subjects researcher. My Walter Reed colleagues supported my research goals and lines of ethnographic inquiry, and asked me to become an Associate Investigator in a number of their studies. In that role I collaborate in data collection, interpretation, analysis, and dissemination (presenting study findings). When I was ready to submit my own proposal for approval and oversight, I secured the support of senior military colleagues who were credentialed at Walter Reed, who became Principal Investigators for my studies, as is required at military facilities. Since then I have continued to collaborate with military and civilian teams of researchers who are conducting research at Walter Reed and collaborating institutions; for example, in a study about the physiologic effect of training service animals, with investigators at the Uniformed Services University of Health Sciences; a study of the relationship of autonomic regulation, gene expression, and mind–body practice with researchers at Harvard University and Mount Sinai Beth Israel Medical Center; and a study of the healing influence of art therapy with teams at Drexel University, PA. Now, as a research program manager at a brain injury clinical research institute at Walter Reed, I also work with investigative and technology teams to capture, codify, archive, and disseminate data, via the Federal Interagency Traumatic Brain Injury Research (FITBIR) registry, housed at the National Institutes of Health (NIH) in Bethesda.

Other anthropologists have conducted work at Walter Reed; for example, medical anthropologist Seth Messinger (2010) has shown (among other findings) the healing benefits of peers' and peer families' interactions with SMs in rehabilitation, and the importance of engaging with and acknowledging the altered physical and social worlds that patients actually inhabit. Messinger's work has come to the attention of policy makers within the US military health care system and has generated calls for further qualitative research among wounded, ill, and injured SMs (Caravalho 2011).

Framework

Because my work is based in the belief that notions of ability (and disability) are socio-culturally constructed and environmentally influenced, I requested permission and have been able to conduct research in a space where being "fit," becoming "unfit," and being rehabilitated are overtly understood, acknowledged, and enacted; i.e. at an MTF. People in this setting offer a geography of marked subjectivities; a space in which I can listen to, observe, participate with, and interview people who expressly acknowledge themselves and consociates by rank, ability, readiness, and resiliency. They mark themselves and others, notice changes, make claims, and enact measures within a highly structured system; a system in which signs and symbols abound and are associated with changes – for better and for worse – in status, and subsequently in ideas about deservedness. The people with whom I work are providers, administrators, coordinators, or recipients of care, and whether they have grasped my role as an anthropologist or not, they say they support my ethnography because they share my interest in understanding the lived experience of SMs whose perceived fitness has been unexpectedly altered, and the under-recognized consequences of having been wounded, become ill, or been injured. At the same time, consociates at Walter Reed are cognizant of and usually expressive about the place and system in which we work: a military base and hospital. The very semiotics I am interested in tracking are central to our varied roles in this space and time; signs and symbols at a military treatment facility are not just prominent; they are essential to identifying – even codifying – and managing change(s) in rank, status, ability, recognition, and access to resources.

Socio-cultural constructions of deservedness may attach eligibility for recognition to facsimiles of able-bodiedness (McRuer 2006). Based on what other researchers and ethnographers have posited, what I observe and collect, what respondents tell me, and what my analysis reveals, it seems that semiotics of posture, gait, uniforms, salutes, medals, and even prosthetics and assistive technologies that mimic able-bodiedness may actively mediate messaging that rewards particular kinds of harm and modes of rehabilitation; in other words, privileged valuations rest on visible and intelligible expressions of corporeal re-integration, such as being able to walk upright. Thus a chain of membership, dis-membership, and re-membering appears to connect particular people, and not others. Some SMs appear or claim to be excluded from widely endorsed and mediated rehabilitative regimens because of their invisible, unintelligible, and "inadmissible" injuries; and they are tacitly constructed as ineligible for, or may be excluded from, the benefits that accrue to others who are granted access on the basis of their visible or "admissible" harm. In addition, when SMs are harmed, they disavow self-identifying as "disabled," distinguishing themselves from others using nomenclature that hierarchizes harm; i.e. as "wounded," "ill," and "injured," the terms-of-art that are replacing the phrase "Wounded Warriors" in many texts.

After September 11, 2001, many US military communications began to include the term "Wounded Warrior," in a rhetorical strategy to reflect the warrior ethos and spirit of wounded soldiers (Krull and Haugseth 2012; Pincus 2012; USAPS 2008; WWP 2011). For a number of years the term "Wounded Warrior" was used in numerous texts to denote people from any of the Armed Forces who had been grievously harmed in combat and were undergoing rehabilitation at MTFs. Based on my data collection and analysis, this term also came to connote "amputee." By 2010 however, in response to patients and their advocates who regarded "Wounded Warrior" as an exclusive term that referred to only a segment of those who had been harmed during active duty, many people and mediated texts began to refer to SMs whose fitness has been adventitiously altered in an array of ways as "wounded," "ill," and "injured"; referring respectively to people who have been harmed in combat, people who have been harmed by disease, and people who have been harmed in, or by, accident(s) (S&NMIECS 2010).

While the genesis of these terms lay in an attempt to be inclusive of all active-duty SMs who have been harmed, as often – or perhaps always – happens, unexpected consequences unfolded, pivoting on a dynamic struggle between structure and agency (Ahearn 2001). I have found that as a result of, or in response to, this more recent rhetorical strategy, SMs who have suffered harm are categorized (by themselves and others) within an animated taxonomy that uses "wounded," "ill," and "injured" to distinguish provenances of harm, degrees of sacrifice and service, and levels of deservedness. By provenances I mean sources of harm: where and how harm occurs and is found – not just corporeo-cognitively, but also geo-physically, as in a combat zone for example; technologically, as in a truck rollover, or via an Improvised Explosive Device; and bio-medically, as in psychological health disorders, cancer, heart disease, or diabetes.

Theoretical Stance

To identify semiotic mechanisms at work in the terrain of an MTF, I use analytical and methodological tools plumbed from Critical Disabilities Studies (CDS) that examine constructions of fitness, power, and socio-cultural reproduction (Adkins 2003; Davis 2010; Ingstad and Whyte 1995; Lindenbaum and Lock 1993; Rapp and Ginsburg 2001; Shuttleworth and Kasnitz 2001). In these catchments, researchers problematize notions of disability and deservedness, positioning fitness and unfitness, and eligibility and ineligibility as textually and socially constructed notions that maintain forces and relations of power via normalization and naturalization. By "normalization" I am referring to foundational work done by critical scholars of stigma in which being (or claiming to be) normal is associated with and co-constitutes inclusion; and by "naturalization" I mean the process by which practices that are broadly condoned become so "obvious" that they also become unnoticed, are tacitly understood, and may remain unexamined (Ablon 1981; Althusser 1971; Brown 2010; Decena 2008; Fairclough 2003; Goffman 1959, 1963; Pêcheux 1982). Identifying, examining, and elucidating how normalization and naturalization occur among people within a space enables reflection, contestation, and equilibration. By expressing and examining usage of the apparently inclusive term "wounded, ill and injured," my respondents and I illuminate unanticipated yet powerful exclusionary work that its operationalization may be doing.

Critical Discourse Analysis (CDA), whose analytical method examines how, when, and in what form language, linguistic constructions, discourses, and texts emerge, are circulated, and gain consent (Fairclough 2003) also informed my scrutiny. CDA looks at processes that mobilize texts, which in turn reify and generate loyalty to perceived conditions and instantiations of sexuality, gender, class, age, and ability.

CDA's scrutiny of talk and text (Abu-Lughod and Lutz 1990) enables the study of meanings and perceptions. CD analysts believe that language is not powerful in and of itself, but is imbued with power as a result of who uses it, how it is used, and the context within which this usage takes place. Discourses do not merely reflect social practices but also constitute or construct them. CDA requires paying attention to specific words, phrases, and locutions, and their relationship within socio-cultural and spatio-temporal contexts. CDA scholarship offers a useful and productive toolkit of methods and analyses that link the textual and the social; and that has been somewhat overlooked within medical research generally, and within research regarding rehabilitation at MTFs in particular (Smith 2007). Its significance for my work lies both in indexing the origins and reproduction of generative discursive mechanisms; and more pointedly, in the (usually) unintended, uneven, and perhaps unjust material and existential consequences that flow from them. Based on what people tell me and what I observe during the course of my ongoing research, orders of deservedness at MTFs are sustained in discourses among SMs, their families, NMAs, and care providers; and these discourses have palpable consequences that are expressed, reflected, experienced, and upheld in spatio-temporal interactions (Howarth and Stavrakakis 2002).

Although points of view vary across their respective epistemological and ontological horizons, most CDA and CDS scholarship poses fundamental questions about eligibility, and offers insights that complicate tests for or measures of recognition and access to resources when these devices rely on ideas about fitness or ability. In turn these questions complicate notions about the ways in which constructions of ability and deservedness are instrumentalized or mediated in human interaction. The socio-cultural effects of these mediations have significance for people; they shape and determine the implementation, or absence, or co-option of socially just policies and practices that influence peoples' lived experience (Lindenbaum and Lock 1993).

In the last two decades' move towards patient-centered medicine within and outside the military, the burden of selecting, adhering to, and sustaining appropriate treatment and recovery regimens increasingly falls to individuals, families, and communities (IOM 2012; PPACA 2010). Underlying this shift in responsibility may be the assumption that patients have the recognition and access to resources that they need to make informed decisions about their own health management. This assumption may obviate the lived experience of people who are not considered eligible to receive and use privileged tools and technologies. Examining and deconstructing uneven if normalized aspects of lived experience among a group of people who are deemed as having been altered by wounds, illnesses, or injuries may help patients, health care providers, and policy makers identify and critically evaluate incommensurable recoveries (or un-recoveries). In turn, thresholds of "eligibility" may be re-examined, and unexpected consequences may be forecast, mitigated, or forestalled.

My ethnography at an MTF continues to show that unless asked and listened to, consociates in rehabilitation at an MTF may not notice or question aspects of their lived experience that could or should be managed differently. My research respondents frequently note (and my ethnographic data express) that civilian and military lives are "different," and that active duty and veteran status are different too; nonetheless, calls and support for bridging gaps between these cultures are burgeoning, including with respect to health care (Cohen 1998; FPCMHC 2012;

Gronke and Feaver 2001; Maddow 2012; PRC 2011; Szayna et al. 2007; USHCVA 2007). An MTF represents an unexpected yet appropriate and complex space for ethnographic inquiry about health care policy and practice; and more broadly, may address and offer insightful solutions for contemporary social concerns, including linkage between disability and deservedness, and misunderstanding between members of the military and civilians regarding equity.

Methodology

Research across the Military Health System (MHS) is conducted by a range of clinicians, social scientists (including anthropologists), therapists, and others (Barton 2008; Engel et al. 2014; Finley 2011; Gariti et al. 2009); in 2014 at Walter Reed over 1,000 active protocols were underway. Each of them was reviewed in three phases – scientific, administrative, and ethical – then approved and overseen under federal strictures regarding human protection. Because military personnel are generally considered vulnerable subjects due to the potential for their coercion, unique human protection guidelines exist for studies being conducted at DOD sites (CITI 2014; DODI 2011). Many studies at MTFs are multi-sited, including military and civilian investigators and participants; and are being conducted at local, regional, national, and even global scales. Their findings influence military medical policy and practice – and affect civilian medical care as well (Moskowitz 2013).

To conduct ethnographic research at Walter Reed, I submit proposals for review and approval in an online tracking system; and solicit letters of support from clinicians and administrators who consider the practical impact of the work I am planning, and permit access to spaces and people over whom they have responsibility. Once study protocols are approved and acknowledged, I recruit potential participants by typical ethnographic means, such as word of mouth, introductions by key influencers, flyers, and by identifying myself and my study aims to people with whom I have permission to mingle – for example, in clinics, eating spaces, recreation facilities, internal hallways, and pass-throughs; outside in gardens; or at events. In addition to the several badges I am required to wear every day at Walter Reed, when recruiting potential subjects I often wear a badge that is associated with the particular study underway, including the study's name and IRB approval number.

In order to receive IRB approval and letters of support I provide details about the people I seek to enroll, eligibility and exclusion criteria, the justification for their particular participation, the questions I will ask; the ways in which I will strive to ensure equal representation in sexuality, gender, class, age, and ability; and how my encounters will be empathetic and respectful. This discussion leads to and promotes interest in and support for the work I conduct: questions that anthropologists ask, and the ethnography we conduct, are persistently fascinating to ourselves and others because we are truly invested in listening to peoples' stories. At Walter Reed, my interest in how people regard themselves and are regarded by others after unexpected changes in their abilities consistently elicits more curiosity, support, and participation than disinterest or resistance. Other researchers have noted that qualitative research study participants report benefit from being able to freely discuss their experiences in a non-judgmental setting, by being seen as representatives of others like them, and by contributing knowledge that may help themselves or others like them (Taylor et al. 2010). When I screen people who are interested in participating, we talk about the fact that while they may not receive direct measurable personal benefit from participating in the study, the knowledge gained with their help will be used to comprehend experiences of wounded, ill, and injured SMs, care providers, families, and NMAs who are undergoing, supporting, or providing rehabilitation; and may positively impact military and civilian health care policy, practice, and patient experience.

In other words, as many anthropologists and ethnographers do, I seek approval for asking people to talk to me, for recording or noting their narratives, participating in or observing their activities, and collecting examples of material culture – objects – at my research site. To gather these data, I ask people in various spaces such as clinic waiting rooms, eating spaces, or events like Town Halls to share stories, or direct me to others who might. I provide my contact info and a flyer or postcard about the study, and inform them of its purposes and potential significance. I request that we conduct confidential interviews in spaces they may recommend that are secure, private, and comfortable in which I will record their comments (and mine). And, I ask people to point me to objects and media that they encounter, create, notice, react to, or wish for.

Findings

Since September 11, 2001, approximately 2,000 active duty SMs have become amputees; while upwards of 400,000 have been diagnosed as having comorbidities of Post-Traumatic Stress Disorder (PTSD), Traumatic Brain Injury (TBI), and Psychological Health issues (PH), and about 49,000 have become ill because of disease or have been injured in accidents (Fischer 2010; Magda et al. 2012; Tanielian and Jaycox 2008). I found that visibility of harm and recovery's attributes (such as missing limbs and prosthetics) appears to be linked with the degree of attention wounded, ill, and injured SMs receive; indeed, visibility and invisibility of harm endured in military service is the subject of much scholarship (Tanielian and Jaycox 2008). What may be under-examined are linkages between provenances (i.e. origins and sites) of harm, obvious and unobvious modes of rehabilitation, and subsequent levels of recognition and access to resources. My examinations reveal that differences in "membership" experiences may result from actions that valorize fitness and re-fitting as key elements of eligibility for recognition and access to resources; and consequences of cognitive, psychological, and physiological "unfitness" may include experiences of "dis-membering," including misallocation of particular modes of rehabilitation, and inappropriate assumptions about being able to return to duty.

SMs who have obviously been corporeally dismembered (i.e. have lost limbs or digits), may more readily experience re-membership during and after rehabilitation. Based on my research, people who are harmed in combat are regarded (and may regard themselves) as more deserving of recognition and access to resources than those who are harmed in accidents or by disease. Furthermore, visibly harmed SMs who are being visibly rehabilitated and whose harm originated in combat get more recognition and access to resources than SMs who are invisibly harmed; i.e. those whose harm (be it by accident, or by disease) originated during training or routine (non-combat) active duty and who are being invisibly rehabilitated (using drug regimens for example, or chemotherapy, or complementary alternative interventions such as acupuncture or meditation). My data indicate that SMs who are visibly harmed and understood to have been wounded in combat are selected to sign on to techno-scientific and athletic models of rehabilitation and appear to be recognized and rewarded in ways that others are not. Respondents inform me of kinds of recognition and access to resources, and I also observe mechanisms of inclusion and exclusion. For example, I notice (and study participants tell me) that people who use prosthetics, state-of-the-art transportation devices (such as Segways®), or service animals receive a lot of attention and praise; while some others who self-identify as having improved their ability to remember names and dates, or reduced their consumption of drugs, or are attaining better scores in cognitive measurements, are unnoticed – even disregarded.

Discussion

While qualitative research among civilian subject populations is routinely conducted by social scientists, particularly anthropologists and ethnographers, most studies about SMs have been conducted by scientists using quantitative methodologies (Moore et al. 2011; Oliffe 2005; Pope 2005). In turn, quantitative research about wounded, ill, and injured SMs often focuses on evaluation from the points of view of medical providers. Relatively little work that aggregates and analyzes qualitative data collected from the patient's perspective has been conducted with SMs who are participating in treatment and rehabilitation at MTFs. Moreover, most qualitative research regarding hospitals in general has focused on and collected data from service "providers" such as medical and therapeutic practitioners, rather than on service "consumers" (patients and their families); and some has privileged providers' points of view (Jennings et al. 2007; Rankin 2003).

Beyond their utility in challenging health care policies and practices for wounded, ill, and injured SMs, my ethnographic research findings may be significant to social justice advocacy for people elsewhere who are unintentionally relegated as undeserving – people who may be excluded or "dis-membered" by naturalized mechanisms of recognition and redistribution. Indeed those who are excluded may not only be dis-membered from their original affiliation as fit members of a specific group within a specific force: they also may not be "re-membered" in the same ways – or at all.

My data show that people at my site and in my studies are galvanized by having their stories heard, by co-identifying multivariate texts that convey powerful normalized messages, and by thinking about their own subjectivities differently. As an anthropologist at an MTF I can gather stories and observe practices in a space that expressly relies on signs and symbols, from a point of view that differs from those of SMs, their family members, care providers, and NMAs. Where my colleagues "see" routine practices, and implement or respond to naturalized policies, my interest in and training as an ethnographer, permit me to see the same data, i.e. the texts that we use and are surrounded by at Walter Reed, differently. In turn, by means of ethnography, study participants and colleagues are able to "see" themselves and their subjectivities – their lived experience – differently too.

Furthermore, my ethnography at an MTF helps us to understand that rehabilitation of wounded, ill, and injured SMs includes more than attending to their corporeal, cognitive, and affective recovery: Walter Reed is more than an MTF. It is also a medical refuge and a state of exception; a space-time in which harms are redressed and things lost and missing are reattached – not just limbs or cognition, but also attributes of membership. At this site consociates jointly work to re-member and rehabilitate both people and ideals such as sacrifice and service. As we solicit, contribute, share, and examine texts together, participants and colleagues find and note to me the remarkable and unremarkable, noticed and unnoticed ways in which their own and others' lived experiences differ and are changed when their fitness for duty is unexpectedly altered, their recovery regimens conferred, and their routines re-established depending on their status as wounded, ill, or injured. Together we find that the site, the source, and the visibility of the harm they have endured, and how their treatments plans are molded, may or may not engender marks of membership and equitable levels of recognition and access to resources.

The invisibility of some bodies whose wounds, illnesses, or injuries are unapparent or unintelligible may not draw "attention" to other consequences of active-duty military membership and service; e.g. disease, chronic pain, accidents, internal damage to organs and tissues, depression, loss of memory or impaired cognition, or suicidal ideation. Rehabilitative regimens and remediations for these "existentialities" and their exigencies may be under-recognized, overlooked, or disregarded; and their deservedness comparatively less valorized, even unredeemed. This is important to understand, as contemporary warfare, advanced modes of rehabilitation and re-integration, and the presence of militarization are felt in communities worldwide (Açiksöz 2012; Ben-Ari 2004; Gusterson 2007; Lutz 2009; Meekosha and Dowse 1997; Nordstrom 2004; Price 2008). In other words, the visible and invisible effects of war, and naturalized meanings of sacrifice and service continue to penetrate all walks and ways of life – socio-culturally, politico-economically, and with respect to health care. Wounds, illnesses, and injuries of war and military service affect SMs and civilians worldwide. The lived experience of rehabilitation at an MTF may differ to some extent from that of veterans and perhaps more so from civilians; yet I find that the span of disregard or erasure for those who cannot be "re-membered" for one reason or another, may be broadly under-recognized.

My ethnography at an MTF provides an example of applied theoretical anthropology. With the generous support of colleagues and research respondents, my participation and observation, interviews and surveys, data collection, and analyses demonstrate that constructions of ability and "dis"ability are socio-cultural as well as environmental; that the effects of these constructions are uneven and poorly understood; and that they require further research (Schneider and Ingram 2005). The lack of mutual knowledge and understanding between civilian and military cultures is divisive and costly at personal, familial, community, and national scales. Understanding the lived experience of military active duty, including rehabilitation, is important to bridging the gap between civilian and military cultures: members of the military are people who are the same and different from civilians, and vice versa. Garnering knowledge about the real and lasting effects of becoming wounded, ill, or injured – no matter the source or visibility – is critical to managing costs and consequences across widening politico-economic, bio-medical, and socio-cultural geographies in military and civilian terrains.

Acknowledgments

The author wishes to acknowledge the unflagging support of COL Sara Breckenridge-Sproat, LTC Meryia Throop, Dr Bonnie Jennings, and Dr Janice Agazio.

Note

1 Non-medical attendant (NMA) is a designation used within the US Armed Forces to signify a designated caregiver. Wounded, ill, and injured service members who are in rehabilitation at MTFs and who do not have or want immediate families (spouse or children for example) to support them in their recovery are permitted to designate other individuals as caregivers. By means of ethnography at Walter Reed in Washington D.C., Wool and Messinger (2011) capture trenchant aspects of NMAs' lived experience.

References

Ablon, Joan. 1981. "Stigmatized Health Conditions." *Social Science & Medicine. Medical Anthropology* B15(1):5–9.

Abu-Lughod, Lila, and Catherine A. Lutz. 1990. "Introduction: Emotion, discourse, and the politics of everyday life." In *Language and the Politics of Emotion: Studies in Emotion and Social Interaction*, edited by Catherine A. Lutz and Lila Abu-Lughod, 1–23. Cambridge: Cambridge University Press.

Açiksöz, Salih Can. 2012. "Sacrificial Limbs of Sovereignty: Disabled Veterans, Masculinity and Nationalist Politics in Turkey." *Medical Anthropology Quarterly* 26(1):4–25.

Adkins, William. 2003. "The Social Construction of Disability: A Theoretical Perspective," accessed August 25, 2009, www.allacademic.com/meta/p107285_index.html.

Ahearn, Laura M. 2001. "Language and Agency." *Annual Review of Anthropology* 30:109–137.

Althusser, Louis. 1971. *Lenin and Philosophy and Other Essays*. New York: Monthly Review Press.

Barton, Thomas David. 2008. "Understanding Practitioner Ethnography." *Nurse Researcher* 15(2):7–18.

Ben-Ari, Ayal. 2004. "Combat, Emotions, and the 'Enemy': Metaphors of Soldiering in a Unit of Israeli Infantry Reserves." In *Cultural Shaping of Violence*, edited by Myrdene Anderson, 165–178. West Lafayette, IN: Purdue University Press.

Benedict, Helen. 2009. "Testimony on Military Culture." Testimony before the House Committee on Oversight and Government Reform Subcommittee on National Security and Foreign Affairs. June 25, accessed October 12, 2009, http://nationalsecurity.over sight.house.gov/documents/20090625172502.

Bourdieu, Pierre. 2003. *Language and Symbolic Power*. Cambridge: Harvard University Press.

Brown, Lerita M. Coleman. 2010. "Stigma: An Enigma Demystified." In *The Disabilities Reader*, 3rd edition, edited by Lennard J. Davis, 179–192. Oxon and New York: Routledge.

Caravalho, Joseph Jr. 2011. "Dismounted Complex Blast Injury." Report of the Army Dismounted Complex Blast Injury Task Force. Prepared by the Dismounted Complex Blast Injury Task Force for the Army Surgeon General. Fort Sam Houston, TX. http://armym edicine.mil/Documents/DCBI-Task-Force-Report-Redacted-Final.pdf.

Chandler, Daniel. 2007. *Semiotics: The Basics*, 2nd edition. New York and London: Routledge.

CITI (Collaborative Institutional Training Initiative at the University of Miami). 2014. "Department of Defense National Capital Region Medical Directorate biomedical human protections requirements," accessed December 28, 2014, www.citiprogram.org/index. cfm?pageID=22.

Cohen, William. 1998. "Remarks at Ohio Wesleyan University Graduation. Delaware, OH, USA," accessed April 24, 2010, www.defense.gov/transcripts/transcript.aspx? transcriptid=1146.

Dahlberg, Karin, Nancy Drew, and Maria Nyström. 2002. *Reflective Lifeworld Research*. Lund, Sweden: Studentlitteratur.

Davis, Lennard J. 2010. "Constructing Normalcy." In *The Disabilities Reader*, 3rd edition, edited by Lennard J. Davis, 3–19. Oxon and New York: Routledge.

Decena, Carlos Ulises. 2008. "Tacit Subjects." *GLQ* 14(2–3):339–359.

DOD (US Department of Defense). 2005. "Department of Defense Base Closure and Realignment Report Volume 1; Part 2 of 2: Detailed Recommendations," accessed January 15, 2011, www.brac.gov.

DOD (US Department of Defense). 2013. "Department of Defense Task Force on the Care, Management, and Transition of Recovering Wounded, Ill, and Injured Members of The Armed Forces: Reference Handbook of Key Topics and Terms," accessed December 28, 2013, http://rwtf.defense.gov/Portals/22/Documents/Reference/fy2013reference.pdf.

DODI (US Department of Defense Instruction). 2009. "Department of Defense Instruction 1300.24. Recovery Coordination Program (RCP)," accessed July 13, 2011, www.dtic. mil/whs/directives/corres/pdf/130024p.pdf.

DODI (US Department of Defense Instruction) 2011. "Department of Defense Instruction 3216.02. Protection of Human Subjects and Adherence to Ethical Standards in DoD-Supported Research," accessed December 4, 2012, www.dtic.mil/whs/directives/corres/ pdf/321602p.pdf.

Engel, Charles C., Elizabeth H. Cordova, David M. Benedek, Xian Liu, Kristie L. Gore, Christine Goertz, Michael C. Freed, Cindy Crawford, Wayne B. Jonas, and Robert J. Ursano. 2014. "Building the Evidence Base for Complementary and Integrative Medicine Use among Veterans and Military Personnel." *Medical Care* 52(12), Suppl. 5.

Fairclough, Norman. 2003. *Analysing Discourse: Textual Analysis for Social Research*. New York: Routledge.

Finley, Erin P. 2011. *Fields of Combat: Understanding PTSD among Veterans of Iraq and Afghanistan*. Ithaca, NY: Cornell University Press.

Fischer, Hannah. 2010. "U.S. Military Casualty Statistics: Operation New Dawn, Operation Iraqi Freedom, and Operation Enduring Freedom." Congressional Research Service 7–5700 RS22452, accessed March 23, 2011, www.crs.gov.

FPCMHC (Federal Patient Centered Medical Home Collaborative). 2012. Catalogue of Federal Patient Centered Medical Home (PCMH) Activities as of October 2012, accessed August 23, 2014, pcmh.ahrq.gov/sites/default/files/attachments/DoD_PCMH_Activities_Public_Final%281%29.pdf.

Gariti, Katherine O., Leila Sadeghi, Sowmya D. Joisa, and William C. Holmes. 2009. "Veterans' Distress Related to Participation in a Study About Detainee Abuse." *Military Medicine* 174:1149–1154.

Goffman, Erving. 1959. *The Presentation of Self in Everyday Life*. New York: Anchor Books Doubleday.

Goffman, Erving. 1963. *Stigma: Notes on the Management of Spoiled Identity*. New York: Simon and Schuster.

Gronke, Paul and Peter D. Feaver. 2001. "Uncertain Confidence: Civilian and Military Attitudes about Civil–Military Relations." Paper prepared for the Triangle Institute for Security Studies "Project on the Gap Between the Military and Civilian Society," Peter D. Feaver and Richard Kohn, Co-Principal Investigators, pp. 1–41.

Gusterson, Hugh. 2007. "Anthropology and Militarism." *Annual Review of Anthropology* 36:155–175.

Howarth, D., and Yannis Stavrakakis. 2002. "Introducing discourse theory and political analysis." In *Discourse Theory and Political Analysis: Identities, Hegemonies, and Social Change*, edited by David Howarth, Aletta J. Norval, and Yannis Stavrakakis, 1–23. Manchester and New York: Manchester University Press.

Ingstad, Benedicte, and Susan Reynolds Whyte. 1995. "Disability and Culture: An Overview." In *Disability and Culture*, edited by Benedicte Ingstad and Susan Reynolds Whyte, 3–32. Berkeley: University of California Press.

IOM (Institute of Medicine). 2012. *Best Care at a Lower Cost: The Path to Continuously Learning Health Care in America*. Washington, D.C.: National Academies Press.

Jennings, B.M., S.L. Heiner, L.A. Loan, E.A. Hemman, and K.M. Swanson. 2007. "What Really Matters to Healthcare Consumers." *Journal of Nursing Administration* 35(4):173–180.

Johnstone, Barbara. 2008. *Discourse Analysis*, 2nd Edition. Malden, MA: Blackwell Publishing.

Krull, Heather, and Matthew Tyler Haugseth. 2012. *Health and Economic Outcomes in the Alumni of the Wounded Warrior Project*. Santa Monica, CA: RAND.

Lancaster, Roger. 2003. *The Trouble with Nature*. Berkeley: University of California Press.

Leap, William. 2003. "Language and Gendered Modernity." In *The Handbook of Language and Gender*, edited by Janet Holmes and Miriam Meyerhoff, 401–422. London: Blackwell.

Leap, William. 2004. "Language, Belonging, and (Homo)sexual Citizenship in Cape Town, South Africa." In *Speaking in Queer Tongues: Globalization and Gay Language*, edited by William Leap and Tom Boellstroff, 134–162. Urbana: University of Illinois Press.

Leone, Mark P. 2005. "Landscapes of Power." In *The Archaeology of Liberty in an American Capital: Excavations in Annapolis*, 63–110. Berkeley, Los Angeles, London: University of California Press.

Lindenbaum, Shirley, and Margaret Lock. 1993. "Preface." In *Knowledge, Power and Practice: The Anthropology of Medicine and Everyday Life*, edited by Shirley Lindenbaum and Margaret Lock, ix–xv. Berkeley and Los Angeles: University of California Press.

Lutz, Catherine. 2009. "Anthropology in an Era of Permanent War." *Anthropologica* 511:367–379.

Maddow, Rachel. 2012. *Drift: The Unmooring of American Military Power*. New York: Random House.

Magda, Jean-Louis, Greg Linch, Whitney Fetterhoff, and Mary Hadar. 2012. "Afghanistan War Deaths." *The Washington Post*. September 2, 2012, A14, accessed September 6, 2012, http://apps.washingtonpost.com/national/fallen.

McRuer, Robert. 2006. *Crip Theory*. New York: New York University Press.

Meekosha, Helen, and Leanne Dowse. 1997. "Enabling Citizenship." In *Feminist Review*. No. 57. Autumn, edited by Pnina Werbner and Nira Yuval-Davis, 49–72. New York: Routledge

Messinger, Seth. 2010. "Getting Past the Accident; Explosive Devices, Limb Loss, and Refashioning a Life in a Military Medical Center." *Medical Anthropology Quarterly* 24(3):281–303.

Moore, M., D. Brown, N. Money, and M. Bates. 2011. *Mind–Body Skills for Regulating the Autonomic Nervous System. Version 2*. Defense Centers of Excellence for Psychological Health and Traumatic Brain Injury, Arlington, VA: DCoE Publications.

Moskowitz, Eric. 2013. "Hospital Visit Inspires Marathon Amputee J.P. Norden," accessed August 23, 2014, www.bostonglobe.com/metro/2013/06/15/hospital-visit-inspires-marathon-amputee-norden/ctWhYEi3BYKL1FC30GpFCM/story.html.

Nordstrom, Carolyn. 2004. *Shadows of War: Violence, Power, and International Profiteering in the Twenty-First Century*. Berkeley: University of California Press.

Oliffe, John. 2005. "Why Not Ethnography?" *Urologic Nursing* 25(5):395–399.

Pêcheux, Michel. 1982. "The Subject Form of Discourse in the Subjective Appropriation of Scientific Knowledges and Political Practice." In *Language, Semantics and Ideology*, 155–170. New York: St. Martin's Press.

Pincus, Walter. 2012. "A Window on the Wounded." *The Washington Post*, April 6, A11.

Pope, Catherine. 2005. "Conducting Ethnography in Medical Settings." *Medical Education* 39:1180–1187.

PPACA (Patient Protection and Affordable Care Act). 2010, accessed December 5, 2014, http://housedocs.house.gov/energycommerce/ppacacon.pdf.

PRC (Pew Research Center). 2011. *The Military–Civilian Gap: War and Sacrifice in the Post-9/11 Era*, accessed August 23, 2014, www.pewsocialtrends.org/files/2011/10/veterans-report.pdf.

Price, David. 2008. "Inside the Minerva Consortium: Social Science in Harness." Published in CounterPunch.org, June 24, accessed July 13, 2008, www.counterpunch.org/price06252008.html.

Rankin, J.M. 2003. "'Patient Satisfaction': Knowledge for Ruling Hospital Reform – An Institutional Ethnography." *Nursing Inquiry* 10(1):57–65.

Rapp, Rayna, and Faye Ginsburg. 2001. "Enabling Disability; Rewriting Kinship, Reimagining Citizenship." *Public Culture* 13(3):533–556.

Schneider, Anne L., and Helen M. Ingram. 2005. *Deserving and Entitled: Social Constructions and Public Policy*, edited by Anne L. Schneider and Helen M. Ingram. Albany, NY: State University of New York Press.

Shuttleworth, Russell P., and Devva Kasnitz. 2001. "Introduction: Anthropology in Disability Studies." *Disability Studies Quarterly* Summer 21(3):2–17.

Smith, J.L. 2007. "Critical Discourse Analysis for Nursing Research." *Nursing Inquiry* 14(1):60–70.

S&NMIECS (Smithsonian & Navy Medicine Institute Ethics Conference Series). 2010. "Wounded Warrior Care Panel Testimony." National History Museum. Washington, D.C., April 28, accessed February 4, 2011, http://nmvaa.org/nmi/media/category.php?cat=healthcare.

Soja, Edward W. 2003. "Writing the City Spatially." *City* 7(3):269–280.

Szayna, Thomas S., Kevin F. McCarthy, Jerry M. Sollinger, Linda J. Demaine, Jefferson P. Marquis, and Brett Steele. 2007. *The Civil–Military Gap in the United States: Does It Exist, Why, and Does It Matter?* Santa Monica, CA: RAND.

Tanielian, Terri, and Lisa H. Jaycox. 2008. *Invisible Wounds of War: Psychological and Cognitive Injuries, Their Consequences, and Services to Assist Recovery*, edited by Terri Tanielian and Lisa H. Jaycox. Santa Monica, CA: RAND.

Taylor, P.J.M., Awenat, Y.M., Gooding, P., Johnson, J.B., Pratt, D., Wood, A., and Tarrier, N. 2010. "The Subjective Experience of Participation in Schizophrenia Research: A Practical and Ethical Issue." *The Journal of Nervous and Mental Diseases* 198(5):343–348.

USAPS (US Army Posture Statement). 2008. "Information Papers: U.S. Army Wounded Warrior Program," accessed November 26, 2010, www.army.mil/aps/08/informationpapers/sustain/US_Wounded_Warrrior_Program.

USHCVA (US House Committee on Veterans' Affairs). 2007. "Full Committee Findings of the President's Commission on Care for America's Returning Wounded Warriors," accessed July 17, 2010, www.gpo.gov/fdsys/pkg/CHRG-110hhrg39452/pdf/CHRG-110hhrg39452.pdf.

VA (US Department of Veterans Affairs). 2011. "Federal Recovery Coordination Program." VA Pub 0802, accessed August 2, 2011, www.va.gov/vapubs/viewPublication.asp?Pub_ID=537&FType=2.

Wool, Zoë, and Seth Messinger. 2011. "Labors of Love: The Transformation of Care in the Non-Medical Attendant Program at Walter Reed Army Medical Center." *Medical Anthropology Quarterly New Series* 26(1):26–48.

Woolhandler, Stephanie. 2007. "Uninsured Veterans: A Stain on America's Flag," accessed November 12, 2015, www.pnhp.org/PDF_files/Woolhandler_Veterans_Testimony.pdf.

WWP (Wounded Warrior Project). 2011. accessed October 11, 2013, www.woundedwarriorproject.org.

3

NAVIGATING THE BOUNDARIES OF AN ANTHROPOLOGICAL EDUCATION IN A NONPROFIT WORLD

Chelsey Dyer

Over a one-and-a-half-year period I worked at two nonprofits, Witness for Peace Southeast (WFPSE), a small international nonprofit that focuses on human rights issues created by United States military and economic intervention in Latin America, and a large environmental organization in Australia, Greenpeace Australia Pacific (GPAP). Though the organizations differed in size, location, and interests, my work at both generated similar queries about how anthropology can be used outside of the academic setting. However, for both roles with the nonprofits, I was not hired as an anthropologist. Instead, it was assumed that my anthropological learnings would bolster my work and creativity throughout the job. I hoped this would hold true. Nonetheless, with both positions I struggled to determine how my studies would amplify my work, as little I learned in school spoke directly to working outside of the field of academia.

My story begins in 2013 when I graduated with a master's in anthropology from George Mason University. When I began graduate school I wanted to use my anthropological education to work from within the US government and better international relationships. My master's was aimed to buttress my passion for humane US policies with the knowledge, skills, and qualifications necessary to pursue my goal, which, simply put, was to help people.

However, as my education continued I quickly decided that I was uncomfortable working within an institution in which the results of my research could be taken piecemeal and used to justify already existing policies that needed alterations. I adhere to the notion that all anthropological work should be published publicly. And so, I decided I wanted to pressure the system from the outside instead of working within it. Getting my master's in anthropology to "further my career" was not about increasing my salary (though I hoped this would be a happy side-effect), it was intended to assist me in finding my niche in the world, to make my daily life more meaningful through an education that gave me the skills and knowledge to make a sustainable change in the ills of the world – specifically the impacts of US militarization in Latin America. Throughout my struggle to find my career, I have slowly learned that my career does not define me. I define my career. My passion, my interests, my love and knowledge of anthropology, and my own need to have a job that I feel pays earth and humankind for my existence, defines what I do.

As I child I always sought as much information about a situation as I could gather. I knew there was always more than one side of a story, usually more than two or three. As an adult, this impetus transferred over into a passion for anthropology's holistic nature. I have always wanted answers, but not the simple ones, the complex, tangled, gray, and messy answers that reflect the veracity of life. To me, anthropology's power lies in its ability to provide these answers, answers that can bring new perspectives to policy debates, social movements, and anything and everything in-between. Anthropology was not just a degree, it was a tool to help me find a career that fills a personal need for meaning, a meaning that I contrasted and nourished throughout my time in the nonprofit field.

The experiences I encountered in the nonprofit world helped me establish my own rules of conduct and ethical protocols as an anthropologist. However, more questions were also created. Is there a uniform definition of anthropology, or is it based on individual application? Where does anthropology end and the nonprofit business world begin? This chapter explores what many graduates and students are keen to know. What is the job hunt like in the nonprofit industry post-graduation? Does an anthropology degree help you find employment in a nonprofit? How do you use your degree at your job? I will relate my personal and professional journey as I exited graduate school, sought nonprofit employment, and arrived at two positions in nonprofit organizations in which I sought to define what anthropology was to me while reconciling the sometimes rigid academic structures of thinking, discourse, and methodology into existing worldviews of nonprofit organizations.

Barriers and Decisions

A few months after my graduation in 2013, with fresh ideas and a desperate pressure to find lucrative employment to pay off my loans, I was left questioning the value of my degree more often than I would like to admit. I knew it was of great personal worth, it allowed me to expand my theoretical understandings and the conceptual framework of my worldview in a myriad of ways. Research has shown that anthropology masters' degrees provide high job satisfaction ratings (Fiske et al. 2010), and in 2012 anthropology was ranked as the second best job for women by *Forbes Magazine* (2012). Yet, I wondered how my degree would help me *find* a job. I was less worried about job satisfaction and more about potential employability. I wanted a job and I wanted to practice anthropology, but I wasn't sure if I could achieve both. Throughout my job search I continued to wonder, if I obtained a job in the nonacademic sectors that advertised for anthropological skills and knowledge, was I still practicing anthropology? Was I still an anthropologist?

I was led to anthropology late in my undergraduate career after focusing on a biological science major for my first three years. While I studied about disease and mechanisms of the body I found myself more interested in the social conditions that perpetuated continual illness, or how doctors dealt with cultural differences in the emergency room. I turned to anthropology because it offered a more holistic explanation, and within its explanation I felt I could find more sustainable solutions to socio-cultural problems like poverty, educational divides, and militarization. Though I chose to pursue a master's because I felt it would provide me with the tools necessary for a career outside of academia, my enjoyment of teaching and research led me to want to continue on to a PhD. However, before I continued with school I wanted to keep on with my education outside of an academic environment. I was keen to do more than write about my research findings, I wanted to apply them in real-world situations, and I could not find an avenue in academia that allowed me to do so.

As anthropologists, we are trained to be objective observers and uninfluential participants. We are not taught how to convey knowledge, unburdened from jargon, to the general public, or organize the population to campaign for change. I wanted to go beyond institutionally sanctioned areas of learning. I wanted to galvanize the public, and create interest among laypeople, not just students. I wanted to show how useful anthropology could be, and I felt I could not do this inside academia. I was committed to influencing change, but I needed the skills and a platform that academia could not provide. When searching for suitable candidates in academia, hiring committees search for those who have published, taught, and researched. There is less of an emphasis on how you have used your research to impact and educate others outside of the academic field. Contrastingly, when searching for work in the nonprofit arena, employers want to know how you have used your skills. Following my master's graduation, I felt limited by academia's expectations and empowered by the nonprofit sector. I loved learning, but I felt learning for the simple pleasure of knowledge and publishing was selfish and unfulfilling. Turning to advocacy through a nonprofit was not my default option after graduate school. It was my progression as an anthropologist. I wanted to use my academic skills in an applied setting, and one day use the knowledge I gained from both environments to create what I never found in academic anthropology – a platform that connects with the public and advocates for holistic solutions to complex socio-cultural and economic issues. And thus while sustaining these beliefs and hopes, job hunting began.

The Hunt

The American Anthropological Association's (2012) website states that "it is a great time to become an anthropologist" because of the growing job market. In addition, The US Department of Labor (Bureau of Labor Statistics 2012) projects "faster than average" job growth from 2012 to 2022 for anthropological positions with an average salary of $57,420 per year. However, the Department of Labor also warns that anthropology's small field indicates that though significant job growth is projected, it only equates to an additional 1,400 jobs. Congruently, competition will be fierce. After a solid year of job hunting, pre- and post-graduation I found advertised anthropological jobs were more common in larger cities and were fraught with competition. However, most noticeably, I discerned that many jobs that might favor anthropological knowledge or methodology fall outside the characterizations of the discipline.

Despite my hesitations, I was one of many anthropology graduates seeking employment outside of the academy. Following a Durkheimian (Durkheim, Mauss, and Needham 1963) nature to categorize, our expanding field has separated and defined different types of nonacademic anthropology under distinct headings: applied, engaged, and more recently "practicing anthropologists" (Borofsky 2000; Mullins 2011; Rylko-Bauer, Singer, and Van Willigen 2006; Singer 2000). Though anthropology has been engaging with the nonacademic market since World War II, as anthropologists elucidated the ethical issues of working outside of the academy (issues such as spying, transparency, and informed consent – made apparent during World War II), the application of anthropology became suspect (Price 2002). Despite this history, in the 1980s an increasing number of anthropology graduates began to enter the nonacademic market. Today the trend has continued and been exacerbated by competition in the academic job market and higher wages offered elsewhere. Now it is estimated that there are more anthropologists working outside academia than within it (Nolan 2013).

Admittedly, at the time of my job hunt I was less concerned about what "type" of anthropology I was practicing – applied, engaged or practicing – and more focused on finding paid employment that fit within my ethical standards. I wanted a job in which I could use my anthropological skills, that was working towards a cause (whether environmental or human rights), and that would teach me new skills that I could not learn in academia. Accordingly, I focused much of my time searching job sites that were targeted towards individuals who desired a career in the not-for-profit sector.

Witness for Peace Southeast

On searching targeted jobs sites geared towards social engagement careers, like Indeed.com, I found a variety of positions that valued an anthropologist's knowledge or methodology, or requested an anthropologist specifically. However, what motivated many of these requests was often a misunderstanding of what anthropology is. Anthropology has entered a new sphere of public and professional involvement, but it is no longer sensationalized or popularized by mainstream academics like Margaret Mead. This lack of visibility coupled with the humanities' decreased social value, has left a void in public and employer knowledge of what anthropology is and the skills it teaches potential employees. As such, outside of academic positions, employers who might advertise for anthropologists or value an anthropological degree have a job description that is not anthropological at all.

However, my time spent with Witness for Peace Southeast (WFPSE), a small international nonprofit that had a regional office in Raleigh, North Carolina, bolstered my conviction that I wished to remain in the nonprofit field. I began volunteering with WFPSE while I was in school. I progressed to their board of directors about six months later. Following my graduate research, I visited Colombia with the organization and was able to see local communities and speak with individuals who are typically off-limits to tourists due to safety concerns. While in Colombia, I was confronted with my own privilege of US citizenry. Because of their class, status, race, and ethnicity, the concerns and struggles of those we spoke with in Colombia were devalued and silenced by the Colombian and US governments. Evolutionist assumptions of US superiority automatically imbued my voice with more resonance, more power. Yet, I didn't want to speak on behalf of Colombians. Their voices, their stories were what I found most empowering and inspiring to myself and others. I did not want to take that away. Instead, I desired to be a microphone, and not let my privilege cloak their voices.

My work with WFPSE was my first attempt to use my anthropological knowledge and skills to further a social and political cause – just US policies in Latin America. The small size of the organization and a dearth of funders meant my work there was unpaid. So whilst completing my thesis and volunteering my time, I continued to search for paid work. During my time with WFPSE I worked at a local office within the US and remotely from Australia. Though the organization is a nationally known nonprofit, with international team members placed throughout Latin America, the regional office in Raleigh, North Carolina consists of only one paid staff member and a host of volunteers and board members whose responsibilities are often congruent to those of paid staff at larger organizations. The small size of the organization lent a unique passion to our work. I was often overcome with frustration at our inability to mobilize more individuals to our cause – just US economic and military policies throughout Latin America. However, the size of our workforce also decreased the bureaucratic melee and opaque transparency that other organizations face. Furthermore, my role as both a board member and worker gave me a unique view of how the organization functioned and of my role within its operations.

In my work within the organization I began managing the Facebook page and drafting a campaign that would focus on the impact of US policies in Colombia. As a small organization, our needs were intertwined with our mission. Likewise, many of our actions had multi-faceted goals – fundraising was meant to grow the capacity of our campaigns and vice versa. WFPSE relies on a primary model of engagement called "transformative witnessing." The organization sends groups of US citizens on delegations across Latin America to witness the economic, social, political, and personal impacts of policies crafted and enforced by US officials. Our model of change is based on the idea that individuals will be so stirred by what they witness on a delegation, that they are unable to return to the US and continue to remain apathetic. Personally, it worked for me. After one delegation I was hooked. Yet, one of the organization's greatest weaknesses was maintaining a relationship with past delegates, keeping them energized, and mobilizing others who were unable to go on delegations. I stayed active within the organization by contacting them and requesting or creating work to help the mission.

I was never hired for my positions within the organization. In many ways I weaseled my way in, learning as I went. Many of my first hours there were spent completing tasks that my anthropology degree did not prepare me for. Writing Facebook posts, editing fundraising appeals, planning events – these aren't things that are taught in class, they are skills you have to learn by doing. Yet, my anthropological training gave me the skills to think critically about how my tasks within the organization connected to our supporters, and gave me fluency in more than one area of work. For example, when I began work on the organization's Facebook page I crafted and disseminated a supporter survey broadly asking those who were interested in the organization what drew them to Witness for Peace, what their personal experience with the organization was, and what types of topics they enjoyed reading about. Had I had more time and resources I would have developed a plan to speak individually with supporters, taken life histories, and implemented focus groups to gather more thorough information. I did not want to simply post information, I wanted to develop a real relationship with supporters while maintaining a carefully crafted message in each post. After about a year, I had increased the page's "likes" by 350%. Without my anthropology training I would not have ruminated and continued to develop creative channels to engage with and understand the organization and its supporters from a fundraising, campaign, and marketing perspective. The structure of the organization, its need for support, and the altruism of those who already worked there allowed me to elbow my way in and make a space for myself. Not only was this something that would supplement my resume, it was an experience that furthered my personal and anthropological growth, and my anthropological knowledge advanced my experience. Anthropology empowered me to think critically about each task I was assigned. As with running the organization's Facebook page, I did not embark on new tasks without thoroughly researching them and how to make them successful. It is difficult to say if I completed the tasks differently or even better than others. I have no comparator, only my own success. However, I can say for certain that anthropology allowed me a greater scope of involvement. My anthropologically driven, thoughtful and thorough approach to each activity allowed me to engage in more areas of the organization. Instead of being inhibited by a more targeted degree, like marketing, I was empowered and able to apply my skills across all fields, from marketing, to communications, to community organizing.

Though I learned how to apply my anthropological knowledge at WFPSE, while in school there was not a class on "applying anthropological learnings in a non-academic job." Although the program at George Mason did not have an applied anthropology focus at the time I attended, the faculty recognized that most students exiting the program would not continue on to academia, but would enter the workforce (and as of 2015 are making adjustments to suit students with applied and academic interests). With more students than in the history of the discipline progressing on to nonacademic jobs post-graduation, the differentiation between specifically applied and academic-geared programs should be unified into one coherent program. After all, each feeds into the other. Despite my lack of formal training in applying my learnings, I subconsciously turned to more humanistic approaches during my work at WFPSE, sending surveys to our supporters about how they viewed the organization, using focus groups and interviews, and strategies more people-centric than number focused. However, the organization's limited capacity and my eager spirit still left me feeling as though I wanted to do more. I felt my suggestions were those a marketing student, communications major, or sociology instructor might make, but they did not have the roots in anthropology that I so valued. At the time, I was correct. My observations and understanding of the organization were still in their nascent phases. I felt that because I could not interview supporters and those we were in solidarity with that I could not help. I was wrong.

Unknowingly, I was in the field the entire time. The office was my field, the organization and how it operated was my study. Slowly, I realized that to increase the impact of the nonprofit I had to understand how the organization's components interacted with one another, not just how the organization interacted with the public. I only grasped this idea when I stopped searching for answers and purely observed, learned, and waited for a path to reveal itself. I was using my anthropological skills all along, and anthropology led me to my most exciting recommendation to the organization. A month after writing this chapter, per my suggestion, I will be leading a new strategic development and organizational restructure workshop with the Board of Directors.

Greenpeace Australia Pacific

While working with Witness for Peace Southeast I did not find another paying position that interested me in Raleigh. I have no doubt that had I been living in Washington, D.C., San Francisco, or another large city, positions of interest would have been manifold. Providentially, in early 2014 I was presented with a personal opportunity to move to Sydney, Australia. One might see it as the perfectly placed love story intermingled in a journey of personal and career-centered discovery – if life were like a movie. However, life is more multi-faceted than can fit on a big screen, and moving to Sydney, though tempered with the excitement of being with the one you love and surrounded by kangaroos, was a challenging relocation for someone such as myself who finds comfort and security in small-town familiarity (how ironic for an anthropologist). In April 2014, I began the job hunt afresh in a new economic, socio-political, and cultural environment. Though I did not arrive in Australia until June, I anticipated several months of job searching. Similar to my search in the States, I used job sites that were geared towards individuals searching for nonprofit work, including Idealist.com and Ethicaljobs.com.au. My career intentions remained the same. If I was not working in academia, I would work in the nonprofit field. However, my visa only allowed me to work with an organization for up to six months at a time. This limited my options, as many companies were only hiring for permanent positions and did not want to sponsor a foreign migrant when there were a myriad of Australian residents equally qualified for the role. Thankfully, anthropology imbued in me skills that were of equal value in most locations. In a sense, my studies globalized my work skills for an increasingly global market. Judy Tso (2013) outlines core competencies required across today's globalized job market. They are:

- Cultural competency – understanding global and international markets and cross-cultural systems
- Understanding complex systems
- Strategic and analytic ability
- Ability to work across disciplines
- Ability to work inductively and from a customer perspective
- Training in ethnographic research methods

I found all of these in anthropology. Yet, while job searching I struggled to communicate the value of the discipline to potential employers. Congruently, Tso emphasizes the importance of "communicating the value of anthropology" to employers by highlighting how your training encompasses these traits. While my anthropological training certainly endowed me with each of the aforementioned skills, to most employers I still lacked the basic professional experience that is increasingly a key facet of today's hirability quotient. So, I continued to apply to a multitude of positions in Sydney, but meanwhile vowed to find employment with Greenpeace Australia Pacific (GPAP) before I left. I was in awe of the size and operating model of the organization, and desired to get more involved to understand how it maintained persistent growth while WFPSE floundered.

Greenpeace is an international environmental nonprofit, well-known for taking non-violent direct action against corporations or governments that pursue environmentally devastating policies. At the time I was in Australia, the Australia office's campaigns focused on climate change, protecting the Great Barrier Reef, and ending fossil fuel energy dependence. Admiration, curiosity, and a dogmatic intent on achieving my goal drew me to apply for four roles with GPAP. After interviewing for two different positions, I was finally granted a position as a "Project Assistant," a largely administrative role.

I accepted the job because I wanted to work for GPAP no matter what the title. However, after the post-hiring glow wore off, I found myself struggling with feelings of frustration over my employability. Six months after graduation and $75,000 in debt, I was discouraged and scared. I had wanted my master's degree to propel me past this introductory role and into a more advanced position where I felt I was adequately challenged. However, I, like many employers, devalued my skills. Though I felt my degree did not matter because I was still in an introductory role, I had blatantly ignored the reality of today's job market in which experience is a key factor in an employer's decision to hire potential candidates. While at first this reality proved infuriating, later it showed its usefulness in allowing me to better acquaint myself with the organization and its operations before advancing. An anthropologist in a foreign land would not immediately participate in a cultural ceremony, but would observe, question, and learn first. By accepting an introductory role in the organization I unknowingly allowed myself time to learn more about how my skills could benefit their mission. In addition, though my master's degree did not immediately elevate me to a higher position, it did allow me to advance faster.

While WFPSE's office housed one full-time person in a tiny room rented from a church, GPAP filled two floors of a bustling office with about sixty permanent, part-time, and contract employees. Arguably the impact of their campaigns was significantly larger than that of WFPSE. I was keen to learn how they operated and apply what information I could glean to the fragile WFPSE office. Along with thorough introductions to each of the departments, during my second week of work I was called into a "coffee and cake" meeting with the CEO. Here, around a small wooden table with chocolate pastries and coffee I'd made using a "plunger" (one of many Australian specialties) I and several other new starters discussed our passions with the CEO while he explained his role in the organization. After the meeting, as the CEO and I walked back to our desks amidst the hum of whirring computers and quiet discussions, he highlighted that he was interested in any feedback I had to give about the organization and suggestions for its improvement. He mentioned that my "fresh eyes" untainted by memory, history, and interactions with the organization, combined with my anthropological mind would surely have some insights. "I mean, that's what you do anyway, you study people!" I settled into my desk, a hint of red crawling up my neck to my cheeks, and proceeded to evaluate what I had so far observed. I felt honored. The CEO recognized the value of my anthropological skills. Yet, intermingled with the naïve pride, was also a feeling of pressure. After only two weeks I felt as though I needed to deliver some grand observation about the organization, and if not then, then certainly sometime during the rest of my employment. I did not even know where all the meeting rooms were yet, let alone the intricacies of how a complex organization operated and what needed to change. When I began writing this chapter I had worked there six months, and I still did not feel able to give a recommendation about how the organization should function. And yet, because I am an anthropologist, for just a moment I thought I should have immediate answers. I should know more in a shorter period of time. I should have great ideas about how to fix things.

I realized that the CEO and I had different conceptions of what anthropology was. My definition was still fluctuating, growing as I decided on what type of anthropologist I wanted to be, and constantly influenced by other's assumptions of what it was. This conversation lit a spark in my mind. I worked for one organization (WFPSE) in which my anthropological skills were not acknowledged and where I felt arrogant to even mention them; and for another organization in which my skills were over-estimated. I realized, if I were to practice anthropology I first needed to clarify what the discipline meant to me. After all, what is anthropology?

And most importantly, how can I better explain it to others? I could not answer the latter question until I answered the former for myself.

Because of my work in the nonprofit sector I now know what anthropology is *to me* and I use my understanding of it to explain it to others, using one of the favorite anthropological tools: thick description. Rattling off a book definition usually does not resonate with someone who possesses the most basic understanding of the discipline. Instead, I found using your own experience, complementing the definition with how it is applied in real life, and how you have used it, helps co-workers, friends, and family expel their own conceptions and absorb yours. There is no "one-size-fits-all" way to explain anthropology, but I have found that people understand my passion and my application more than any rote definition I have to offer.

What Is Anthropology?

So what is anthropology to me? It is an amalgam of zooming in and zooming out on the minutiae of life, connecting the dots, asking questions that are answered with more questions. It is observing. It is participating without judgment. It is writing and explaining what you see. It is seeing all of humankind as equals while being fascinated by our differences. It is everyday and it can be in everything. But, academia did not teach me this. My experiences in the nonprofit world did.

When I began my anthropological office work, my subconscious was still ingrained with the trite stereotype of anthropologists conducting fieldwork in a foreign land or community, not in the stiff comfort of an office chair. Yet, slowly, I learned by doing. At first I was just a new employee, a new traveler in a foreign land, but over time I became an anthropologist. The office became my Trobriand Islands. I became immersed in the culture and impassioned by new discoveries. I learned the unique language, social networks, hierarchies, values, and history of GPAP and WFPSE. I developed clearer pictures of how the organizations operated. And over time, I realized that if I wanted to effect change in the wider world, perhaps I first needed to learn about the organization that was trying to enact it. Like all anthropology, this process takes time and lies in the fluidity of the organization.

However, my position at GPAP allowed me access to multiple facets of the organization and permitted me to learn more. I took minutes in a variety of meetings, from confidential management meetings to organization-wide strategy meetings. After each meeting I was tasked with clarifying my notes and distributing them to meeting attendees. Such a simple duty was often surprisingly challenging and enlightening. I had to learn to properly recap information without eliminating any aspect of the speaker's message while also grappling with terms and information that I did not know or understand. While doing this for both management and general staff I slowly learned how people conceptualized the organization, and of divides in thought between management and staff.

"Let's Go Save the World"

Sitting around a small wooden desk before a meeting a few co-workers and I engaged in casual conversation. I sat down and was asked by my supervisor "what I would do if I wasn't saving the world." I hesitated, confused, and returned the question to those at the table. Replies of "working with animals and teaching" came back to me followed by laughs and a "but the world won't save itself so I'm here." And I realized that to them working at Greenpeace was a calling to literally save the world, the planet, from destructive human practices. This huge, empowering, and crushing thought was at the crux of most disagreements I saw within the organization. The majority agreed on the mission, but a consensus had yet to be found on how to accomplish it, especially between management and staff.

About five months into my time at GPAP I found myself taking minutes in a Finance Committee meeting of the Board of Directors. The organization had been going through a transitional period in which new roles were being created and old roles where being discarded. Naturally, this had created tension amongst many of the employees who chafed at the prospect of change, were disheartened at losing long-time colleagues, and were wondering about their own job security. This was a half-day long meeting in which the financial motivations for some of the recent disturbing decisions were being discussed. About ten of us were seated around a twenty-five-person table. The room was long, thin, and windowless with walls decorated with posters of the smiling faces of activists on boats and atop buildings basking in the success of their missions. Though the table was long and the room the biggest in the office, the lack of windows and the sparse air filtering through an aircon unit on one wall made the space seem distinctly airless and dense. One half-day of talking about GPAP's finances was an adequate amount of time for one's brain to drift off into a dense fog. I sat in the middle of the table with the committee members, the Chief Operating Officer, and the CEO surrounding me. I was flanked by power. The meeting began with a brief opening and then the board secretary began projecting a variety of documents on the screen in front of us, charts, graphs, descriptions – the financial value of people's positions. Watching the numbers flash in front of me and documenting the conversation that ensued, for the first time since the organizational shift had been announced I understood the reasoning behind it. The committee members were thoughtful, clear, and concise and believed that this would make the organization stronger. However, this meeting was confidential. I could not go and explain to my peers the reasons why their long-time colleague was losing their job. Instead I would listen as they expressed understandable frustration at the process and their coinciding feelings of devaluation as employees. In this meeting I realized, just like at WFPSE, through all of my tedious tasks and frustrating days at work, I had been using my anthropological skills. Along with specific methodologies and theories, anthropology also trained me to suspend judgment, listen more than I speak, respect diversity and difference, and resist conclusions until the data are all in. But it was not until this meeting that I had an "aha" moment in which I recognized the divide between management and staff and its impact on how the organization functioned. When my contract ended and I had my informal exit interview, I described this moment in detail to my boss. I explained both sides of the tension within the organization with the hope that a greater understanding would lead to more acceptance. In a sense, I verbally published my findings. As my time at the organization ended I felt I had made a meaningful insight, but I still did not achieve my goal of connecting anthropology with the wider populace, and I wondered – Without theory was this anthropology? Had I truly been practicing anthropology all along?

I sought to answer my own question and found that most arguments against applied or practicing anthropology highlight ethical issues. Yet, few have asked if what is being practiced is anthropology at all. Morris and Bastin (2004) argue that anthropology is "based conventionally in a methodology of long-term field-work of a small-scale, face-to-face kind, and founded in theoretical orientations which are sensitive to cultural and social difference." Accordingly, I believe anthropology is a fusion of a multitude of facets. These include:

- Long-term fieldwork
- Theory
- An unbiased and reflexive approach
- Recognition of positionality
- Participant observation
- Presentism/a recognition of change
- The concept of relativity – asking not "What makes it better?" but "What makes this work for them?/Why do they do it this way?"
- Understandings and inquiries into power relations and how this affects our work
- Transparency
- Ethics – do no harm to those we work with
- Synchronic and diachronic perspectives

So I was practicing anthropology? To be honest, I'm still not sure. I was using my skills, I was acting as an anthropologist, but was I practicing anthropology? I believe anthropology has all of the above-mentioned characteristics, with long-term field-work, participant observation, theory, and ethics as the pillars of our discipline. As such, it is not possible to practice anthropology in every setting. To me, anthropology without long-term fieldwork is not anthropology. Observing without participating, knowing the "what" but not the "why," is not anthropology. Being unable to release your findings for academic or social review is not transparent and it is not anthropology (Low and Merry 2010; Sillitoe 2007). My time working with these two nonprofits showed me both what anthropology is, and what it is not to me, because perhaps it is something a little different to everyone.

Anthropology is passionate, political, difficult, and fulfilling. It is not just a job. It is a way of thinking, acting, and living. I learned how to use anthropological skills in a workplace setting, and my work taught me how to use anthropology. However, what I originally sought to find does not yet exist – a unified anthropology that bridges academia with practice, the academy with the public. And yet I maintain my quixotic belief that this is the direction in which anthropology is going. We just need to stop and remind ourselves who we are, and who we can be to the public, before we move forward.

The Divide

My greatest concern with the literature I have read to date which argues on behalf of applied or practicing anthropology is the hostile undertone I detect from applied, engaged or practicing anthropologists towards academia. In their endeavor to justify the existence of a new type of anthropology, academic anthropology has become the "other," often connoted as less admirable than the applied field due to its disconnect with everyday society (Nolan 2013).

While in Sydney I was granted the opportunity to present a discussion about the strengths and weakness of applied anthropology at a conference on working with indigenous peoples. I highlighted potential limitations of working in an applied setting including ethical concerns, inability to have transparency or control over what is done with your work, and the implications of serving client needs. Meanwhile, academia is limited by the requirement to publish jargon-filled narratives inaccessible to the public, limited funding, and at times a paralytic elevation of relativity that impedes action (James 2004). While the benefits of applied anthropology include the ability to actively apply your work and engage with the public. However, many within the audience did not endorse my critique of applied anthropology.

As I stood wearily in front of a room of about thirty anthropologists, the dim light from the PowerPoint slides mercifully hiding the red perfusing up my cheeks, I fielded an array of comments demeaning academic anthropology as a rebuttal to my applied critique. One middle-aged man felt particularly disturbed by the idea of informed consent. He argued vociferously that if a community denies your request to study them, you could still observe them from the outside. I swallowed a quickly approaching tactless response and replied by noting that observation was not anthropology and highlighted the breech in ethics his course of action would entail. He remained firm in his opinion. However, the reaction my critique garnered spoke to the divide in our discipline, a divide that is still fresh and sensitive to criticism. We should not be attacking each other but recognizing each other's strengths and weaknesses. Applied anthropology needs more theory to support its work. Academic anthropology needs to uncloak it findings from pedantic jargon and engage with the public. And both need to clarify what anthropology is so we can explain it to ourselves, our bosses, and the public.

Where Do We Go from Here?

The pedantic jargon and the elitist ivory tower stereotypes about academia that pervade public imagination leave laypeople uninterested and unconvinced by anthropological theory. Today's consumerist and narcissistic environment leads to citizens who are often only interested in topics that affect them in their day-to-day lives. And the anthropology of today does not energize and inform the public as to why the topics we study are important to those outside of academia. The discipline is in danger of becoming irrelevant – not because it is not necessary, but because it is not understood. This is what I discovered while in the field.

I did not discover what anthropology is. I discovered what it could be. Shrouded behind business models, profit margins, and pedantic publications, the public does not see what anthropology can be, should be, and is in the process of becoming – a conduit for information, unification, and positive social change. We as a discipline can change this. We can write op-eds, connect with local nonprofits that do work we are interested in, and replace our jargon with vocabulary understandable to all to attract a nonacademic base of readers. If the public is not interested in our work, if they are not knocking on our doors asking for more information, we should bring our knowledge to them. We can host a community event or a house party informing others about our research. Anthropology taught me to think creatively and analytically. I was able to apply these skills in my nonprofit work to engage with supporters and solve problems. We, as a discipline can do the same. We can use our ingenuity to move our discipline back into the minds others. If we want a horizontal movement, one that unites people on equal terms around a common goal, we need to start viewing people equally – including our anthropological colleagues. Right now we are running two different movements and I am stuck in the middle, between the ivory tower and the grassroots movement, the academic and the applied anthropologist. My journey post-graduation showed me that just because I call myself an anthropologist does not mean I am doing anthropological work. However, if we close the divide between the sub-disciplines, clearly delineate what anthropology is, and are able to explain it to others we can create a space and opportunities for full-bodied anthropological work in academic and nonacademic settings. There are a multitude of ethical, pertinent, and important causes that would benefit from hiring anthropologists – fieldworking, theory-creating, ethical, participant-observing anthropologists – the organizations that fight for them just do not know it yet. So was my master's in anthropology worth the time, money, and effort? Yes. Though it has been a difficult journey, one that does not suit everyone, I have found personal and professional value in my degree. I am an anthropologist. It is exhausting, challenging, fulfilling, and right where I want to be.

References

American Anthropological Association. 2012. *Anthropological Careers*. Accessed February 5, 2015. www.thisisanthropology.com/anthropological-careers.

Borofsky, Robert. 2000. "Public Anthropology. Where To? What Next?" *Anthropology News* 41(5):9–10.

Bureau of Labor Statistics. 2012. *Anthropologists and Archaeologists*. Accessed February 5, 2012. www.bls.gov/ooh/Life-Physical-and-Social-Science/Anthropologists-and-archeologists.htm#tab-1.

Durkheim, Émile, Marcel Mauss, and Rodney Needham. 1963. *Primitive Classification*. Chicago: University of Chicago Press.

Fiske, Shirley J., Linda A. Bennett, Patricia Ensworth, Terry Redding, and Keri Brondo. 2010. "The Changing Face of Anthropology: Anthropology Masters Reflect on Education, Careers, and Professional Organizations: AAA/CoPAPIA 2009 Anthropology MA Career Survey." Accessed February 3, 2015. www.aaanet.org/resources/departments/upload/Changing-Face-of-Anthropology-Final-2.pdf.

Forbes Magazine. 2012. "The 10 Best Jobs for Women in 2012." Accessed February 3, 2015. www.forbes.com/pictures/lmj45hmij/best-jobs-for-women.

James, Craig R. 2004. "Criticizing the Impunity? Bridging the Widening Gulf between Academic Discourse and Action Anthropology in Global Health." In *Expert Knowledge: First World Peoples, Consultancy and Anthropology*, edited by Barry Morris and Rohan Bastin, 2. New York: Berghahn Books.

Low, Setha, and Sally Engle Merry. 2010. "Engaged Anthropology: Diversity and Dilemmas." *Current Anthropology* 51(S2):S203–S226.

Morris, Barry, and Bastin, Rohnan, eds. 2004. *Expert Knowledge: First World Peoples, Consultancy and Anthropology*. New York: Berghahn Books.

Mullins, Paul R. 2011. "Practicing Anthropology and the Politics of Engagement: 2010 Year in Review." *American Anthropologist* 113(2):235–245.

Nolan, Riall. 2013. "Introduction." In *A Handbook of Practicing Anthropology*, edited by Riall Nolan. Oxford: John Wiley.

Price, David. 2002. "Lessons from Second World War Anthropology." *Anthropology Today* 18(3):14–20.

Rylko-Bauer, Barbara, Merrill Singer, and John Van Willigen. 2006. "Reclaiming Applied Anthropology: Its, Past, Present, and Future." *American Anthropologist* 108(1):178–190.

Sillitoe, Paul. 2007. "Anthropologists Only Need Apply: Challenges of Applied Anthropology." *Journal of the Royal Anthropological Institute* 13(1):147–165.

Singer, Merrill. 2000. "Why I Am Not a Public Anthropologist." *Anthropology News* 41(6):6–7.

Tso, Judy. 2013. "Job Hunting in the Twenty-First Century." In *A Handbook of Practicing Anthropology*, edited by Riall Nolan, 37. Oxford: John Wiley.

4

THE FAIR MONEY COLLECTIVE

Michael Scroggins

This chapter describes the activities of the FAIR Money collective, a project that explicitly encourages amateur participation in social research;[1] research that encompasses Conrad Arensberg's (1981) understanding that "personalized ethnography" encompasses both empirical and conceptual work; research that owes a debt to Sol Tax's action anthropology.[2] In this sense, FAIR Money is a polemic whose existence argues that working with unexpected consociates, or on problems of local interest, need not mean abandoning conceptual development.

The FAIR Money collective, to date, has been animated by an interest in payday lending within Silicon Valley.[3] The existence of two financial systems, one with beneficial terms for the upper and middle class and another with punitive terms for the working class, is especially apparent in Silicon Valley. Due to the brute fact of credit scoring in 21st century America, this difference has a ramifying effect on social mobility.

The brute fact of dual financial systems is obvious to anyone driving from East Palo Alto to the Stanford campus. And as the drive might suggest, the solution to this problem is often stated in terms of the presence, or lack, of knowledge; in terms of who is, and who is not, financially literate. This speaks to a wider pattern in American life of producing and creating (and exporting) educational initiatives as solutions to social problems.[4] FAIR Money has eschewed assumptions about the presence or absence of knowledge, in favor of starting with an empirical description of the ordinary financial life of its research participants.

My initial involvement with the FAIR Money collective stemmed from a long-held interest in collectives, hackerspaces, and amateur scientific societies and has been sustained by the intellectual appeal of working with my FAIR Money consociates. The collective form of organizing demands that all aspects of the FAIR Money's research are subject to deliberation and debate at each step. In this sense, the slow, deliberate pace of FAIR Money's research has a strong affinity with the tempo of traditional anthropological fieldwork. In contrast to much hastily done ethnographic work within NGOs and in corporations, the analysis and conceptual development flowing out of FAIR Money's fieldwork is allowed time to develop and deepen through debate and deliberation. If the project appears radical it is only because field research in the anthropological tradition retains the power to render visible both the unexpected and the uncomfortable.

This chapter is organized into three sections. The first section addresses the organization and history of the FAIR Money collective. It begins with a brief overview of the collective's organizing principles, then narrates a longer history of FAIR Money from its inception to the present day and ends with a discussion of participating in the project. The second section presents a synopsis of FAIR Money's research on predatory lending in Silicon Valley. The chapter closes with a brief reflection on the history of practicing anthropology with unexpected consociates.

What Is FAIR Money?

First, FAIR Money is a collective. A collective is a form of horizontal organization eschewing the formation of strict hierarchies. In recent history, horizontalism has come to the fore through its use in the 1999 Seattle WTO protests, the 2001 Argentine financial crisis, and in the recent Occupy movements. While FAIR Money is not explicitly associated with protest movements, nor affiliated with other organizations, horizontalism has served as a sturdy and practical form of organization, which encourages member participation in all facets of FAIR Money, ensures that FAIR Money's research agenda is controlled by members, that its analytic categories develop from its own research, and that FAIR Money remains a small, volunteer-led project. A side effect of this form of organization is that FAIR Money cannot raise money or be forced into organizing along lines dictated by the demands of accounting for external funding. FAIR Money is, through a choice mandated by its organizational form, small, locally focused, egalitarian, and uninterested in a more formal or legally binding kind of organization.

Second, FAIR Money is a creed in two parts. The first is a statement of the problem FAIR Money is interested in:

> FAIR Money's mission is to find effective ethical alternatives to crippling consumer debt, from oppressive student loans to payday loans and other forms of predatory credit, with the ultimate goal of giving individuals more choices to participate in American life on their own terms.

The second is a statement about the kind of solutions FAIR Money will pursue:

> FAIR Money's Work towards a Solution: FAIR Money conducts qualitative and ethnographic research to reach a deeper understanding of the financial blight in the lives of the 99% and identify potential solutions that can give

low-income Americans a better chance to participate on their own terms and to rely more on each other and less on businesses that take advantage of the mismatch between income and aspirations that is built into the fabric of American culture for all but the very top wage earners.

The creeds can be, and have been, revised on several occasions. These creeds live on the FAIR Money website (http://fairnetwork.org) and are part of the public face of the FAIR Money collective. While these two statements are public, there is also a private creed members of FAIR Money must adhere to – that the work of FAIR Money should be enjoyable and carried on, even when serious, in a spirit of fun. Fun indexes both the enjoyable nature of research – the simple pleasure of curiosity – and an attitude of care towards fellow members, research participants, and FAIR Money's audience. Because FAIR Money is sustained by the interest of volunteers, personal connections and working relationships are vital and the maintenance of these relationships is given priority over efficiency.

A History of the FAIR Money Collective

The history of the FAIR Money collective begins with hearing an NPR radio story in November 2012 during the founding member's[5] commute to work in Silicon Valley. The story described the financial struggles of a middle-aged man with two daughters in college and a wife fighting cancer. In the midst of the blizzard of medical and educational bills, he took out a small (few hundred dollars) payday loan to make ends meet. When he could not pay the loan back immediately, the high interest rate on his payday loan and the aggressiveness of the payday loan company began to have an outsized effect on his finances. He ended up paying back thousands of dollars on a loan of a few hundred dollars. For the founder of FAIR Money, the news story served as an ethical call to action, which was soon translated into a practical research agenda aimed at looking for a solution to the problem of predatory lending in Silicon Valley. Further, the framing of the story, in that it assumed the man was ignorant of the potential consequences of the payday loan, foreshadowed a key theme emerging from FAIR Money's research.

What started as a small personal project in early November 2012 grew by early December 2012 to include a pair of additional researchers, drawn from the founding member's personal network. In late December 2012, a call for participation in the emerging project was put out through the anthrodesign mailing list.[6] I, along with several others, joined the FAIR Money collective in January 2013 after responding to the anthrodesign post. By mid-January 2013 FAIR Money had half a dozen design researchers, anthropologists, and designers working on solving the problem of predatory lending in Silicon Valley. Primary research continued with this initial group of researchers through the spring of 2013, with the last set of participant interviews occurring in early May 2013.

At this time, FAIR Money's work was strongly centered on the idea of deriving a design solution for a user need: tools to facilitate identifying short-term credit at better terms than payday loans. If research had proceeded at the torrid pace of design projects in industry, designing a smart phone application is likely where FAIR Money would have stopped. However, due to the intermittent nature of the work schedule, FAIR Money moved at a much slower pace, a pace more often found in academic anthropology than industry research. FAIR Money never produced an application but through the slow analysis of data demanded by the intermittent pace, FAIR Money moved from taking a client-centered view of the problematic situation towards a broader, more indirect set of solutions to what was emerging as a complex knot of social, personal, and economic forces rather than a simple problem of individuals lacking access to equitable credit instruments (though the latter remains important).

In the summer of 2013, FAIR Money released its initial findings to an audience drawn from the anthrodesign mailing list. In the following months, FAIR Money made two key decisions. The first decision was not to seek nonprofit status with its reporting requirements and legally ordained structure or to raise external financing, but rather to remain small, slow, informal, self-organized, and loosely structured. The second decision was to conceptualize student loans and mortgages alongside payday loans. Taken together, these decisions intentionally turned FAIR Money away from relying on problematics, timelines, or categories deemed important by potential funders and left control of the project fully in the hands of its members. And it was decided by the members to continue with the egalitarian, and intentionally inefficient, method of organization and slow pace because the project was personally and intellectually rewarding.

In keeping with its focus on predatory lending and debt, FAIR Money planned a comparative study of student debt practices at San Jose State University and California State University (CSU) Fresno in August 2013. These two institutions were selected because they both have comparable student populations and the former sits in Silicon Valley while the latter sits in the Central Valley. Again using the members' networks of personal contacts, plans were made to partner with one anthropology fieldwork class at each institution.

A funding cut at San Jose State canceled the class that was supposed to be partnered with and scuttled Fair Money's comparative research plan. However, FAIR Money was able to work with a class at CSU Fresno in the fall of 2013 on a study of student debt. One member visited an undergraduate fieldwork class at CSU Fresno to give a pitch about the project and ask for student volunteers to work on the project in the first weeks of the semester.

The pitch was a success, and in Fresno, a working group of six students, supervised by Dr James Mullooly, spent the fall semester studying the experience of applying for and receiving financial aid. A key finding from that fall was the effect of reported family information on the financial aid reward. The formula used to determine financial aid rewards yielded entirely different outcomes depending upon how a family situation was described. In Silicon Valley, members of FAIR Money conducted a series of interviews with students in debt, visited financial aid offices at several universities, and put into conversation the research conducted at CSU Fresno and research conducted by FAIR Money. Analysis of the data from this collaboration was conducted in Google Docs, which, with Dr Mullooly's expertise, was turned into an ad hoc and collaborative qualitative data analysis program so that students at CSU Fresno and FAIR Money members could perform a joint analysis.

In March 2014, FAIR Money organized a panel at the Society for Applied Anthropology (SfAA) conference in Albuquerque, New Mexico with students at CSU Fresno. At the SfAA, FAIR Money presented findings from its spring 2012 study of predatory lending along with findings from the fall 2013 study of student debt as part of a panel focused on FAIR Money's organization and work.

The period following the 2014 SfAA conference was one of contemplation over the future direction of FAIR Money. Some members argued in favor of continuing to study student debt and others for conducting a more thorough analysis of FAIR Money's work on payday lending in Silicon Valley. After some weeks of deliberation, it was collectively decided that FAIR Money would pursue a close analysis of their spring 2012 study on predatory lending and write a report detailing FAIR Money's findings.

The upshot of FAIR Money's wanderings into student loan research was a deeper and more nuanced view of the complexities of debt and income inequality. During this time, FAIR Money members read widely and discussed theoretical works on debt and inequality and critically examined various policy initiatives aimed at alleviating debt and poverty. In this sense, FAIR Money served as an informal seminar group. The slow speed at which FAIR Money moves allowed the time necessary to develop a conceptual, as well as empirical, critique of approaches to predatory lending.

Over its brief life, members have come and gone but FAIR Money has maintained a core group of five to seven members at all times. Though FAIR Money started with a single person spurred to action, today it has grown into a self-maintaining organization with the distinctive form of organization mentioned previously and a distinctive theoretical viewpoint: turning design problems, such as creating a financial app to help users avoid predatory loans, inside out. That is, starting the design process not from the perspective of the designer's, or a sponsoring institution's, assumptions or desires, but from the perspective of the potential user. While this is the goal of human-centered design, the institutional constraints imposed by profit and funders too often conspire to foreshorten this process. The organization of FAIR Money, in contrast, allows this slow process a place to unfold over an extended period of time.

Structures of Participation in FAIR Money

FAIR Money has, to date, been a collection of anthropologists, designers, design researchers, economists, and business owners with varying interests in predatory lending and varying levels of participation in the project. To date, participation in FAIR Money has revolved around four axes: monthly meetings, research, writing, and outreach. Each will be briefly described below.

There is a standing meeting at a private residence on the first Saturday of the month with additional meetings held via videoconference as needed. To date, the monthly meeting has occurred over lunch at a member's home. Decisions on the direction FAIR Money will take are made in person at the monthly meeting. Normally, a monthly meeting lasts three hours, though meetings have been both longer and shorter. Monthly meetings are the most formalized aspect of FAIR Money and a monthly meeting follows a strict, though entirely unwritten, three-element structure described in Table 4.1. As was mentioned previously, the meeting structure is oriented towards sociality and maintaining relationships rather than efficiency. It is important to note here that all decisions are open to debate and revision.

Out of the monthly meetings flows FAIR Money's research agenda. FAIR Money's research methods to date have drawn heavily from the field of design research.[7] Many of the methods employed in design research assume participation in the research process by non-researchers and are designed to facilitate this participation. Initial analysis is generally performed as a group with the Post-it note method of analysis common to design research, in full awareness of the method's limitations (Nafus and anderson 2009). Doing analysis in this way distributes the initial work of analysis across the group, keeps everyone on the same page, and yet allows for deeper analysis by individual members. FAIR Money's public documents have been written collectively using Google Docs as the writing tool. Track changes and comments are used as in any other word processor, the only difference being that multiple authors can work on the same document at the same time. As with any collaborative writing process, maintaining a consistent tone of voice across multiple authors is a challenge, but a consistent set of editorial norms is slowly emerging.

TABLE 4.1 The Structure of a Monthly Meeting

Activity	Duration	Activity
Gathering	30 minutes	The member in whose home the meeting is held cooks lunch while other members bring dessert and snacks. The meeting never starts until lunch is ready, the table is set, and the meal is served. Eating is prior to working.
Personal Updates	30 minutes	The meeting opens with a round of personal updates. Stories of personal success or failure are heard by the group, and cheers and/or advice are given.
FAIR Money Work	90–180 minutes	Only after small talk, personal updates, and the consumption of a meal is the meeting agenda addressed. Decisions on the course of the project are made at this time via deliberation and discussion by the members gathered around the table. No formalized consensus procedure is used.

Outreach for the project has been driven by the initiative of individual members. Deciding upon a consistent outreach strategy and correct outreach targets has been one of the more difficult parts of the FAIR Money project, as it involves meta-deliberation over the direction of project. Collaborations undertaken to date have included joint research projects with the Institute for Public Anthropology at CSU Fresno, a panel at the 2014 SfAA conference, and presentations about payday lending to several local organizations in Silicon Valley.

In an unanticipated development, a few members have also used experience gained working with FAIR Money to change careers or apply to graduate school. FAIR Money has also developed into an informal apprenticeship program where novice researchers work in concert with more experienced researchers. In keeping with general FAIR Money practice, there is no formalized apprenticeship program, just the invitation to participate in some aspect of FAIR Money.

FAIR Money's Work on Payday Lending

In this section, I will present a brief synopsis of FAIR Money's spring 2012 research project on predatory lending in Silicon Valley and discuss how its initial empirical research into everyday financial lives led to a conceptual argument contra financial literacy training as a way to mitigate predatory lending. FAIR Money set out not by assuming the correctness or incorrectness of either payday lenders or those who seek them out, but rather sought to describe and understand the conditions which lead people to seek out payday loans. The end point of this research is an argument against financial literacy education as a solution to predatory lending.

Payday loans do not exist in a vacuum. They exist in relationship to other formal financial services, such as banks, credit unions and credit cards, which many of the study participants have been locked out of, as well as to informal financial services, such as borrowing from friends and family, and to activities like pawning goods, yard sales, and informal businesses. The existence of, and sometimes necessity of, payday lending is an unfortunate fact of American economic life for those without access to other sources of credit. For many, payday loans are the lender of last resort and a place to turn to when better options have been exhausted.

One currently ascending approach to alleviating payday lending, financial literacy, conceives of the problem as one of ignorance: One takes a payday loan because one does not know better. However, FAIR Money's empirical work demonstrated quite early on that the participants did know better, and those who took payday loans did so under a specific set of circumstances, which had little to do with the presence or lack of knowledge. Hence, what started as a straightforwardly empirical project quickly confronted the necessity of conceptual work.

Conceptualizing Silicon Valley

It is a commonplace to regard Silicon Valley as having attained the very pinnacle of economic success. It has spawned imitations around the globe as well as a burgeoning academic literature detailing its history, present, and possible future. By all the usual quantitative measures – even those that take into account the human cost of economic development and measure something other than purely economic output – Silicon Valley is at the very peak of economic success both materially and imaginatively.

For example, according to "A Portrait of California," an application of the human development index to the state of California, Silicon Valley scores higher than any region of the United States on the human development index.[8] The area is buoyed up by high scores for post-secondary education, educational opportunities, and health care. The authors divide California into five levels of human development, placing "Silicon Valley Shangri-La, comprising 1% of CA population" at the top of the index. They write, "Extremely well-educated, high-tech high-flyers living in Silicon Valley – entrepreneurs and professionals fueling, and accruing the benefits of, innovation, especially in information technology. Highly developed capabilities give these Californians unmatched freedom to pursue the goals that matter to them."

Built around Amartya Sen's (2000) capabilities approach, the human development index ties economic development to an accumulation of human capabilities. Success can then be understood not purely in economic terms but as living a life of "choice and value." Such outcomes are seen as the product of both internal and external factors. While it is believed that the measure of human development is an advance over GDP, it still obscures the extremely uneven distribution of opportunity and choice across all residents, as was evident in the research participants' lack of access to the very advantages Silicon Valley is assumed to confer.

In contrast to "A Portrait of California," a recent *Atlantic* piece, "Not Even Silicon Valley Can Escape History" (Madrigal 2013), compares Silicon Valley to Detroit. Using a rare book published in the mid-1980s, *Rich's Guide to Santa Clara's Silicon Valley*, Richard Schmeider takes a road trip to the geographical heart of Silicon Valley. There, he finds a collection of service businesses and incubation spaces, which serve as a contrast to manufacturing plants found in the *Guide*. Gone are the manufacturing jobs with their middle-class incomes; in their place are low-paying service jobs and high-paying technology jobs. The move from industrial to post-industrial landscape has inscribed into the landscape both a legacy of industrial pollution and a legacy of economic inequality. The technological breakthroughs and globalized economy so rewarded by consumers have not seen the rewards distributed as equally. Yet, even a post-industrial landscape is reliant upon traditional blue-collar workers. Buses must have drivers, schools must have teachers and custodians, coffee shops must have baristas, and buildings must have maintenance workers. It is this post-industrial Silicon Valley, not the utopian Silicon Valley of the "Measure of America," that FAIR Money encountered through its fieldwork and conceptualized in its findings.

The Methods and Mechanics of FAIR Money's Fieldwork

Here, I will take a closer look at the mechanics of the spring 2012 study on payday lending in Silicon Valley. Exploratory fieldwork was carried out in November

2011 by the founding member and a close consociate. Formalized fieldwork began in January 2012 following the public instantiation of FAIR Money on the anthrodesign mailing list. As was mentioned earlier, the study followed a style of research common to design research, a style of research that allows for easy collaboration. Following a standard commercial procedure, FAIR Money used Craigslist as a recruiting tool and offered a generous gift certificate for participation in the study.

From a pool of 223 potential participants who responded to the Craigslist advertisement, ten respondents were recruited to participate in the study. The ease of attracting potential participants was underscored by comments from several participants, who said that they often volunteer for research in order to earn extra money.

The main research method consisted of a pair of two-hour interviews conducted in the participant's home, bracketing a thirty-day spending diary, which asked the participants to record all of their expenditures during the thirty-day period. Interviews conducted during the initial home visit followed a standard protocol, while the return visit questions were formulated from a combination of data from the initial visit and the diary study. During the return visit, the participants were asked to draw a map of their financial relationships detailing how money flows into and out of their life; charting where it comes from and where it ends up. The interviews were videotaped and each member of the research team either participated in or viewed every interview. FAIR Money members also visited several payday lending establishments in the study area. No attempt was made to link specific payday lenders to specific participants; rather the intention was to understand the experience of payday loan shopping.

The main finding from the spring 2012 study was that the participants, despite incomes ranging from just over the poverty line to well into six figures, were unable to meet their financial obligations. In some cases at least, this was due to individual choice, but a broader pattern was evident. Incomes have simply not kept pace with the cost of living – educational costs, housing costs, transportation costs, or the costs of raising a family within Silicon Valley. Across income levels, all participants felt the pinch of insufficient income. In short, they faced conditions of economic scarcity rather than surplus.

All employed a variety of tactics (de Certeau 1984) to make ends meet. Many were moonlighting, or being entrepreneurial, to varying degrees of success. Others had become bargain hunters and worked to save on everyday expenses. More importantly, the participants' use of debt reflected this reality. Some were engaged in informal lending networks and served as bankers for, or debtors to, friends and relatives. Others were forced into using the array of expensive subprime financial services to pay their rent and other bills.

One tactic used in times of extreme need when other resources were exhausted was the payday loan. An example of taking out a payday loan occurred when one participant's car broke down and the participant was faced with a choice between missing work and taking out a payday loan for car repairs. In this case, the short-term pain of the payday loan, despite its high cost, ensured the long-term financial maintenance of the household. This was clearly not an act performed out of ignorance of the way the financial system works, but a logical act aimed at preserving the more important resource.

Seeing Money from the Inside Out

Contra the variety of ingenious tactics deployed by the participants, an increasingly common approach to alleviating payday lending is through financial literacy education.[9] The financial literacy approach assumes that those who avail themselves of payday lending do not know how to handle money in a responsible manner. The assumption is that to work a full day is to earn an adequate income and to be capable of generating a surplus. Further, it elides the tremendous amount of work and skill necessary to simply maintain a toehold against a receding economic tide in a post-industrial landscape like Silicon Valley.

Assuming that people earn enough money to have a surplus carries damaging political consequences for those laboring under conditions of scarcity. Earning comes first in the financial literacy conception[10] and allows for the accumulation of a surplus, which the other elements of the financial literacy conception rely upon for support. Absent earning power, any theory of financial literacy as a route out of poverty falls on its face. None of FAIR Money's participants earned enough money to allow the other tenets of financial literacy to work and hence, cannot be said to be "financially literate." In an inversion of the financial literacy tenets, the participants borrowed money, rather than saved money, to protect their most precious resources.

However, everyone in the study, regardless of income, education, social position, or financial situation, reported that they are "good with money." Even participants who have inconsistent income, a high debt load, poor credit, and are unbanked consider themselves savvy money managers. The concept "good with money" indexes a range of moral and ethical ends not taken into consideration by either rational actor theory or the financial literacy curriculum.

For example, it is possible to be "good with money," even with a damaging credit history, if you are able to support your family's immediate needs for food and shelter and maintain aspirations to a better life. To be "good with money" does not mean to be good at accumulating money or deploying your resources in the most rational manner when viewed from a financial literacy perspective, but rather to be skillful in using whatever money can be earned to maintain close relationships and keep the hope for a better tomorrow alive.

Though money often arrives at irregular intervals, bill payments come due at regular intervals. To this point, the participants reported an order to the way bills get paid. Sometimes the order is chronological, but as money grows tight, it is often based on the bill's importance. Utilities, including electricity, internet, and cable television, rank highest in importance. All of the participants showed a very strong work ethic and demonstrated great ingenuity in making extra money, yet most still struggled to make ends meet.

In other words, "being good with money" has little to do with accumulating money in the name of financial security, or the conventional or "approved" use of credit and debt, such as college and house mortgages. Further, the participants were fully aware that their use of payday loans was contrary to conventional financial practice, but they generally had rational and pressing reasons for using them. Those struggling in poverty know an immense amount about money. They are not ignorant of the financial system and the manner in which it operates, nor can they escape its grasp on their possible futures.

Discussion: Anthropology with Unexpected Consociates

This chapter started by asserting that amateur participation is something that needs to be encouraged within social research and implying that amateur participation need not rule out theoretical development. The figure of the amateur anthropologist, interested in local issues and attached to local organizations and accountable to local institutions, is often written out of the history of anthropology. The impetus for purging amateurs from anthropology within American anthropology stemmed from Boas's (Stocking 1960) efforts to professionalize anthropology around a shared theoretical viewpoint. It was argued by Boas, in an argument with McGee over inclusion in the newly formed American Anthropological Association (AAA), that professionalism was the only way to ensure the steady conceptual development of the field.[11]

However, within applied anthropology, professionalism has often taken on a meaning very different than Boas intended. For instance, Van Willigen (2002) has claimed, in a textbook introducing applied anthropology to undergraduates, that anthropology lacks a distinctive conceptual viewpoint and is rather a set of methods in the service of "client problems." Similarly, Nolan (2013), writing for those planning a career in applied anthropology, has argued that anthropological practice requires solving the problems of "external clients," who supply both the problems and the criteria for a solution to those problems. To be professional, in these recent formulations, means precisely to cleave conceptual development from practice.

When Sol Tax wrote his call to an action anthropology, he demanded that anthropology's responsibility was both do something *and* to learn something. This call was an explicit rejection of the unreflexive application of theory to problems, in particular problems set and measured by external clients. It was also an affirmation of the Boasian concern with the problem of new knowledge. But, whereas Boas was concerned with purging unexpected consociates from the organization of anthropology, Tax, writing sixty years after Boas, saw that this was not possible. Anthropology would have to face unexpected consociates yet keep anthropological concerns at the center of practice.

In an important sense, the organization of the FAIR Money collective finds a historical antecedent in the pluralistic scientific associations, conversation clubs, and intellectual associations of 19th century America (Menand 2002). Like many of those associations, FAIR Money draws problematics from local issues, researchers from local pools, and is addressed primarily, but not exclusively, to other local organizations and institutions with an interest in the same problematic, such as local charities, financial institutions, and service organizations. FAIR Money's local focus and collective form of organizing, however, has not kept FAIR Money from adhering to Tax's injunction to both do something and learn something.

The next step for FAIR Money started with the March 2015 release of *Good with Money: Getting By in Silicon Valley*, a report on predatory lending in Silicon Valley. With the release of the report, FAIR Money is transitioning from a closely held collective organized around kitchen tables to a public group organized around open meetings in the San Francisco Bay Area. Expanding the circle of unexpected consociates while retaining the relationships that allow FAIR Money to keep going will be the next challenge. But, expansion will be accompanied by the debate, deliberation, and ensuing slow pace which has made the work of the FAIR Money collective intellectually rich and satisfying. This is the same commitment to slow and careful deliberation that has animated the last century of anthropological fieldwork and continues giving anthropology the ability to produce unexpected knowledge.

Notes

1 In the late 19th century, anthropology in America was only loosely institutionalized. Early research projects were initiated on the basis of personal, rather than disciplinary, interest and were often initiated by interested amateurs. The first hint of change came with J.W. Powell's tenure as director of the Bureau of American Ethnology during which he outlined a broad course of research for the emerging discipline. However, the issue of disciplinary formation versus amateur participation came to a head during the debate between McGee and Boas during the formation of the American Anthropological Association (AAA) (Stocking 1960). Boas famously tried to restrict access to a group of forty professional anthropologists while McGee argued for a much broader basis of participation, which included interested amateurs. While a complete history of local ethnological organizations is beyond the scope of this chapter, it should be noted that the dynamic embodied in this founding argument over the organization of anthropology, which was won by McGee, runs through the history of anthropology.

2 In his 1980 AAA presidential address, Conrad Arensberg (1981) lamented the separation of applied anthropology and academic anthropology that he and Chapple created: "We misnamed this move 'applied anthropology' because it was a new turn to contemporary scenes. It was no longer concerned only with tradition. This misnomer, too late corrected to *Human Organization*, our journal's name, lost for us the understanding of the profession that the new broadened, personalized ethnography fed back into theory and still does." Here, forty years after founding the Society for Applied Anthropology (SfAA), Arensberg reconsiders the idea of an unreflective application of anthropological theory to social problems. While Arensberg's lament came towards the end of a long career, Sol Tax (1975, 515) formulated action anthropology in the 1950s as an explicit reaction to applied anthropology. On the position of the action anthropologist, contra the position of the applied anthropologist, Tax wrote, "He wants to help a group of people solve a problem, and he wants to learn something in the process. He refuses ever to think or to say that the people involved are for him a means of advancing his knowledge; and he refuses to think or to say that he is simply applying science to the solution of those people's problems."

3 A payday loan is a short-term loan, typically less than $500.00, with a fixed dollar fee that translates into an annual interest rate of 300% or higher. Here it is also a shorthand for any loan with similarly punitive terms.

4 The historian of American education, Lawrence Cremin (1965) wrote, "One of my friends likes to remark that in other countries when there is a profound social problem there is an uprising; in the United States we organize a course!" Similarly, Willis (2011) has recently argued that financial literacy courses, despite their demonstrated ineffectiveness, serve to prevent effective financial regulation.

5 I use member here as a shorthand for participation in FAIR Money, and particularly for attendance at the monthly meetings. There are no formal membership criteria or requirement outside of participation in some aspect of the project. Nor is there a concept of a former member of the collective. However, to participate in FAIR Money's decision making requires participating in the monthly meetings.

6 The anthrodesign mailing list primarily caters to anthropologists and researchers in allied fields who work closely with designers and product managers in industry. Though the mailing list has an international audience, it has a large audience of Silicon Valley-based researchers.

7 Design research is a field that overlaps considerably with applied anthropology, especially the aspect concerned with "wicked problems" (Rittel and Webber 1973) that cut across technical and social boundaries. Though, having been developed in the years following World War II (Cross 2007), it lacks the particular political connotations that applied anthropology carries. It also shares with anthropology the peculiar quality of not clearly belonging to either the sciences or the humanities.

8 "A Portrait of California" (Burd-Sharps and Lewis n.d.) is part of the Social Science Research Council's "Measure of America" series of reports. The reports are a modified application of the human development concept, commonly used by the United Nations, to the United States. The "Measure of America" combines data from the Centers for Disease Control and the US Census into three high-level indicators of human development – A Long and Healthy Life, Access to Knowledge, and A Decent Standard of Living.

9 The history of the term financial literacy as told through Google N-Gram reveals that the term received wide adoption starting in 1987. A more detailed history is beyond the scope of this chapter, but it would be a worthwhile pursuit.

10 While a history of financial literacy schemes is beyond the scope of this chapter, a representative financial literacy schema can be found at www.mymoney.gov. It consists of five tenets – earn, save and invest, protect, spend, borrow – which build on each other. In this schema, earning is the most important tenet and the tenet on which the rest of the hierarchy relies. Without enough earnings to create a surplus, financial literacy is impossible.

11 Professionalism in the Boasian formulation meant national organizations. But, consider the proliferation of local anthropological societies shortly after the formation of the AAA. For instance, the Southwestern Anthropological Association was founded in 1929 and the Central States Anthropological Society in 1921. Both of these societies expressly invite interested local amateurs to attend and participate in their meetings.

References

Arensberg, Conrad. 1981. "Cultural Holism through Interactional Systems." *American Anthropologist* 83(3):562–581. doi:10.1525/aa.1981.83.3.02a00040.

Burd-Sharps, Sarah, and Kristen Lewis. n.d. "A Portrait of California – Measure of America: American Human Development Project." www.measureofamerica.org/california.

Cremin, Lawrence A. 1965. *The Genius of American Education.* University of Pittsburgh. Horace Mann Lecture, 1965. Pittsburgh: University of Pittsburgh Press.

Cross, Nigel. 2007. "Forty Years of Design Research." *Design Studies* 28(1):1–4. doi:10.1016/j.destud.2006.11.004.

de Certeau, Michel. 1984. *The Practice of Everyday Life.* Berkeley: University of California Press.

Madrigal, Alexis C. 2013. "Not Even Silicon Valley Escapes History." *The Atlantic* July 23. www.theatlantic.com/technology/archive/2013/07/not-even-silicon-valley-escapes-history/277824.

Menand, Louis. 2002. *The Metaphysical Club: A Story of Ideas in America.* 1st edition. New York: Farrar, Straus and Giroux.

Nafus, Dawn, and ken anderson. 2009. "Writing on Walls: The Materiality of Social Memory in Corporate Research," in *Ethnography and the Corporate Encounter: Reflections on Research in and of Corporations*, Melissa Cefkin, ed., 137–157. London: Berghahn Books.

Nolan, Riall, ed. 2013. *A Handbook of Practicing Anthropology.* 1st edition. Chichester; Malden, MA: Wiley-Blackwell.

Rittel, Horst W.J., and Melvin M. Webber. 1973. "Dilemmas in a General Theory of Planning." *Policy Sciences* 4(2):155–169. doi:10.1007/BF01405730.

Schmeider, Richard. 1985. *Rich's Guide to Santa Clara's Silicon Valley.* Los Altos, CA: Business Directories Inc.

Sen, Amartya. 2000. *Development as Freedom.* Reprint edition. New York: Anchor.

Stocking, George W. 1960. "Franz Boas and the Founding of the American Anthropological Association." *American Anthropologist* 62(1):1–17. doi:10.1525/aa.1960.62.1.02a00010.

Tax, Sol. 1975. "Action Anthropology." *Current Anthropology* 16(4):514–517.

Van Willigen, John. 2002. *Applied Anthropology: An Introduction.* 3rd edition. Westport, CT: Praeger.

Willis, Lauren E. 2011. "The Financial Education Fallacy." *American Economic Review* 101(3):429–434. doi:10.1257/aer.101.3.429.

5

ON EMBEDDED ACTION ANTHROPOLOGY AND HOW ONE THING LEADS TO ANOTHER BY CHANCE

Jonathan L. Zilberg

What is the practical and theoretical value of following up on unexpected, or serendipitous, information during fieldwork? That is the question this chapter explores. In reflecting back upon how three successive applied ethnographic research projects of mine led from one to another I revisit the literature on serendipity in anthropology and other fields and consider the theoretical, practical, and pedagogical consequences those conceptual models might have for an anthropology of the unexpected. Conducted in Indonesia, each project came about and led directly from one to the other by pure chance, thus the term "linked ethnographic serendipity." In each case, a single short comment immediately caught my attention as significant and worth investigating. Simply put, a red flag or critical datum surfacing in one research context led to a different applied activist project in a very different context.

In the process of discovering the literature on serendipity, I came to realize that there is an enormous difference between simply recognizing an obvious research topic worth investigating and the serendipitous datum. First one has to realize that the typical understanding of serendipity as merely an unexpected chance interesting observation is not serendipity (Rond 2014). Chance is an event while serendipity is a capability dependent on bringing separate events, causal and non-causal together through an interpretive experience put to strategic use (Makri and Blandford 2012a, 2012b). Thus serendipity turns out to be a more complicated concept than one would otherwise imagine from its usual currency as merely being something unexpected. Simply put, in its modern definition by Horace Walpole in *The Three Princes of Serendip*, and dating back to Amir Khusrau's *Hasht Bihasht* of 1302, a tale about the Persian King Bahram V of the Sassanid Empire (420–440), the term refers to "the combination of accident and sagacity in recognizing the significance of a discovery" (Remer 1965, 6–7).

There is specific consequence in being aware of the literature on serendipity for graduate school pedagogy as George Marcus (2009) emphasizes for an era of disciplinary transition in which students are by and large ahead of the discipline, though this is not uniformly the case (Hale 2008). Apparently, graduate students today are typically more interested in applied and activist agendas than their older professors and the students trained in graduate anthropology programs in the 1980s and 1990s. An analytic awareness then of serendipity and the literature on unexpected and unanticipated consequences will be of particular value for students interested in applied anthropology. Though the value of serendipity in qualitative research has been clearly shown (Fine and Degan 1996) and though there is an emergent appreciation in anthropology of it as a subject of vital concern (Hazan and Hertzog 2012; Rivoal and Salazar 2013) my purpose here is to extend current thought by calling for a greater attention in anthropology to the theoretical work on the topic in other disciplines, specifically to two illuminating models of the "serendipity pattern" as presented by Lawley and Tompkins (2008) and modified by Makri and Blandford (2012a, 2012b). There are other relevant studies, for instance on intuition by Klein (2013), and a history of work in sociology on unexpected and unanticipated consequences by Calhoun (2010), Portes (2000), and Merton and Barber (2004). The work on innovation and knowledge diffusion by Swan, Scarborough, and Robertson (2003) and Rogers (2003) is equally pertinent. Above all, there is the critical foundational work by Andel (1994), though the literature on the role of the unexpected and serendipity in science (Roberts 1989; Corneli 2012) and economics is for reasons of space and focus barely referred to in this chapter, except to mention in passing the irreverent best seller *The Black Swan* (Taleb 2007).

To be sure, as George E. Marcus (2009, 22) highlights, the surprise or serendipitous datum in anthropological research has the status of being virtually a disciplinary trope. Nevertheless, as Hazan and Hertzog (2012) emphasize, the phenomenon and its importance for the discipline has remained theoretically unexamined. We are returned again then to Hortense Powdermaker's acute observation that "Little record exists of mistakes and learning from them, and of the role of choice and accident in stumbling upon significant problems, in reformulating old ones, and in devising new techniques, a process known as serendipity" (quoted in Fine and Degan 1996, 444–5). As Marcus calls for, and as Hazan and Hertzog (2012) illustrate, there is theoretical and practical value to be had in incorporating an appreciation for the ubiquity and consequence of serendipity into graduate training, and there Robert Willim (2013) notes that we should even embrace a sense of events in fieldwork as being outside of our control, never mind capitalizing on failure (Le Feuvre 2010). The idea is at hand then that graduate students should be trained to sagaciously take advantage of the changes of course that the unexpected offers during research. A familiarity with the phenomena and research could allow them to establish connections between data towards generating new anthropological insight into the nature and importance of serendipity (Le Courant 2013; Giabiconi 2013; Dalsgaard 2013).

There is a world of difference between careful planning for conducting anthropological research projects on specific problems in graduate school and what happens when one discovers unexpected topics during research and then seizes the opportunity offered by the serendipitous observation that stands out as a potent metaphor. In fact, anthropological research is particularly well suited for investigating the unexpected, so much so that Daniel Miller noted at the 2012 EASA Young Scholars Forum that "it is important to cultivate a certain willingness to seize unforeseen opportunities" and if necessary set aside previous research plans and methods (Rivoal and Salazar 2013).[1] There, in its fullest significance to the discipline, serendipity is seen as an engine for anthropological research with the potential to advance both method and theory (Hazan and Hertzog 2012, 183) in the context of post-1980s disciplinary changes (Marcus 1999, 2002, 2008).

The Data and the Contexts

The three projects spanning the last decade that inform this chapter are only introduced in cursory detail here as the purpose of this chapter is to merely use them as anchors for reflecting on the literature on the unexpected, towards conceptualizing serendipity patterns to be explored in future analysis. Instead of outlining each project's practical and political agendas I simply note the unexpected way in which one project led to another. The first project was in Banda Aceh, Aceh, the second in Jakarta, Indonesia's capital located in West Java, and the third in the city of Jambi and nearby village of Muarajambi, in the province of Jambi, Sumatra. The first project focused on the Aceh Tsunami Museum (Syahril 2008; Samuels 2012; Zilberg 2009), the second on the Museum Istiqlal, effectively the National Islamic Museum (Zilberg 2010, 2011), and the third on the archeological site museum in Muarajambi (Kausar 2013; Kausar and Zilberg 2013; McGhee 2013). The first project began in the background context of my ongoing work on Indonesian museums (Zilberg 2007, 2014) and in that project in Aceh I collaborated with cultural activists at a local activist organization, Tikar Pandan (Idria forthcoming). In the second project I worked with the curator at the Museum Istiqlal.[2] In the third project I collaborated with graduate students from the IAIN Jambi (the State Islamic University of Jambi) who also worked at the Jambi Arts Council (Dewan Kesenian Jambi) and separately with local activists in an arts and culture research organization, Padmasana. During the first project I was successively associated with the Faculty of Economics at the University of Indonesia, Monash College, Jakarta, and the Jakarta Institute of the Arts (IKJ), while during the second and third projects in Jakarta and Jambi I was affiliated with the graduate school at the Universitas Islam Negeri Syarif Hidayatullah (a State Islamic university in Jakarta). The final project took place in the applied context of the Governor's Jambi Melayu Cultural Revitalization Project and culminated in the First International Conference on Jambi Studies (ICJS) in 2013 (Zainul 2013).[3] The goal in all these applied projects besides the specific activist outputs realized and unrealized, expected and unexpected, has been to encourage the production and dissemination of local knowledge and to stimulate informal network formation outside of the policy-oriented activity occurring in the Indonesian Knowledge Sector, as it is termed in the development community (McCarthy and Ibrahim 2010). It also has provided me with an embedded context for studying the nature of the connected problems in the Indonesian university system and related institutions such as libraries, archives and museums (Hull 1994; Suryadama and Jones 2013).

Here are the critical unexpected events or incidents, the three serendipitous data. The first datum surfaced during an informal discussion on a wholly different subject in the National University of Singapore, the idea for developing an international program for Institute Kesenian Jakarta, the Jakarta Institute of the Arts. I learned there by chance about the plans for the new Tsunami Museum which I immediately opposed. The second datum emerged during an interview with the head of the planning committee for the Tsunami Museum in which he recalled how he had specifically told the government that he would only participate in the Tsunami Museum project if the mistake of the Museum Istiqlal was not repeated again. The third datum emerged during a field visit with museum personnel organized by the Jambi Arts Council to the archaeological site of Muarajambi in West Sumatra in which I learned that the information on Candi Teluk I and II had been removed from the site museum in case it might have embarrassed the then President during a recent visit. Each resulted in extended case studies which emerged as a consequence of action research, with the third case study as yet incomplete.

The Model: Expect the Unexpected and Cultivate Sagacity

Pek van Andel (1994, 644) writes in the "Anatomy of the Unsought Finding" that the reason why serendipity is typically underestimated is because realities such as the non-rational and accidental, the unsought, etc., are deliberately expunged in publishing theoretical and experimental research, that is eliminated by a process of rationalization. As Gary Klein (2013) explores in *Seeing What Others Don't: The Remarkable Ways We Gain Insights*, serendipity is a basic factor in the history of highly original research just as it is in the evolution of creative academic research careers over the medium and long term. While this is no surprise to anthropologists it is apparently not something that has been seriously taken into account during graduate training. Thus Marcus (2009) emphasizes the importance of generating an awareness of this at the proposal writing stage so as to incorporate rather than limit the potential of the unexpected discovery during field research. And similarly, Hazan and Hertzog (2012), in *Serendipity in Anthropological Research: The Nomadic Turn*, point out that in some anthropological quarters, serendipity is being placed at the methodological center, as an engine for anthropological research and theory, particularly in applied anthropology. There is indeed a practical value in being primed to be on the alert for chance observations that offer up significance, for being sagacious enough and nimble enough to seize rather than resist the opportunity to pursue the unanticipated datum. One has to be bold enough to depart from a previous planned course of action.

Not only can it be useful to embrace the opportunity to go with the flow opened to us by the unexpected but there is something else at hand too for those with applied interests. For if we engage frictions (Karp et al. 2006), if we emotionally, practically, and politically engage the kind of deeply problematic issues that researchers often automatically avoid (Hale 2008), as they surely spell trouble, then fieldwork can yield unexpected practical productive consequences despite the risks. While current models of serendipity focus on the "auspicious" or positive aspect of insight in a prepared mind, I propose that it would be sagacious and useful to incorporate critical, negative dimensions as well as unachieved and negative outcomes into the current models, for there is virtual certainty of failed, unrealized or only partly realized outcomes and wholly unexpected discoveries and results in working in applied contexts.

Fine and Degan (1996) emphasize that the theoretical value of paying attention to serendipity depends upon the masterful synthesis for the sake of insight. Extending this Hazan and Hertzog (2012) emphasize that we need to pay attention to sagacity as a basic component of serendipity, for we do not really discover a new datum in that it is our background knowledge and interests that open us up to recognizing in a flash the significance of that datum point, its connections and potential utility. Yet there is a temporal aspect to this too in that it is only after investigating it and its relation to other data that the true significance of the datum impresses itself upon us and then acquires its full anthropological and theoretical significance. In this, coupling sagacity with serendipity can be used as a research tool and process to create novel concepts and explain phenomena and not merely as a concept referring to how observations unfold. Ultimately, the goal is no less than to create "an alternative paradigm of ethnographic method as legitimate as the traditional one" (Marcus 2002, 198 in Hazan and Hertzog 2012, 181). It involves "a journey for exploring unexplored issues that leads us to question 'what the discipline is all about'" (ibid., 179). The challenge is that anthropology should be about action and interaction and that the elementary principle in anthropological research should be to generate expanding contexts of abduction.[4] The idea in the literature as yet still somewhat outside of anthropology is to establish connections and significances by reflecting back upon successive incidents of linked serendipity, that is through a conscious process of examining the iterative cycle (backward and forward projection) in the serendipity pattern (Lawley and Tompkins 2008; Makri and Blandford 2012a, 2012b).

In a foundational article "Anatomy of the Unsought Finding," the biologist Pek van Andel (1994, 645) describes how the successful researcher should have "one eye open for sought findings and another eye for unsought findings." There Andel defines serendipity as "the art of making an unsought finding" in which the researcher has to be sufficiently sagacious as to be able to link together two unexpected and superficially unrelated and apparently innocuous data to make a significant observation, that is to draw from them a valuable understanding or conclusion. Robert Merton subsequently described this as a process in which "the unanticipated [read unexpected], anomalous and strategic datum" forces the inquisitive creative investigator into new directions and to either extend their pre-existing theoretical views or conceptualize new theoretical horizons (Merton 1948, 56; also see Merton and Barber 2004). For "serendipitists," it is a matter of lucky timing, background knowledge, and sagacity. Again, above all, one has to be sagacious enough, willing to seize upon unsought opportunities and even abandon prior research if necessary when the moment and the datum presents itself.

Ugo Fabietti has provided a most compelling analysis of the centrality and crucial methodological centrality of the discovery principle in anthropological research in the opening chapter "Errancy in Ethnography and Theory: On the Meaning and Role of 'Discovery' in Anthropological Research" in Hazan and Hertzog (2012, 15–30). There he writes:

> We hardly ever recount the way in which we came into possession of certain apparently insignificant information which nevertheless helped us to make progress in our fieldwork. Or, if we do, we tend to present the matter in an incidental manner without problematizing and discussing the exact role of such events in the process of our understanding.
>
> *(Fabietti 2012, 16)*

Fabietti makes three key points: 1) observing an unanticipated, strategic datum, an "unexpected fact," the discovery of something that one had not been seeking, can allow one to develop a new theory or to extend previous theory; 2) the datum should be surprising in that it must be inconsistent with prior theory and facts; and 3) the datum must be strategic in that the aim of this research is not about the datum itself but what the discovery brings to the datum. Simply put, the abductive process of establishing the significance and value of the linked datum is intuitive and is based on inference. But it is not accidental as typically imagined, for not only does the researcher's background make the incidental observation possible but it establishes the background in which the datum's significance lies. In correlation with the other datum then the serendipity pattern can confirm a dynamic that had not been observed before, and this is especially important as it can ultimately reconfigure the relevant political relations in those particular networks and beyond.

What I have learned by reflecting back on these three projects, and only later discovering the literature on the theoretical consequence of taking serendipity seriously as a research method, is this. Successively following up on serendipitous data provides for expanding circles of abduction (Hazan and Hertzog 2012, 3) in which reflective iteration or "iterative circularity" (Lawley and Tompkins 2008, 4) allows one to progressively clarify the significance of the data. In that context, the positive and negative outcomes of the events, the unrealized and partially realized goals, constitute expanding event horizons for future anthropological work. Though I find Makri and Blandford's (2012a, 2012b) "empirically grounded process model" of serendipity compelling as commented upon below, I prefer the original event focus of the Lawley and Tompkins sequence and suggest that for applied anthropology we add the dimensions of the skeptical prepared mind and negative outcomes, and the cumulative value of successive linked projects.

To begin with, and to return to the point made at the beginning of this chapter, as Mark de Rond (2014) writes in "The Structure of Serendipity," it is critical to emphasize that the typical perception of the term serendipity simply as something unexpected is erroneous.[5] As he pithily puts it returning as all authors necessarily do to Merton (1948), serendipity is the identification of paired meaningful but not always causally related events that are then strategically used. And as he and the scholars who study serendipity are at pains to clarify there are four kinds of serendipity, two of these constitute "true" serendipity and two "pseudo-serendipity." One has to keep in mind these differences for analytic reasons as they have consequences for explanation and thus ultimately theory. No doubt, the issue of serendipity, its temporal, relational, and situational dimensions, is then not as simple as it sounds.

In the instances referred to in this chapter, in each case the project came about due to a red flag, that is, a critical datum or "critical incident component" (Makri and Blandford 2012a and 2012b; Flanagan 1954; Rous and McCormick 2006). They were not insights per se as much as moments of discovery and recognition that an important issue and connection had just surfaced, which deserved attention. It is perhaps critical to highlight again that the aims in each case were not to produce ethnography, nor were they concerned with method and theory, though that turns out to be one of the unintended consequences. In the first case, the connection made was very simple, that if any money was to be spent on a museum it should have been spent on the provincial museum which had survived the Tsunami completely intact, keeping in mind the state and nature of Indonesian museums (Zilberg 2014). The second insight was that there was an emerging history of linked problems in museums, and the third insight was that all three critical datum points were ultimately about power and politics and deeply revealing of center–periphery relations.

In exploiting connections then, in maximizing the value that can result from serendipity, the outcomes are only valuable in so far as they advance knowledge, have a long-lasting impact, are timely, and result in a jump in understanding. As the models show we make "backward facing reflections" on the value of the outcomes, this is the role of the iterative component advancing this component of the model as in Lawley and Tompkins (2008). Next we use those reflections to project further value gained from the data and connections until the values, and analytical, practical, and theoretical consequences, become clearly apparent. In my case, I see these three successive linked serendipitous projects as three concentric circles of expanding abduction in which, through action, I progressively understand the constraints and politics hindering institutional performance in Indonesia, though that must be elaborated upon elsewhere.

In the context of the literature on the methodological and philosophical value of serendipity, it is a given that one can only recognize the unexpected because one's prior concerns and research make it possible to do so. It is what one brings to the datum rather than the datum itself that is theoretically significant. It is not enough then to simply argue that by being open to the serendipitous we can seize upon interesting new sites and topics for fieldwork. What the study of serendipity tells us is that by practicing sagacity we discover unforeseen connections between the data. These instances lead us to appreciate the particular and the general so as to tell us something important about the universal, and why such research matters not only to citizen and subject but to the discipline. In short, in Fabietti's perspective, an ethnographic discovery is a datum that allows one to shift one's perspective on a particular theme or problem and allows one to advance understanding and knowledge about a research topic.

Research as Revelation: Using the Literature on Serendipity to Bridge Disciplines

During the course of the research itself, I become so committed to the idea of research as revelation and of the value of an activist serendipity that I promoted the anthropology of the unexpected as an important methodology that young researchers should consider if they are seeking to make original and creative contributions. For instance, I introduced and elaborated upon this idea as an explicitly mystical Sufi practice at a workshop on qualitative methods in social science at *Rumah Kitab*, an Islamic study organization in Jakarta. But it is only now on reflection that I realize to what degree I have throughout my anthropological career been cultivating the intuitive, a practice of being open to chance in which a problem suddenly presents itself during the flow of fieldwork and calls out for critical attention (Zilberg [1995] 2003). The topic always comes to me and not the other way around, completely unsought – the next research topic – kapow! Perhaps it is a matter of being acutely aware, of being there in the moment. The simple result is that one project seems to lead to another by pure chance. Not only have I fostered the idea in the Indonesian context that this is the best way to find an interesting research topic, an effective strategy for finding something original and creative to study, but more importantly – if one has applied and activist interests – for actively contributing to building a more open society.

More broadly, I believe that it might be theoretically and practically productive to more-systematically bridge research on serendipity, creativity, and innovation across the disciplines (Fine and Degan 1996; Johnson and Kaplan 1987; Le Feuvre 2010; Merton and Barber 2004; Rickards, Runco, and Moger 2009; Portes 2000; Schneider and Wright 2013; Shavinina 2003; Andel 1994; Zelizer 2010). In that broader context, for instance in bridging an anthropology of the unexpected with Gary Klein's (2013) triple-pathway model and Swan, Scarborough, and Robertson's (2003) modeling of innovation episodes, knowledge, and networking for instance, we might well find productive common cause. By being familiar with such literature, graduate students in anthropology could be hyper-primed for discovery during the preparation phase of their careers. As graduate students are bound to experience the unexpected datum during anthropological research, they should be trained to feel secure enough about seizing the opportunity to transform their projects as needed, to go with the flow. Quite separately, by deepening the conceptual clarity and potential of these innovation processes and serendipity patterns as they are known, these meta-models, mainly from outside the discipline, potentially add to the trans-disciplinary empirical value of anthropological research and its application. Hence, instead of providing an anthropological analysis of the three projects concerning what significances one could bring to bear on these three linked Indonesian data, as was my original intention in writing this chapter, my concern has shifted to simply providing a synthetic view of these models and the promise they hold for anthropology.

There is a powerful literature on the unexpected in sociology which offers far more developed macro-theoretical case studies and discussion than currently exist in anthropology concerning serendipity (Merton 1948; Portes 2000) and these are important as they concern explanation and hypothesis building. For instance, the most fundamental issue raised by the consequence of serendipity is that it radically problematizes linear models of goal-oriented human action (outputs, results, intended consequences). Thus Portes advances Merton's work "The Unanticipated Consequences of Purposive Social Action" by showing the range of possibilities that can exist in which goals can be achieved by a "fortuitous concatenation of events" (Portes 2000, 7). But a word of caution perhaps, for if we do not differentiate types of serendipity to begin with and keep in mind Eco and Seboek's (1983) and Peirce's (1958) work on abduction at the same time, then we simply will lack the clarity required to generalize towards any middle-range theory.

To be fully conscious of the processes involved in generating insights on a cognitive level consider for instance Klein's (2013) triple-pathway model. Klein advances a four-stage model of insight – preparation, incubation, illumination, and verification. In doing so he shows how triggers (red flags, critical incidents, or the serendipitous datum), activities, and outcomes vary depending on whether one is following up on one of three types of experiential pathways, namely contradiction, connection, or creative desperation. Just as in the process of gaining unexpected anthropological insights, in the realm of applied psychology Klein shows that the common experience across these three paths of seeing what others have not is an open and alert mind. What we need to do is increase the "swirl" of ideas and information for it is only when there is sufficient turbulence that fortuitous accidental connections can be made (ibid., 185). Equally useful here is Rond's (2014) observation of how important the chance encounter of minds has been in science, and the utility of mixing up the systematic and serendipitous as revealed in the relevant literature in applied business studies with the application of the jazz metaphor or "controlled sloppiness" (ibid., 21). And to return to anthropology, by pure chance of random comments and information passed or discovered in the context of work and research, in network collaboration and in the constant practice and expansion of wide-ranging interests including hobbies, the unexpected can have major impacts not only on one's research itself (Causey 2012) but on one's career as well. Perhaps by becoming familiar with the study of serendipity in those other research traditions and their applications, and in conducting comparative analysis of how insights have been gained in anthropology, graduate students could be trained to be strategically open to sagaciously seizing the advantage offered by the datum that will present itself when they find themselves in the right place at the right time.

Towards conclusion a few final notes on the literature on serendipity are in order. First of all, as Andel (1994, 644) cautions, it "should not be underestimated or exaggerated." Serendipity should complement systematic research, and there the significance of the connections created and insights made ultimately lies in their diffusion, social impact, and creative novelty (Evans 1995; also see Rogers (1983) 2003). Equally significant is Lawley and Tompkins's (2008) statement that what happens before the datum is as important as what happens after, that it is the preparation and the existence of "anticipatory schema" (Evans 1995) that itself produces the conditions for serendipity to occur. The mind has to be prepared to recognize the auspicious datum in the first place. It does so through making connections involving a combination of unexpected circumstances and insight, which serve a need coupled with a valuable outcome (Makri and Blandford 2012a, 2012b), a "unique and contingent mix of insight coupled with chance" that has a purpose (Fine and Degan 1996, 436). In short, there is a practical value to framing one's accumulating data and experience within a model in which systematic empirical research and serendipity complement and reinforce each other (Andel 1994, 644).

Conclusion

The consequence of how one unexplored issue leads to another is a form of nomadology (Hazan and Hertzog 2012). Serendipity forces us to question what anthropology is about, and it arguably has a special relevance to the next generation of graduate students. In turning to serendipity we might well participate in legitimizing an alternative paradigm in ethnographic method in which a centrality is placed in cultivating the preparedness and sagacity required to make the most of the chance discovery. In that context an elementary principle in such anthropological research could be to generate expanding contexts of abduction for iterative reflection in an endless productive process and career-long professional transformation (Gottlieb 2012). And there we might ask as O'Dell and Willim (2011) do – might the concept of "the field" itself have no beginning and no end?

Writing this chapter has allowed me to begin the process of conceptualizing temporal, relational, and analytical aspects of serendipity in my own fieldwork, never mind life, and to realize that my own methods are not as "irregular" as I had assumed in my relative isolation, having been essentially permanently in the field since completing my dissertation twenty years ago. In that time, anthropology has become to me more than anything else about action and interaction, and here I have found common ground with the longstanding ideas in the field, that anthropological theory should derive energy from engagement with rather than insulation from messy political issues and public debates (Hale 2008). As for the unexpected, the insights made by the contributors to the Young Scholars Forum mentioned at the start of this chapter are fitting to return to by way of conclusion. Stefan Le Courant (2013) has considered how serendipity is related to "a continuous oscillation between different researcher personalities" and Julia Giabiconi (2013) has revealed how the unease created by the tensions between the personal self, the ethnographic self, and the academic self can be used as a heuristic tool for generating new forms of anthropological knowledge. Steffen Dalsgaard (2013) has elaborated upon how fieldwork is "temporally constituted," how the relationships between fieldworker and field changes serendipitously over time. This emerging work on serendipity has unexpectedly allowed me insight into my own particular path and personality. It has been transformative for how I now understand my own ethnographic research on museums and on other institutions in Indonesia in the post-Soeharto period, and on social change here more generally. I imagine that if any anthropologist were to reflect upon their own work and career with these ideas of serendipity patterns, specifically oscillation, tension, and time, in mind I am sure each and every one would find interesting significances and patterns they had not been so consciously aware of before, or at least, able to clearly articulate.

In that, perhaps the ideas and literature referred to here might be useful to anthropologists who are struggling to make sense of the ultimate significance of the twists and turns, the unexpected outcomes, the realized and unrealized goals in their research, applied or not. For instance, as regards the serendipitous and peripatetic evolution of my own anthropological career and tendency to embrace unexpected possibilities, had I not met in graduate school and married a fellow anthropologist, an Indonesian activist, Sandra Hamid, now the Indonesian Country Representative for The Asia Foundation, I would not have shifted my primary research from Africa to Asia nor have ever remotely considered such action-oriented embedded anthropological work.

Acknowledgments

At the University of Illinois at Urbana-Champaign, my US institutional research affiliation, I thank Elizabeth Sheehan for bringing the literature on serendipity to my attention and Angelina Cotler for providing me with additional materials. In Indonesia I thank in particular the following people who have variously facilitated these research projects through affiliations or collaboration: the Ahmad family of Muarajambi, Abid Husnul, Ali Akbar, Azyumardi Azra, Bambang Harymurti, Devi Kausar, Jumardi Putra, Lies Marcoes, Ratna Dewi, Reza Idria, Rizki Syahril, Sandra Hamid, Sardono Kusumo, Suadi Asyari, and Yusuf Rahman.

Notes

1 In the normal graduate research context, at least in historical sociology, Charles Tilly (2008) cautions against high-risk but high-consequence research, that it is best left for post-graduate research or what George E. Marcus (2009) refers to as Second Projects.
2 For an instance of the high quality of published research by one Indonesian curator, see Ali Akbar (2015).
3 ICJS was a deliberately strategic conference designed to bring attention to and support the Governor's agenda for a Melayu cultural revival.
4 As summarized by Andel (1994: 636) referring to Peirce's ideas on abduction as the logical process through which explanatory hypotheses are formed. Furthermore, according to Umberto Eco there are three levels of abduction to account for, over-coded, under-coded and creative (Eco and Seboek 1983).
5 One of the most interesting aspects of Rond's article on the definition of true serendipity as "the junction of a causal but meaningful relation" is the literature cited. Besides the foundational references to Andel (1994) and Merton and Barber (2004), we are introduced to a selection of parallel literature in science and business by-and-large uncited in the anthropological and sociological literature.

References

Akbar, Ali. 2015. "The Influence of Ottoman Qur'ans in Southeast Asia through the Ages." In *From Anatolia to Aceh: Ottoman, Turks and Southeast Asia*, edited by A.C.S. Peacock and Annabel Teh Gallop, 311–334. Oxford: Oxford University Press.

Andel, Pek van. 1994. "Anatomy of the Unsought Finding. Serendipity: Origin, History, Domain, Conditions, Appearances, Patterns and Programmability." *British Journal of Philosophy of Science* 45(2):631–648.

Calhoun, Craig J. 2010. *Robert K. Merton: Sociology of Science and Sociology as Science*. New York: Columbia University Press.

Causey, Andrew. 2012. "Drawing Flies: Artwork in the Field." *Critical Arts* 26(2):162–174.

Corneli, Joseph, Alison Pease, Simon Coulton, Anna Jordanous and Christian Guckelsberger. 2012. "Modelling serendipity in a computational context." *Cognitive Computation* 4(3):246–279.

Dalsgaard, Steffen. 2013. "The Field as a Temporal Entity and the Challenges of the Contemporary." *Social Anthropology* 21(2):213–225.

Eco, Umberto, and Thomas A. Seboek. 1983. *The Sign of Three: Dupin, Holmes, Peirce*. Bloomington: Indiana University Press.

Evans, Peter. 1995. *Embedded Autonomy: States and Industrial Transformation*. Princeton: Princeton University Press.

Fabietti, Ugo. 2012. "Errancy in Ethnography and Theory: On the Meaning and Role of 'Discovery' in Anthropological Research." In *Serendipity in Anthropological Research: The Nomadic Turn*, edited by Haim Hazan and Esther Hertzog, 15–30. Farnham, Surrey: Ashgate Publishers.

Fine, Gary, and James Degan. 1996. "Three principles of Serendip: Insight, Choice, and Discovery in Qualitative Research." *Qualitative Studies in Education* 9(4):434–447.

Flanagan, John C. 1954. "The Critical Incident Technique." *Psychological Bulletin* 51(4):327–358.

Giabiconi, Julia. 2013. "Serendipity … Mon Amour? On Discomfort as a Prerequisite for Anthropological Knowledge." *Social Anthropology* 21(2):199–212.

Gottlieb, Alma. 2012. *The Restless Anthropologist: New Field Sites, New Visions*. Chicago: Chicago University Press.

Hale, Charles R. 2008. *Engaging Contradictions: Theory, Politics, and Methods of Activist Scholarship*. Berkeley: University of California Press.

Hazan, Haim, and Esther Hertzog. 2012. *Serendipity in Anthropological Research: The Nomadic Turn*. Farnham, Surrey: Ashgate Publishers.

Hull, Terence. 1994. "Institutional Constraints to Building Social Science Capability in Public Health Research: A Case Study from Indonesia," *Acta Tropica* 57:211–227.

Idria, Reza. forthcoming. "Muslim Punks and State Sharī'a." In *Islam and the Limits of the State: Reconfiguration and Authority in Contemporary Aceh*, edited by Michael Feener. Brill: Leiden University Press.

Johnson, Robert J., and Howard B. Kaplan. 1987. "Corrigendum: Methodology, Technology and Serendipity." *Social Psychology Quarterly* 50:352–354.

Karp, Ivan, Corrine A. Kratz, Lynn Szwaja, and Tomas Ybarra-Frausto. 2006. *Museum Frictions: Public Cultures/Global Transformations*. Durham: Duke University Press.

Kausar, Devi Rosa Krisnandhi. 2013. "Heritage, Tourism and Development: Synchronizing Global, National and Local Narratives." *The First International Conference on Jambi Studies*, 39–50. Jambi: Dewan Kesenian Jambi.

Kausar, Devi, and Jonathan Zilberg. 2013. "Community Based Tourism and Conservation in Muarajambi Temple, Indonesia." Paper presented at *Tourism and the Shifting Values of Heritage*, National Tapei University, Tapei.

Klein, Gary. 2013. *Seeing What Others Don't: The Remarkable Ways We Gain Insights*. London: Nicholas Brealey Publishing.

Lawley, James, and Penny Tompkins. 2008. "Maximizing Serendipity: The Art of Recognizing and Fostering Potential – A Systematic Approach to Change." Paper presented to The Developing 7 Group, June 2008. www.academia.edu/1836363/maximizing_Maximizingserendipity_the_art_of_recognizing_and_fostering_potential. Posted May 18, 2011. Accessed March 9, 2015.

Le Courant, Stefan. 2013. "What Can We Learn from a 'Liar' and a 'Madman'? Serendipity and Double Commitment during Fieldwork." *Social Anthropology* 21(2):186–198.

Le Feuvre, Lisa. 2010. *Failure.* Cambridge, MA: MIT Press.

Makri, Stephann, and Ann Blandford. 2012a. "Coming Across Information Serendipitously – Part 1: A Process Model." *Journal of Documentation* 68(5):684–705.

Makri, Stephann, and Ann Blandford. 2012b. "Coming Across Information Serendipitously – Part 2: A Classification Framework." *Journal of Documentation* 68(5):706–724.

Marcus, George E. 1999. *Critical Anthropology Now: Unexpected Contexts, Shifting Constituencies, Changing Agenda.* Santa Fe: School of American Research Press.

Marcus, George E. 2002. "Beyond Malinowski and after Writing Culture: On the Future of Cultural Anthropology and the Predicament of Ethnography." *The Australian Journal of Anthropology* 13(2):191–199.

Marcus, George E. 2008. "The End(s) of Ethnography: Social/Cultural Anthropology's Signature Form of Producing Knowledge in Transition." *Current Anthropology* 23(1):1–14.

Marcus, George E. 2009. "Notes Towards an Ethnographic Memoir of Supervising Graduate Research through Anthropology's Decades of Transformation." In *Fieldwork Is Not What It Used to Be: Learning Anthropology's Method in a Time of Transition,* edited by James D. Faubion and George E. Marcus, 1–34. Ithaca: Cornell University Press.

McCarthy, John, and Rustam Ibrahim. 2010. *Review of Social Science Capacity Building Support in Indonesia's Knowledge Sector.* Canberra: AUSAID.

McGhee, Annie. 2013. "Going North to the Land of the Snows: Muara Jambi, Serlingpa, Atisha and Tibetan Buddhism." In *The First International Conference on Jambi Studies,* 365–396. Jambi: Dewan Kesenian Jambi.

Merton, Robert K. 1948. "The Bearing of Empirical Research upon the Development of Social Theory." *American Sociological Review* 13(5):505–515.

Merton, Robert. K., and Elinor Barber. 2004. *The Travels and Adventures of Serendipity.* Princeton: Princeton University Press.

O'Dell, Tom, and Robert Willim. 2011. "Irregular Ethnographies: An Introduction." *Ethnological Europaea* 45(1):5–14.

Peirce, Charles S. 1958. "A Neglected Argument for the Reality of God." In *Collected Papers: Selected Writings,* edited by Phillip Weiner, 358–379. New York: Dover.

Portes, Alejandro. 2000. "The Hidden Abode: Sociology as Analysis of the Unexpected. 1999 Presidential Address." *American Sociological Review* 65:1–18.

Remer, Theodore, G. 1965. *Serendipity and the Three Princes.* Norman, OK: Oklahoma University Press.

Rickards, Tudor, Mark A. Runco, and Susan Moger. 2009. *The Routledge Companion to Creativity.* London: Routledge.

Rivoal, Isabelle, and Noel B. Salazar. 2013. "Contemporary Ethnographic Practice and the Value of Serendipity." *Social Anthropology/Anthropologie Social* 21(2):178–185. https://lirias.kuleuven.be/bitstream/123456789/356652/2/Contemporary+ethnographic+practice+and+the+value+of+serendipity.pdf. Accessed March 8, 2015.

Roberts, Royston M. 1989. *Serendipity: Accidental Discoveries in Science.* New York: Wiley.

Rogers, Everett M. (1983) 2003. *Diffusion of Innovations,* 5th edition. New York: Free Press.

Rond, Mark de. 2014. "The Structure of Serendipity." *Culture and Organization*. http://dx. doi.org/10.1080/14759551.2014.967451. Accessed March 8, 2015.

Rous, Beth, and Katherine McCormick. 2006. "A Critical Incident Technique: A Valuable Research Tool for Early Intervention," Research Spotlight, National Early Childhood Transition Center, May 2006. www.hdi.uky.edu/nectc/Libraries/NECTC_Rearch_ Spotlights/Critical_Incident_Technique.sflb.ashx. Accessed March 8, 2015.

Samuels, Annemarie. 2012. *"After the Tsunami: The Remaking of Everyday Life in Banda Aceh, Indonesia."* Doctoral thesis, Leiden University.

Schneider, Arnd, and Christopher Wright. 2013. *Anthropology and Art Practice*. London: Bloomsbury Academic.

Shavinina, Larisa V. (ed.) 2003. *International Handbook on Innovation*. Oxford: Elsevier Science Limited.

Suryadama, Daniel, and Gavin W. Jones. 2013. *Education in Indonesia*. Singapore: ISEAS.

Swan, Jaqueline, Harry Scarborough, and Maxine Robertson. 2003. "Linking Knowledge, Networking and Innovation Processes: A Conceptual Model." In *Handbook of Innovation*, edited by Larisa V. Shavinina, 680–694. Oxford: Elsevier Science Limited.

Syahril, Rizki K. 2008. "Tsunami Museum: Collective Memory, Destruction, Disaster, and History." *Syndicate Dokarim*. https://sindikatdokarim.wordpress.com/2008/12/03/tsunami-museum-penhancura-ingatan-kolektif-bencana-dan-sejarah. Accessed March 8, 2015.

Taleb, Nassim N. 2007. *The Black Swan: The Impact of the Highly Improbable*. New York: Penguin.

Tilley, Charles. 2008. "Selecting a Dissertation Topic: Range and Scope." http://essays.ssrc. org/tilly/resources. Accessed March 8, 2015.

Willim, Robert. 2013. "Out of Hand: Reflections on Elsewhereness." In *Anthropology and Art Practice*, edited by Arnd Schneider and Christopher Wright, 81–88. London: Bloomsbury Academic.

Zainul, Aris A. 2013. "ICJS Sangat Strategis Bagi Provinsi Jambi." *Jambi Tribune*. Thursday 21 November. www.newskpkjambi.com/.../523-icjs-sangat-strategis-bagi-provinsi-jambi. Accessed March, 2015.

Zelizer, Viviana, A. 2010. "Culture and Uncertainty." In *Robert K. Merton. Sociology of Science and Sociology as Science*, edited by Craig J. Calhoun. New York: Columbia University Press.

Zilberg, Jonathan. (1995) 2003. "Yes, It's True: Zimbabweans Love Dolly Parton." First published in *Journal of Popular Culture. Special Issue: Anthropology and Popular Culture* 29(1):111–125. In *Readings from the Disciplines: Research Models for Writers*, 1st edition, edited by Christine Hult. Reprint, 3rd edition. New York: Allyn and Bacon.

Zilberg, Jonathan. 2007. "Traditional Textiles of Indonesia: Today and in the Future." *Proceedings of the Second International Textile Conference at the National Museum of Indonesia, Jakarta, 21–22*. Edited and with an introduction by Jonathan Zilberg. Unpublished manuscript. Jakarta: National Museum of Indonesia. www.academia.edu/10917547/Traditional_Textiles_of_ Indonesia_Today_and_in_the_Future. Accessed March 8, 2015.

Zilberg, Jonathan. 2009. "Memorials, State Domination and Inclusion versus Exclusion: The Case of the Tsunami Museum in Banda Aceh." *The International Journal of the Inclusive Museum* 2(2):99–110.

Zilberg, Jonathan. 2010. "An Anthropological Visit to the Museum Istiqlal." *Suhuf* 3(2):251–275.

Zilberg, Jonathan. 2011. "The Museum Istiqlal: The Case of an Indonesian Islamic Museum." *Suhuf* 4(2):341–357.

Zilberg, Jonathan. 2014. "Is the Museum in Indonesia a Colonial Relic?" Paper presented at the Center for International Studies, Cornell University, Ithaca, New York, October 21.

6

FACULTY DEVELOPMENT AS APPLIED EDUCATIONAL ANTHROPOLOGY

Lauren Miller Griffith

Although I worked for two years in a faculty development center, I did not receive any formal instruction in educational anthropology. My primary interest when I started graduate school was in the anthropology of performance, with a regional focus on Latin America. My secondary interests in tourism and how people learn developed in service of my primary focus. As I pursued this topic, I found that while the anthropological and educational bodies of literature often talked past one another, there was a great deal of complementary material to be found in each corpus. This helped me develop my personal philosophy on teaching and learning in higher education, which I have used in my own teaching and in my work as a faculty development specialist.

I conducted the bulk of my international field research on the Afro-Brazilian martial art *capoeira* during 2008, just as the economy was entering a major recession. I still remember the day I went to the ATM and realized that the exchange rate between the Brazilian *real* and the US dollar was less than two to one. I immediately realized the implications this would have for how much research I could afford to conduct, but was slower to realize what this meant for my prospects as a job candidate. According to research conducted by the National Science Foundation, job prospects for new PhDs continue to decline, having reached their lowest point in more than a decade (June 2014). Although the outlook is slightly better for those in social science than in other disciplines, this is worrisome news for those approaching graduation. Today, there are fewer tenure-track positions open to new PhDs and some are skeptical that such job opportunities will ever rebound to pre-recession levels; therefore, many individuals will by default have to find employment outside of academia (Patel 2015). This problem is not limited to the US; governments throughout the world are encouraging reforms aimed at improving the employability of new PhDs (see Cuthbert and Molla 2015 for a review of Australia's work in this area).

Given the state of the job market that awaited, I was grateful that I had not only begun delving into the literature on the anthropology of education, but had also held a graduate assistantship in my university's teaching center. Although many colleges and universities are shifting toward the use of contingent, rather than tenure-track, faculty, meaning there are fewer secure positions available, these same institutions continue to invest in administrative and professional positions. My experiences as a graduate student opened my eyes to faculty development as an alternative academic career that would ultimately sustain me during a few lean years on the tenure-track job market. Although I have now left behind the world of faculty development for an assistant professorship at a small liberal arts college, I continue to fervently believe that there are a number of problems in higher education today that anthropologists are particularly well suited to address. Anthropologists are good at understanding the lived experience of people who are at the heart of a social phenomenon – in this case, students. We are also good at being cultural mediators. Just as we can understand student culture, we can also understand faculty culture and help the two groups find common ground, which leads to a more productive learning environment. Therefore, this chapter will focus on how anthropologists can help faculty assess the effectiveness of their teaching, contribute to curriculum design, improve campus climate for underrepresented student populations, and make sure faculty and students avoid the potentially paternalistic pitfalls of service learning.

When looking for a job outside of a traditional anthropology program, job seekers have to be their own public relations agents. Very rarely will a job advertisement include the word "anthropologist," so the applicant must make the case that his or her training in anthropology provides the ideal background for a faculty development specialist. This career path may at first seem like a radical deviation from one's original intent to become an anthropologist. After all, because the majority of an anthropologist's professional training takes place in academic settings, students rarely encounter models of nonacademic career paths. Furthermore, many students pursue graduate training in anthropology because of their fondness for academic research and desire to be in the field. Yet, as I will argue in this chapter, it is possible to maintain one's scholarly agenda and build a publication record while working in a faculty development center.

Faculty Development: An Overview of the Field

Faculty developers are tasked with providing ongoing professional support to instructional staff. Faculty developers find employment in both higher education and K–12 settings, though this chapter focuses specifically on the former. In some institutions, this will be a full-time, often twelve-month, salaried position in which one's sole duty is to provide pedagogical support to the faculty. In other institutions, this may be a part-time specialization that one takes on in addition to another instructional or administrative role. In this section, I will explore four common tasks undertaken by faculty development specialists: assessing and improving teaching, assisting with curriculum design, improving campus climate, and fostering the growth of service learning. In each of these areas, the training one receives as a graduate student in anthropology can be immensely beneficial.

Assessing and Improving Teaching

Assessing and improving the quality of teaching on campus is the primary duty of faculty developers. New faculty developers should expect to spend the majority of their time conducting consultations with faculty, observing and evaluating teaching, and preparing workshops, webinars, or other materials that will support faculty members' professional development. Many people are under the impression that teaching is a natural talent you either have or you do not. In reality, teaching is a skill that must be learned and refined over time, just like any other skill. Yet the academy tends to reinforce this myth by cultivating the research skills of graduate students without paying much if any attention to their skills as teachers (Pace 2004).

There are two primary ways to address this issue. The first, often seen as more important by the administration, is helping faculty members adopt more active learning techniques in their own teaching. The second approach, which is becoming increasingly popular at institutions with graduate students, is to interrupt the cycle of under-preparedness by creating a program that teaches graduate students how to be more effective in the classroom. A full exploration of the second is outside the scope of this chapter; a forthcoming edited volume provides a comprehensive overview of ways that developers can help prepare graduate students to become faculty members (Border, forthcoming).

Assessing teaching involves a significant amount of fieldwork on the part of the faculty developer. In my own experience, a faculty member found his or her way into our center via one of two possible paths. Ideally, the faculty member would approach us because he or she was intrinsically motivated to improve the learning experience for his or her students. In other cases, however, the faculty member might be referred to us by a department chair or dean who had noticed an alarming trend in the faculty member's teaching evaluations or had otherwise been alerted to a problem in the classroom.

In either case, the first step is to have an initial meeting with the faculty member to discuss his or her goals in having an outside evaluation conducted. Oftentimes this involves reviewing the quantitative and qualitative feedback the faculty member has received from past student evaluations. Generally, I have found that a rapid, interpretive analysis of this data is sufficient to determine what to focus on in the actual classroom observation. Granted, there may be times when a more in-depth, statistical analysis of this data is warranted, but faculty developers rarely have the luxury of devoting this much time to a single client.

After reviewing this data and discussing the faculty member's impressions of his or her teaching, the faculty developer must make a plan for gathering data that addresses these concerns. Some investigations will be quite general and others will be more targeted. Perhaps the most common form of data collection used in faculty development is the "small group instructional diagnosis" or SGID (Lenze 2012). In its most basic form, a SGID is conducted by dividing students into small groups and having them consider three questions:

1. What is the professor/instructor doing that is *helping* my learning?
2. What is the professor/instructor doing that is *hindering* my learning?
3. What changes could this professor/instructor make to improve my learning?

Then, if time allows, each small group shares their findings with the class and the faculty developer takes notes on their discussion. In actual practice, depending on the size of the class, I often skipped the small-group step and had students do this activity as a class. The skills needed to run a successful SGID are no different from running a focus group, a skill many anthropology graduate students already have or can easily develop. Anthropologists often find focus groups useful when wanting to gather a large number of responses in a relatively short amount of time regarding why people hold certain perspectives or how they make decisions (see Bernard 2006), which is precisely the kind of information faculty developers are trying to learn from a SGID.

It is important that the faculty member not be present for the SGID because his or her presence might inhibit students' comments. The entire process generally takes fifteen to twenty minutes and I prefer to do it at the end of a class period so that I can dismiss the class but invite any of them who want to add additional information to stay. On occasion, I have found that students who might be afraid to reveal a concern in front of their peers will stay behind and tell me these things privately. After the SGID, the faculty developer can perform a content analysis of the notes gathered and present the data to the faculty member.

Another data-collection technique, which can be used in isolation or in conjunction with the SGID, is the classroom observation. Here the anthropologist's training in participant observation can be quite useful. Having determined the focus of the observation through the initial consultation with the faculty member, the anthropologist can focus on potential problems in the faculty member's performance as well as how the students respond to the instruction. While an SGID is certainly faster and allows the faculty developer to gather targeted information, as anthropologists know, observations allow the researcher to witness participants' behavior in as natural a setting as possible.

There may also be situations that call for the use of additional methodologies like surveys, interviews, or focus groups conducted outside of the regular class meeting time. For example, I worked with one faculty member who was teaching a large, introductory class with nearly 200 students. This professor had been in an administrative position for several years and this was his first semester back in the classroom, so he wanted to check in and see how his students thought things were going in class. An SGID would have been difficult to do in such a large group and a single, fifty-minute observation would not have been sufficient to develop an understanding of how all 200 students were responding to the instruction.

Therefore, after discussing the faculty member's specific concerns, I created a customized survey focused on student engagement. I was able to quickly analyze the data and provide a summary to the faculty member within just a few days.

Another way that faculty developers help faculty members improve their teaching is by leading workshops. While there is some debate about whether workshops are as effective as one-on-one interventions based on data collection, many teaching centers continue to provide workshops because they offer economies of scale. Twenty faculty members or more can be reached in the same amount of time as a single data-collection session. Anthropologists who have gained teaching experience, either as a grader, teaching assistant, or even field supervisor, will be able to put their pedagogical skills to use in this area. Another popular approach is that of the faculty learning community in which faculty regularly gather to discuss a topic of their choosing with the assistance of a faculty development specialist who serves as a facilitator in much the same way that a professor might facilitate a graduate-level seminar (see Cox 2004).

Curriculum Design

Depending on the size of the institution, a faculty developer may or may not be involved in curriculum design and assessment. At the institution where I worked, there was a separate curriculum office that dealt with university-wide curricular issues, especially curriculum assessment; however, our unit was occasionally called upon to help departments that were in the process of revising their curriculum. In these cases, the faculty developer is not expected to be a content area expert, but to help facilitate the department's discussions about the curriculum. For example, when one department in the natural sciences wanted to completely redesign their curriculum, individuals from our office attended their meetings to help them articulate learning objectives and determine which courses would address each objective.

There is a structured approach to course and curriculum design (see Wiggins and McTighe 2005), which anyone moving into the faculty development field should be familiar with, but assisting a department with curriculum design requires interpersonal skills in addition to just knowing how to build a curriculum map. It is not uncommon for faculty members to become emotionally invested in the courses they teach, and curriculum revision may feel threatening to individuals who think their interests will not be represented in the new curriculum. The rigid hierarchy of academic positions also complicates these meetings, with instructors and assistant professors often feeling like they have less of a voice than their tenured counterparts. It takes a skilled facilitator to navigate these dynamics. Anthropologists who have been involved in any kind of community development work or participatory research projects will be well suited to facilitating these meetings diplomatically.

When working with departments that are in the process of proposing new programs, faculty developers may be called upon to do research on competing programs at other schools. For example, one department at the institution where I worked was considering proposing a master's program. At one of their initial meetings, I presented an overview of the programs available at nearby institutions as well as those in our peer group. Although the program was ultimately not pursued, this research enabled them to see what they would need to offer if they wanted to be competitive, and helped them think about the specific niche they could fill within this market. The data I used for this task came from program websites rather than scholarly journals, but the steps of data collection, synthesis, and evaluation were essentially the same ones I would use when creating a literature review.

Improving Campus Climate

One of the hallmarks of anthropology, or at least one of its ideals, is our ability to build rapport with individuals from cultural backgrounds different from our own. As institutions of higher education become increasingly diverse, this skill becomes particularly marketable. The norms of college teaching continue to reflect the white, male, middle- to upper-class backgrounds of those who created the system (Smith and Wolf-Wendel 2005). Students from other backgrounds are often forced to assimilate to these norms, which frequently compromises the student's sense of self and their efficacy (ibid.). This often manifests itself in lower rates of achievement for students from underrepresented backgrounds as well as higher rates of attrition. Unfortunately, many faculty members, particularly those in the science, technology, engineering, and math (STEM) fields, are either unaware of this problem or do not see it as something that they should be expected to address. Working in the capacity of faculty development specialists, anthropologists have the opportunity to open faculty members' eyes to how their teaching unintentionally replicates these norms and contributes to the marginalization of underrepresented students, which is an extension of the participatory methods and empathetic representations that our discipline has long used in the service of building cross-cultural understanding.

Some institutions have a separate office of diversity and inclusion. Diversity programming may be provided to faculty through this office, but most diversity officers are not trained in inclusive teaching methods. Therefore, even when a campus does have a separate diversity office, it may be beneficial for the teaching center to co-sponsor a workshop or speaker series on inclusive pedagogies. This is precisely what I did at my prior institution where the director of diversity education was also, interestingly enough, an anthropologist. Together we created a five-part workshop series. Importantly, we took turns hosting these workshops so that neither office was seen as having a monopoly over the topic of inclusive teaching.

One of the problems we found in running this workshop series was that it tended to attract individuals who were already sympathetic to the issue of diversity in the classroom. These conversations were nonetheless beneficial, and we received high ratings on our workshop evaluations, but we struggled to get the message out to the audience that needed to hear it the most. Therefore, one thing an anthropologist working in this capacity can do is to make sure that inclusive pedagogies are integrated into *all* workshops hosted by the teaching center. By using these methods during workshops and calling attention to them, faculty who would not seek out opportunities to learn about diversity will nonetheless be exposed to some key principles. When a teaching center happens to be in charge of new faculty orientation, this can also be an opportunity to present information about the diversity of the student body and the importance of using inclusive pedagogies so that all students have an opportunity to succeed.

Service Learning

Another area in which anthropologists might find a special niche is in promoting service learning. By service learning, I mean a mutually beneficial partnership between a specific class and a community partner in which what the students learn in class can be put into practice in the community, and what they learn through their service is brought to bear upon the classroom experience. These kinds of learning experiences that extend beyond the classroom are often recommended as best practices for education because they involve authentic learning tasks that demand active engagement and collaboration (McKinney et al. 2004, 44).

While I agree that service learning can have a positive outcome for students, it can also have unintended, negative consequences for members of the community (see Mitchell 2008). When college students enter a community trying to "fix" a problem that they are experiencing, it can have paternalistic overtones. The students generally do not have the lived experience necessary to truly understand the problem(s) facing the community. Anthropologists can help by working with the faculty member designing the service-learning course as well as with the students, to help them understand the importance of listening to the community concerns and being responsive to those needs rather than imposing their worldview on the community. Acting as a liaison between the faculty member and the community partner can also be beneficial, because the anthropologist working in a faculty development center is not constrained by the same rigid timeline as is the professor and students whose work has to be completed within the course of the semester. Faculty developers typically work year-round, so they will have more time to build relationships with the community partner, follow up with the partner after the students' work is complete, and bring subsequent groups of students up to speed on what work has already been done and what is yet to be completed.

Maintaining an Active Scholarly Agenda

Many of us pursued doctoral degrees because we enjoy conducting research and find value in sharing the results of that research. Pursuing an applied career does not have to mean an end to one's scholarly writing. Although a faculty developer's daily duties will probably be more focused on consultations with faculty and curriculum development projects at the local level, publication in scholarly journals is often encouraged. There is an entire field known as the Scholarship of Teaching and Learning (SoTL) that focuses on this kind of work.

Some SoTL projects are modest, focusing on a teaching innovation that took place in one instructor's classroom. Others are more theoretical, attempting to explain how people learn. SoTL studies can be qualitative or quantitative, based on a single case or a longitudinal study of intellectual development. The breadth of topics that can be studied within SoTL should feel quite comfortable to most anthropologists. Anthropologists' commitment to holism has gradually developed into a willingness to embrace interdisciplinarity as we engage with scholars working in "cultural studies" writ large (see Marcus 1992). This ability to read beyond the confines of our field prepares anthropologists to work in SoTL, a relatively young, interdisciplinary field whose parameters are still being defined (see Boyer 1990).

The direction of an anthropologist's research will likely change when he or she becomes part of the faculty development community. The topics pursued will be constrained by a number of factors including the current needs of the faculty and/or administration, the problems facing students on campus, and the degree of academic freedom granted by the director of the teaching center or administrators who oversee the division. For example, when I first joined the faculty development center at my previous institution, I was assigned to work with a group of teachers who were trying to improve student engagement by integrating technology into large lecture courses. This was not an area that I previously had any experiences or interest in; however, I approached it as I would any other new project. I began with participant observation, sending my field notes to the professors after each class so they could benefit from what I was seeing. Once I had a sense of some of the reasons why students were disengaging, I worked with our center's educational technologist to develop a survey that could be completed in class with the aid of classroom-response devices or clickers. We also shared this information with the faculty members in charge of the course. Then, based on my field notes and the survey data, the two of us led several focus group interviews to gain more in-depth information about several of the themes that had intrigued us. In the end, we were able to conclude that incorporating a new technology without evaluating and improving the overall course design would "be limited at best and distracting at worst" (Griffith and Roberts 2013, 307).

Although our work on this project began as an assignment from the director of our teaching center, and the dean of the college in which this large lecture course was taught had also requested our support, we ultimately published our findings in an edited volume on technology in higher education (Griffith and Roberts 2013). However, this was not as simple as it sounds, and anyone hoping to continue building his or her curriculum vitae while also filling the requirements of a faculty development job should be prepared for some challenges related to trying to simultaneously perform the roles of employee and researcher. For example, serious questions had been raised about the sustainability of staffing this course and an individual in the administration asked for our data so that it could be used in making personnel decisions. This raised questions about who "owns" the data from research being conducted by a member of the teaching center. In most cases, teaching centers are intentionally absent from evaluative decisions about issues like retention, tenure, and promotion so that the teaching center can be viewed as a "safe space" where faculty go when they need help. Being asked for our data to make a personnel decision not only violated the charter of our center, but it violated my ethics as an anthropologist. My co-author and I refused to share our data and while this initially caused some tension with the administrator who oversaw our center, it was the right thing to do. When we published our findings, we took care to protect the identities of the faculty involved as much as possible so that there would not be negative repercussions of our work.

As in any field, there is a hierarchy of SoTL journals in which one might publish work. The most reputable journals are, of course, peer-reviewed. However, I found that when I was on the job market, looking for a tenure-track position in anthropology, many departments were uninformed regarding SoTL. In such cases, the burden of explaining what SoTL is and how it can be evaluated relative to disciplinary journals falls to the applicant. Job seekers should be prepared to dispassionately explain both the peer-review process in SoTL and why SoTL work *is* anthropology. If an applied educational anthropologist can find a home for this kind of scholarship in the more traditional academic journals, he or she should absolutely do so. I have done this by applying concepts from my faculty development work, like problem-based learning, to my earlier field studies on *capoeira* (see Griffith 2014). I have also found it useful to search for calls-for-papers online, which has increased my awareness of lesser-known anthropology journals and edited volumes. Although the most prestigious anthropology journals rarely publish pedagogy pieces, our discipline has traditionally been interested in issues of how people learn (i.e. enculturation) and journals may be receptive to the idea of a special issue on this topic, which would create an opportunity for anthropologists working in faculty development to share their work.

Even if one decides to publish exclusively in SoTL journals like *College Teaching*, it is advisable to find other ways of maintaining a connection with anthropology journals. For example, *General Anthropology* includes a regular column on teaching, which can be a great outlet for more practical, applied pieces. Another option is to consider writing an occasional book review for a journal like *Anthropology & Education Quarterly*. While a junior scholar would not want to write too many of these, as it suggests he or she lacks unique research to publish, it is a way to stay connected to anthropology as a discipline.

Anthropologists working in faculty development should also look for parallels between what they are doing and larger theoretical discussions in the discipline. Good anthropological theory crosscuts specific field sites, so the college classroom should be treated as just another field site. If the research conducted by a faculty development specialist is not suitable for an anthropology journal, it may still be possible to present this research at anthropology conferences as long as the abstract stresses the theoretical issues that make the work relevant to others in anthropology. The annual Society for Applied Anthropology meeting is an excellent venue for this kind of work.

Preparing for a Career in Applied Educational Anthropology

Although some people today are entering the field of faculty development after receiving graduate training in education leadership programs, this is not a requirement. Many individuals who become involved in faculty development came to it from other disciplines; however, there are some courses within these programs that can be useful for graduate students considering alternative academic careers. Prospective faculty developers should also make use of the workshops being offered for instructors on their campus. Not only will this provide exposure to more of the information about how learning works, it may also give prospective faculty developers ideas for the kinds of workshops they would like to create in the future. Because job finalists are often asked to give a sample workshop as part of their campus visits, it is very important to have experience with these kinds of workshops. With or without access to formal classes and workshops, future faculty developers should educate themselves about how people learn. Fortunately, most of the literature on college teaching was intended to be interdisciplinary and is therefore relatively free of specialized jargon.

Attending conferences and participating in professional organizations is another way to prepare for a career in this field. The Lilly Conferences on College and University Teaching and Learning in the US are particularly well respected and attract faculty members from a wide variety of institutions as well as leaders in the field of faculty development. The intimate environment of these conferences makes networking with established faculty development professionals relatively nonthreatening for junior colleagues. The International Society for the Scholarship of Teaching and Learning (ISSoTL) also hosts an annual conference. Whereas the goal of the Lilly conferences is to give faculty and faculty developers alike exposure to new teaching techniques that can immediately be applied in the classroom, the ISSoTL conference feels more like a traditional academic conference in that its focus is on dissemination of scholarly research on teaching and learning. These conferences are hosted in a different location each year, rotating between the US, Canada, and the United Kingdom. In Canada, the Society for Teaching and Learning in Higher Education also hosts an annual conference. The International Consortium for Educational Development is made up of national faculty development organizations and holds a conference every other year in cities around the globe. Recent events have been held in Stockholm, Bangkok, and Barcelona. Similarly, the International Conference on Improving University Teaching is held in a different country each year, which increases the accessibility of these conferences to scholars.

Another important organization with which to become familiar is the POD Network, the primary professional organization for faculty development specialists in the US. This organization hosts an active listserv and members are extremely willing to support their junior colleagues' development. They too host an annual conference, which is geared primarily towards faculty development specialists rather than faculty members. A benefit of attending this conference is its "job fair" event, which is a relatively informal meet-and-greet period in which candidates looking for a position in the field of faculty development can meet with potential employers.

Another way for individuals to become familiar with the field of faculty development is to begin doing research on their own teaching. The article of mine that gets the most attention, at least based on informal metrics from academia.edu, is an article I wrote based on a teaching innovation I developed for my own class before I became a faculty development specialist and long before I had a tenure-track position. I developed this classroom exercise because my colleagues and I noticed that students found Bourdieu to be particularly difficult to understand (see Griffith 2012). When I created this activity, I did not intend to publish it, but I did so at the urging of the faculty development specialist at the institution where I was teaching. Working on the literature review forced me to deal with a new body of scholarship that I had not encountered previously, which became a starting point for the development of a workshop series I delivered on campus.

For graduate students who are already considering an alternative academic career like faculty development, there may be opportunities to work with their faculty advisors and other mentors on the development of similar projects. If considering this, it is important to find a faculty member who respects the SoTL tradition. I was fortunate in this regard, but in a series of interviews collected by a research team of which I was a part, we found that many advisors actively discouraged their students from focusing on teaching. While this may make sense for graduate students who are preparing for a career at R1 institutions,[1] the truth is that most PhDs will *not* work in such places. Conducting SoTL research is a great way to prepare either for a faculty career in a teaching-intensive institution *or* for a career in faculty development.

Individuals interested in this kind of research might also see what kind of work is already being done on campus and look for ways to get involved. The best place to start is with the campus teaching center. As a student, I had a paid research assistantship with our faculty center, which allowed me to learn many of these skills and familiarize myself with the literature on teaching and learning while working. However, not every teaching center will be as well supported financially. When I became a faculty developer myself, I worked with several students who were able to negotiate informal internship opportunities with our center's director. These were short-term, project-based appointments that may not have been lucrative, but did allow the students to develop an understanding of the kind of work we did. In several of these cases, the students were able to participate in data collection or analysis, which is important in building the kind of resume needed for a faculty development career.

When applying for faculty development positions, applicants should use examples from their own teaching selectively. This is not a teaching position for which one is applying, it is a consultant position, so the applicant will need to show that he or she has the skills to assess and improve others' teaching. The committee is not likely to be swayed by anecdotal evidence of student satisfaction. They will be more impressed by evidence that an applicant has conducted assessments of student learning, in his or her own classes or in someone else's, and that the applicant has made or recommended changes based on those assessments. The committee will also want to know whether or not an applicant has the facilitation skills required to successfully work with faculty members and administrators in an often politically charged environment.

Becoming Comfortable in This New Role

In the interest of full disclosure, there is a reason that I am no longer employed in faculty development. While I did feel that my research was making a significant difference for the students and faculty that I worked with, I missed having my own classes and I mourned the loss of the "anthropologist identity" that came with being academic staff rather than faculty. Whether accurate or not, I felt that many of my colleagues in the anthropology program at my school did not see me as a "real" anthropologist and that caused me a great deal of frustration. My advice to anyone who is considering a job in faculty development is to establish his or her professional identity early on and in no uncertain terms.

If I could do it all over again, here are some things that I think would have made me more confident in my sense of self. If a job candidate wants to teach a course in the anthropology program or have a courtesy appointment in the anthropology department, he or she needs to inquire about this before signing any contractual documents. It must be in writing. I received a verbal assurance that this would not be a problem, but it was more than a year before I was able to get a single course as an adjunct. If at all possible, candidates should arrange to meet with the anthropology department chair during their interview or have a phone conversation with him/ her during contractual negotiations. Again, it is important that candidates be very clear about their goals and candid to all parties involved about what it will take to get him or her to accept the job. Even if told, "we'll figure this out when you get here," candidates should know that changes to their appointment or workload will be more difficult after the paperwork is signed. It may be helpful to remind administrators that the more years a faculty developer spends removed from the classroom, the less credible his or her advice on teaching and learning will seem to the very faculty they are trying to help. Therefore, I argue that teaching *at least* one course per year, if not one per semester, is crucial to the mission of the teaching center.

There may be some flexibility in the actual job title associated with this career. Whereas some people are called "faculty development specialists," others are called "learning consultants" or "instructional designers." Using the title "applied educational anthropologist" or having this language included in the job description, reinforces one's disciplinary connections and increases scholarly legitimacy with the faculty. Even if it is a symbolic action, having this title on a business card may also help applied anthropologists feel as though they "belong" at conferences and disciplinary gatherings.

As soon as possible, applied educational anthropologists should talk to their supervisors about what counts as appropriate professionalization. As discussed previously, there are many valuable conferences on teaching and learning, but it is also important to maintain a connection with anthropology. I encourage new developers to argue that attending anthropology conferences should be part of their regular professionalization, but not expect that one's supervisor will immediately understand the value of these conferences. It may help to prepare for that conversation by compiling a list of papers and panels from previous conferences that would be of benefit to the teaching center. Applied educational anthropologists can also offer to report to the rest of the staff about how they can apply what they learned to the teaching center's goals.

Conclusion

Given the unpredictability of the academic job market, it is important to consider alternative careers. Unfortunately, most graduate programs are focused on cultivating research skills in PhD students and pedagogical training is often treated as an afterthought, if it is addressed at all. The idea that some people are born teachers and others are not is a myth that I hope this chapter can dispel. Teaching is a skill like any other that can be refined with practice and attention to feedback from students. Anthropologists have developed a broad skill set that can be used to gather data about student learning and transform this into a set of recommendations for faculty hoping to improve their teaching.

The field of faculty development is particularly well suited to anthropologists. Not only do we have the skills necessary to collect data from students that will contribute to the improvement of teaching and learning, there are also several subsets of the faculty development field that are ideal for anthropologists. As specialists in intercultural understanding, anthropologists can make a significant contribution to improving campus climate. As our campuses become increasingly diverse, it is important to educate faculty members on inclusive pedagogies that will help all students accomplish their academic goals. Similarly, anthropologists with experience in community development and participatory research are ideally positioned to improve the quality of service learning projects.

Undertaking this line of work does not mean forsaking one's interest in academic advancement. Many teaching centers encourage faculty developers to publish their findings on how people learn. Oftentimes these studies are appropriate for publication in SoTL journals, though some might be presentable in anthropological forums. If a faculty developer should want to transition to an academic appointment in a traditional discipline, it is important to continually add items such as these to his or her curriculum vitae.

It is important for anyone considering going into this field to have a good sense of how administrative and professional academic appointments work. While it is possible to request a teaching appointment in addition to one's other duties, such an appointment is not guaranteed. Successfully balancing one's roles as an academic and as a college/university staff member can be challenging, but this can be a fulfilling career path for individuals who enjoy conducting fieldwork and seeing the results of those findings being applied in an educational setting.

Acknowledgments

I would like to thank the faculty and students with whom I worked as a faculty developer for opening their classrooms to me.

Note

1 The term Research 1, or R1, refers to research-intensive universities that offer a full range of undergraduate degrees and award at least fifty doctorates per year.

References

Bernard, H. Russell. 2006. *Research Methods in Anthropology: Qualitative and Quantitative Approaches*. 4th edition. Lanham: AltaMira Press.

Border, Laura. forthcoming. "Preparing for College and University Teaching: Competencies for Graduate and Professional Students." Thematic issue, *Studies in Graduate and Professional Student Development* 16.

Boyer, Ernest L. 1990. *Scholarship Reconsidered: Priorities of the Professoriate*. San Francisco: Jossey-Bass.

Cox, Milton D. 2004. "Introduction to faculty learning communities." *New Directions for Teaching and Learning* 97:5–23.

Cuthbert, Denise, and Tebeje Molla. 2015. "PhD Crisis Discourse: A Critical Approach to the Framing of the Problem and Some Australian 'Solutions'." *Higher Education* 69:33–53.

Griffith, Lauren Miller. 2012. "Bourdieu's Game of Life: Using Simulation to Facilitate Understanding of Complex Theories." *College Teaching* 60:147–153.

Griffith, Lauren Miller. 2014. "Signature Pedagogies in the Afro-Brazilian Martial Art *Capoeira*: Why Problem Based Learning Produces Better Performers." *Theatre Annual* 67:1–22.

Griffith, Lauren Miller, and Brian A. Roberts. 2013. "Learning Tool or Distraction: Student Responses to the Use of iOS Devices." In *Increasing Student Engagement and Retention Using Classroom Technologies: Classroom Response Systems and Mediated Discourse Technologies*, edited by Patrick Blessinger and Charles Wankel, 307–336. Bingley: Emerald Group Publishing Limited.

June, Audrey Williams. 2014. "Doctoral Degrees Increased Last Year, but Career Opportunities Remained Bleak." *The Chronicle of Higher Education*, December 5.

Lenze, Lisa Firing. 2012. "Small Group Instructional Diagnosis (SGID)." In *Practically Speaking: A Sourcebook for Instructional Consultants in Higher Education*, edited by Kathleen T. Brinko, 46–52. Stillwater, OK: New Forums Press Inc.

Marcus, George E. 1992. "Introduction." In *Rereading Cultural Anthropology*, edited by George E. Marcus, iv–xiv. Durham: Duke University Press.

McKinney, Kathleen, Karey Vacca, Maria A. Medvedeva, and Janice Malak. 2004. "Beyond the Classroom: An Exploratory Study of Out-of-Class Learning in Sociology." *Teaching Sociology* 32(1):43–60.

Mitchell, Tania D. 2008. "Traditional vs. Critical Service-Learning: Engaging the Literature to Differentiate Two Models." *Michigan Journal of Community Service Learning* 14(2):50–65.

Pace, David. 2004. "The Amateur in the Operating Room: History and the Scholarship of Teaching and Learning." *The American Historical Review* 109(4):1171–1192.

Patel, Vimal. 2015. "New Job on Campus: Expanding Ph.D. Career Options." *The Chronicle of Higher Education*, January 12.

Smith, Daryl G., and Lisa E. Wolf-Wendel. 2005. "The Challenge of Diversity: Involvement or Alienation in the Academy?" *ASHE Higher Education Report* 31(1):1–100.

Wiggins, Grant P., and Jay McTighe. 2005. *Understanding by Design*. Alexandria, VA: ASCD.

7

ISLAM AND DYING IN THE UNITED STATES

How Anthropology Contributes to Culturally Competent Care at the End-of-Life

Cortney Hughes Rinker

I was on a conference call with hospital administrators, health care providers, consultants, and researchers from the North and Mid-Atlantic States involved in developing a proposal for federal funding that addressed the need to keep patients from being re-admitted to the hospital within thirty days of discharge. This proposal was in response to the 2010 US health care law that authorized the government to fine hospitals "because many of their patients are readmitted soon after discharge" (Rau 2012). This is "part of a multipronged effort by Medicare to use its financial muscle to force improvements in hospital quality" (Rau 2012). On the call it was concluded that the surveys provided to patients in the hospital before discharge about the care they will receive at home and discussions with nurses and medical staff about discharge instructions were inadequate; we needed to understand what was happening at home and in their communities in order to provide a better picture as to why patients are being re-admitted within one month.

As the only anthropologist in the group, I believed that it was critical to realize that patients do not stay in the hospital and, therefore, we needed to better understand how culture and social circumstances impact whether or not they follow their discharge instructions and if they do, to what degree. It is also important to realize that non-compliance is a choice that people are able to make (Campbell et al. 2001). In this instance, many of the involved hospitals' re-admissions were due to class issues and the fact that several of the patients relied on public health care and did not have a private family physician to follow up with after discharge. They often used the emergency room as primary care even though critical care is very costly. At that point I realized the importance of culturally competent health care and taking into consideration people's backgrounds when caring for them and when designing treatment plans. At the time, I was a postdoctoral fellow working with a health care organization in rural Virginia where many of the patients qualified for government assistance. In working with administrators and physicians to improve the quality of primary care, I did more research on cultural competence in health care and how we could apply it. In this, I realized that class was not an issue often addressed in practice and discovered that the term is frequently used in a very narrow sense to refer to the treatment of ethnic minorities, rather than in a more robust sense that encourages providers to offer treatment and home care instructions that take into consideration issues such as religion, gender, sexuality, and class in addition to ethnicity.

Cultural competence has become a buzzword in the health care system in the United States and internationally (Baker and Beagan 2014; Catalano 2012), but there is not a single definition for it. In the United States, much of the literature on culturally competent health care focuses on the need to address health disparities among ethnic minorities. Kelly Baker and Brenda Beagan write, "Although the term 'cultural competence' has been expanded beyond its initial definition in order to include gender, social class, and sexual orientation, in practice it tends to still be equated with ethnicity and race" (Baker and Beagan 2014, 580). According to the Centers for Disease Control (CDC 2014), "some minorities experience a disproportionate burden of preventable disease, death, and disability compared with non-minorities" making it imperative to design health care programs and treatment regimens that take into account cultural and social factors so that they are successful. The CDC (2014) encourages health communication to take the culture of a population into consideration and to have "behaviors, attitudes, and policies come together in a system, agency, or among professionals to enable people to work effectively in a cross-cultural situation." Culturally competent health care requires,

> a commitment from doctors and other caregivers to understand and to be responsive to the different attitudes, values, verbal cues, and body language that people look for in a doctor's office *by virtue of their heritage*. The concept of tailoring health care is not a new one; we already have medical specialties based on age and gender. Cultural sensitivity is one more dimension of that kind of refinement
>
> *(Goldsmith 2000, 53, emphasis added)*

We can see that this definition of cultural competence stresses the need to understand "heritage" and thus leaves out other attributes like religion, gender, sexuality, and class that could have an impact on health decisions and behaviors.

Joseph Betancourt et al. (2003, 294) state that an essential part of cultural competency is the interactions between patients and the health care system. They write:

> A "culturally competent" health care system has been defined as one that acknowledges and incorporates – at all levels – the importance of culture, assessment of cross-cultural relations, vigilance toward the dynamics that result from cultural differences, expansion of cultural knowledge, and adaptation of services to meet culturally unique needs ... The movement toward cultural competence in health care has gained national attention and is now recognized by health

policy makers, managed care administrators ... providers, and consumers as a strategy to eliminate racial/ethnic disparities in health and health care. There is, however, an ongoing debate as to how to better define and operationalize this critical yet broad construct.

Betancourt et al. (2003) recognize that cultural competence is to help eradicate "racial/ethnic disparities" in health care – certainly vital in being able to provide high-quality care to all patients – but, also acknowledge that there is disagreement as to how to actually define the term and what it includes. Cultural competence has been described as a method to increase the quality of care patients receive and to help that care fall in line with their particular cultural and social values. It has also been said to be a business strategy for medical providers to attract new patient populations. Cultural competence has been incorporated more and more into medical education in the United States (Kripalani et al. 2006) as a way "to help prepare health practitioners for working with culturally diverse and minority populations" (Baker and Beagan 2014). A physician at a large hospital in a suburb of Washington, D.C. explained to me that the Muslim doctor on their team will often get called when a Muslim patient enters their unit because the non-Muslim providers are unsure of how to handle the situation. This doctor said she sometimes feels guilty for always turning over Muslim patient cases to the Muslim physician, and all providers should have some training in religious medical ethics so as to be able to discuss difficult medical issues in an appropriate manner. This was an important issue for her, and even though cultural competence is a buzzword in the US health care system and there is a need for it, there is not a coherent or consistent definition or application of the concept across providers, medical specialties, and organizations, which can cause the term to be reduced most often to racial/ethnic minorities, thus leaving out the cultural and social factors that may impact treatments and care planning. Providing culturally competent health care does not mean just matching providers and patients in terms of nationality, ethnicity, gender, or religion, for instance, but rather taking a patient-centered approach and trying to understand the world from patients' points of view given that their "situated knowledges" are created through their positions in society (Haraway 1989, 581).

Academic/Applied Research: Anthropology and Cultural Competence

This chapter examines the role of anthropology in operationalizing culturally competent health care through sketching out data that I have collected for my current ethnographic project on Islam and end-of-life care in the Washington, D.C. area. Part of the objective of my research is to argue for a more robust approach to culture within the health care system and to dispel the idea among health professionals, educators, and organizations that culture is simplistic, and that a single approach to providing culturally competent care will work for all groups given that there are cultural differences between and within groups. Building on critiques by anthropologists and non-anthropologists alike of cultural competence and how the term culture is used in medical education (Carpenter-Song, Nordquest Schwallie, and Longhofer 2007; Kleinman and Benson 2006; Smith-Morris and Epstein 2014), I suggest that cultural competence is often too narrow in practice. As Baker and Beagan (2014) rightly observe, it has been frequently reduced to reference ethnic and racial minorities, which leaves out cultural and social factors and excludes populations that may need special considerations in care. Furthermore, it denies the fact that "individuals belong to multiple cultures, but those cultures are neither coherent, static, nor do they always join together seamlessly" (Baker and Beagan 2014, 581). Arthur Kleinman and Peter Benson write, "One major problem with the idea of cultural competency is that it suggests culture can be reduced to a technical skill for which clinicians can be trained to develop expertise" (Kleinman and Benson 2006, 1673). In the example I gave at the start of the chapter, medical providers needed to consider class in designing treatment plans and follow-up care for many of the patients so that they were not re-admitted to the hospital, and yet this factor was not considered. In addition, just focusing on ethnicity reduces people's identities to a single attribute and simplifies the ways they experience the health care system and society. Identities and experiences are based on a complex network of characteristics including ethnicity, gender, class, religion, sexual orientation, citizenship status, nationality, etc. (Crenshaw 1991; Hall 1996), and people can belong to more than one culture at once or move between cultures with and without ease – all of which can have an impact on health practices and choices.

I address the ways that anthropological approaches can contribute to a broader and more robust understanding of cultural competence in health care and offer a critique of the notion that culture can be "reduced" to a simple skill. To do so, I will discuss some of my interviews and observations with diverse Muslim communities in the D.C. area as well as my work with national organizations that focus on Islamic medical ethics. In this I will disentangle how Islamic beliefs about death, illness, and the body intersect with the US model for end-of-life care, which anthropologists have noted champions technology and views death as a failure for the health care system and medical providers involved in the case (Chapple 2010; Kaufman 2005). My interest in studying Islam and end-of-life care grew out of the fact that there is a rich and burgeoning scholarship on Islamic medical ethics (Brockopp and Outka 2003; Clarke 2006; Gatrad and Sheikh 2001; Moazam 2006), but there is less work on how theological points and ethics are turned into practice in medical settings, particularly in the United States. Detailing religious ethics is not enough if providers are going to truly deliver religious and culturally appropriate care to patients at the end-of-life. It is not productive to assume that there is a coherent Islamic theology, but rather I argue that a more productive ethnographic starting point is to explore the multiple interpretations and ideas that exist among Muslim communities and to allow the discrepancies and differences to come to the fore; this will provide a more holistic analysis of how Muslims understand what Islam says about death, illness, and the body and help illustrate that a general approach to defining cultural competency may be insufficient. Through detailing my research, I will elucidate some of the deeper meanings attributed to medical practices in end-of-life care for diverse Muslim patients and their families and demonstrate how ethnography has enabled me to examine the ways Muslims' understandings of death and interpretations of sacred texts are put into practice within a health care setting in the D.C. metropolitan area.

Caring for Muslim Patients: Methodology and Background

My primary site for this research study is the Washington, D.C. metropolitan area, which includes parts of Maryland and Northern Virginia. This is an excellent setting given the region's diverse population and the number of Islamic Centers. As of 2011, there were sixty-two mosques in Virginia, seven in the District of Columbia, and fifty-four in Maryland (Bagby 2011). Virginia ranks in the top ten states in terms of the number of mosques. The majority of Muslims who reside in Virginia and Maryland live in the counties surrounding D.C. (ASARB 2010). The role that religion plays in Muslims' health decisions and practices in the United States must be understood within the context of the anxieties about health care and the end-of-life that proliferate in the political, medical, and public realms.[1] The United States is an aging society. The Administration on Aging predicts that between 2009 and 2030 the population of those over sixty-five will increase from 13% of the population to 19%. The age group of eighty-five plus will increase by 350% in this time (Wiener and Tilly 2002). This trend places added pressure on publicly funded programs for seniors, the health care system, and long-term care facilities. Also, the Pew Forum on Religious and Public Life (2011) estimates that the number of Muslims in the United States will double between 2010 and 2030. Approximately 50,000 Muslims earned permanent residency status in the United States in 1992, and in 2009 this number had increased to 115,000 (Inhorn and Serour 2011, 936). Currently, 65% of the Muslim population in the United States was born abroad, but this number will decrease to 55% as the number of native-born Muslims increases (Grossman 2011). Adult Muslim children will be seeking medical care for aging parents that "is judged to be 'religiously appropriate'" (Inhorn and Serour 2011: 935) and will be making choices about end-of-life care in upcoming decades.

Since 9/11 Islam has garnered a great amount of media attention, and even more so in 2015 with the rise of Islamic State (ISIS), Boko Haram, and the end of the wars in Iraq and Afghanistan. Coverage often frames the religion as repressive and against innovation and modernization. Marcia Inhorn and Carolyn Sargent argue that Islam is generally misunderstood in the West, "In the aftermath of ... [9/11] the lack of Western understanding of Islam ... has become abundantly apparent ... [Islam is] a religion that can be said to encourage the use of medicine, biotechnology, and therapeutic negotiation and agency in the face of illness and adversity" (Inhorn and Sargent 2006, 1). Lisa Henry (2010, 46) writes, "Histori-cally, critics comment, the media has treated Islam as violent and backwards and for Islam to be modern was inconceivable." Lance Laird et al. (2007, 922) note, "Media reports, political rhetoric and legislative action ... increasingly focus on

Muslims as an out-group, promoting negative stereotypes of Muslims and Islam. Yet few sources ask how such attention affects the health of Muslims." Laird et al. (2007) ask a key question about how the negative images we see of Islam in the United States impact Muslims' relationships with health care. One female Muslim physician told me that she has had patients who faced discrimination when seeing non-Muslim doctors. In addition, they point out that all Muslims seem to be placed in one group – the "out group" – and little attention is given to the diverse interpretations among Muslim communities in the United States, some of which fall directly in line with many of the policies and best practices in the US health care system.

This is the place where I believe I can contribute the most as an anthropologist and ethnographer – a better understanding of how culture and personal circumstances impact health decision making and practices at the end-of-life for Muslims. Highlighting the diverse ways that Islam informs choices and behaviors can also combat the assumption that populations "have a core set of beliefs about illness owing to fixed ... traits" (Kleinman and Benson 2006, 1673). The D.C. area has extremely diverse Muslim communities, and so for my research I have been working primarily with those who have immigrated to the United States and identify as Sunni.[2] Sunnis make up the majority of the Muslim population worldwide comprising 80–90% of the faith's followers (Inhorn and Serour 2011, 935). I conducted extensive ethnographic research in Morocco between 2005 and 2009 on Islam, development initiatives, and reproductive health care for my dissertation (see Hughes 2011, 2013; Hughes Rinker 2013a, 2013b), but upon completion of my PhD I took a postdoctoral fellowship at Virginia Tech and was quickly brought on board to develop projects alongside a health care organization that were aimed at improving the quality of care in rural southwest Virginia. This was a long way from my research in Morocco, but partially due to personal reasons – most notably my partner being settled in the Washington, D.C. area – I limited my job search to the region. The position's advertisement stated, "experience in working in a clinical environment is desired," which my ethnographic research in three health care clinics in Morocco certainly provided me. It also called for someone who is "committed to improving ... clinical outcomes." Even though the required research was quite different than my dissertation research, I found the position invaluable because it helped me develop a commitment to improving care for individuals and opened up my eyes to the challenges people face in seeking health care. I continue to cherish this trait as a researcher even after my postdoctoral fellowship ended, and I still promote it to my students as a professor of anthropology and as a mentor (see Hughes Rinker and Nahm 2013).

As is happening in many hospitals across the United States, the health care organization I worked with found that one of its hospitals in particular, located in Appalachia, had a high rate of terminally ill patients without advance directives – documents in which patients' wishes are spelled out (a living will) or a proxy is identified (a power of attorney) – when they were admitted.[3] This is a Critical Access Hospital (CAH), meaning that it is located thirty-five miles or more from any hospital or other CAH or located more than fifteen miles from any hospital or other CAH on secondary roads with no highway access (CMS 2014). Given its rural location, the majority of its patients attended one of the three primary care practices in the county, two of which are also owned by the health care organization. There was no specialty care within a reasonable distance. I developed a project to figure out how to make discussions about end-of-life care happen more often within the primary care practices so that when individuals ended up in the hospital at times of serious illness, they would already have documented their wishes and discussed them with their family doctors and loved ones. I collected preliminary data for this study through visiting the hospital and informally interviewing physicians and social workers, interviewing pastors in the local area who provided spiritual care to patients in the hospital, observing hospice nurses as they made home visits in the county and nearby areas, and visiting the two family practices and informally interviewing doctors and nurses when possible. It was while I was conducting this research that I realized the importance of anthropological and ethnographic research to improving health care and creating health policy and to have my work contribute to both scholarly and public discussions. For instance, I discovered that even though the hospital would allow its beds to be turned into hospice beds for a time, the hospice nurses used a completely different electronic medical record (EMR) than hospital personnel. This meant that neither one could view each other's notes about patients, which caused miscommunication between hospice, doctors, patients, and their families. I left the position before the project really got underway, but since then have remained committed to research on health care that is academic, but inherently applied in nature. Following this goal, I wedded my interest in studying Islam and health – as I had for my dissertation research that turned into my monograph and a few peer-reviewed articles – with my newfound interest in end-of-life care in the United States.

I started this project in January 2013[4] just a few months after I began a tenure-track position in anthropology at George Mason University. Given my academic position and my commitment to improving the quality of health care, I decided to design this project so that I can contribute both to scholarly conversations surrounding death, religion, medicine, and ethics and to public debates concerning the end-of-life and Muslim identities in the United States. This means publishing strategically in the future in both academic and professional outlets and being willing to take the time to discuss my project at length – without the academic jargon – with health care providers and administrators. It also means that I have to develop an "elevator pitch" for my project that is suited for those from multiple disciplines and fields and captures my audience's attention in a short amount of time; I have learned in working with medical professionals that is typically all they can spare in their already jam-packed days. This chapter includes data that I collected in 2013 and 2014 primarily through interviews with physicians located throughout the United States who are involved with a national organization, but with international reach, that is dedicated to Islamic medical ethics; practicing Muslim physicians; Imams in the local region; Muslim community members; and observations of a presentation at a local hospital for medical residents on Islam and palliative care.[5] Other aspects of my ethnographic research include interviews with bioethicists, gerontologists, and Islamic scholars; attending conferences on aging, end-of-life care, death, religion and spirituality, and ethics; reviewing relevant literature in anthropology, public health, religious studies, medicine, and other closely related fields; collecting and monitoring popular media on debates surrounding the end-of-life; interviews and observations at a hospital;[6] and a textual analysis of websites and message boards focused on Islam and dying and of information distributed by health care organizations in the D.C. area on end-of-life care. Ultimately, I suggest that anthropological research on the experiential nature of end-of-life care and on how Muslims view medicine as interfacing with their religious understandings has a critical place in discussions of cultural competency, and in actuality should be made central to academic and public debates about culturally appropriate death.

An Ethnographic Project on Islam and End-of-Life Care in the United States

Through my interviews and observations in my research on Islam and end-of-life care in the Washington, D.C. area, I have found that many contradictions exist. One afternoon I attended a thoughtful and informative lecture given by a Muslim palliative care physician to medical residents in internal medicine at a hospital. The physician discussed some of the major Islamic tenets that the residents should be aware of while caring for Muslim patients as they are nearing death. I sat in the back of the room next to another physician and a few other staff members. The room was full with about twenty-five residents in attendance. The physician explained that he had given this lecture several times to hospice providers and other medical staff at the hospital given that there are a relatively large number of Muslim patients who seek care there. In reading literature about the hospital, I have discovered that it aims to treat the entire person including his or her spiritual needs during a health crisis or just routine health care, so it recognizes that providing culturally competent care can be a way to increase patient and family satisfaction, a means to provide higher-quality care, a way to design treatment plans that people will follow and thus have a higher-quality life and not be re-admitted, and a method to attract new patients. In addition, administrators recognize the ethnically and culturally diverse nature of the local region and therefore, lectures like this one by the physician have a key place in its mission and goals. This whole person approach has been said to lead to better clinical outcomes and higher patient satisfaction (Stewart et al. 2000), thus demonstrating the importance of anthropology (and its methods) to better health practices and management.

At this lecture, the physician recalled a time when an older Muslim male patient was in the hospital with a terminal illness. He was unresponsive. He was not going to return to the quality of life he once had and was being kept alive through machines. This physician was called for a palliative care consultation. He spoke to the patient's wife who was by his side. He asked her why she kept her husband alive through the machines. She explained that if she took her husband off of life support it would be considered murder in the eyes of God. The physician returned several times to speak with the patient's wife about different care options to make sure the patient was comfortable and free of pain. He told me that many times patients, or the Imams who will visit the hospital to counsel Muslims patients and families, believe that once life support is started, a patient cannot be removed from it because it would be just like killing the person. This is because it is only God who decides when it is the right time to die. Another physician who used to practice abroad and in the United States but now works full time at a mosque in Virginia explained to me in our interview that the role of the medical provider is to carry out God's wishes. He said, "And the doctor ... the patient is God's patient ... And God is sending the mercy to him through me [the physician], I'm a carrier in God's mercy, my knowledge ... I have no way, I can't withhold it." Several of the Imams and other Muslim physicians that I interviewed for this project all agreed that for every disease God has made a cure, and therefore, all life is God's and we as humans cannot decide when it will end. This is why life support cannot be removed once it is initiated.

During the lecture, the physician recalled that he told the patient's wife that God does not want to burden people and that her husband had physically suffered enough. A verse from the Qur'an states, "God does not charge a soul with more than it can bear" (2, 286). Not only had the patient suffered, but his wife had also had additional emotional and mental stress from seeing her husband's health decline. After several meetings, the wife decided to finally let him be removed from the ventilator and pass away during the Holy Month of Ramadan that year. According to the physician, letting her husband be at peace by unhooking him from the machines was also allowing him to receive extra blessings from God since he was to die during Ramadan. What is interesting in this situation is that what the wife initially understood Islam to say about the timing of death when her husband entered the hospital was the complete opposite of her final action – removing him from the ventilator and allowing him to pass away at the hospital. But, this act did not contradict what the Muslim physician believes about death in Islam. He sees relieving patients' pain and suffering at the end-of-life as an act of compassion if they would never be able to live without the use of machines or would remain unresponsive to stimuli. One Imam I interviewed at a mosque in Virginia, held a similar opinion to the physician if patients are suffering from a terminal illness as compared to having had an accident or experienced an unexpected injury that resulted in them being unresponsive. He recalled one of his worshippers discussing what to do when her aging father fell into a coma after battling cancer,

> So she said what do you think, and [I] said pull the tubes out. Your father is not going to recover. The ICU is for someone who had a motorcycle accident that [may recover] ... This is old age. Keeping him like that and you sitting next to him ... You stopped your life. That's $10,000 a day [referring to potential

earnings from a job she left]. Islam does not tell you to waste your money. Take the tubes out. If he [is] meant to live, he will live. If not, that's God's will.

Instead of viewing the removal of a ventilator as murder, if it is medically acceptable it is also a way for God to provide peace to patients and families who have suffered through terminal illnesses or other severe injuries that prohibit the patients from returning to the quality of life they once had.

Another physician at a hospital in Northern Virginia said that one Muslim family told her that the use of opiates to relieve pain often associated with terminal illness was very much against their religion. Imams in the D.C. area have also said this to me. They state it is against Islam to take any type of medication such as morphine because it can alter your state of mind and you may lose your sense of self. They mentioned that when you take narcotics you may not feel like yourself and you may feel "out of it." One Muslim doctor said that while he may not completely agree with this, he understands their line of thinking. You may curse God if you are out of sorts while on medication and blame God for pain or suffering. If you do not feel like yourself, you may speak out against God, which could have ramifications in the future. Another Imam said to me that Muslims are to take nothing more than Tylenol and to try to treat things as naturally as possible. He said,

Islam does not prohibit medicines ... we say yes, but find natural ways of doing it. If I tell you take a Tylenol or take a spoon of honey ... [and] both will do the same thing, which one would you prefer? So the honey would be better [because it is natural].

In addition, this Imam emphasized the power of prayer, "So you need a ... powerful, powerful prayer ... so if he raise [sic] his hand and said, 'Oh my Lord cure my body,' he will cure. This is a given ... no exception." However, a Muslim man in his twenties originally from North Africa explained to me that Islam is not against any type of medicine, even those that are considered to be controlled or only by prescription if they are intended to take away pain. Alleviating physical pain is a way for God to unburden Muslims in his opinion and to provide them with some sort of comfort as they deal with approaching the end-of-life. In my research, I have found that there are two major ways of thinking about pain medication. On the one hand, pain medication is against Islam because it could make a person lose a sense of self and potentially speak out against or blame God. (I also found this sentiment among some people in Morocco where I am engaged in a similar project on pain management and palliative care at the end-of-life and Islam.) Moreover, since God has created every disease, he has created a cure. He has provided natural cures and responds to prayer. One the other hand, pain medication is a way for God to help relieve some of the burdens and suffering that Muslims bear during end-of-life care.

The general consensus among Imams that I have worked with is that medical providers are to do everything to try to save a person if they are unresponsive. This includes using feeding tubes and ventilators if necessary. Muslim physicians have told me that sometimes it is difficult to have patients complete a DNR (Do Not Resuscitate)[7] order even though the medical treatments may be more of a physical burden than the actual illness. One Imam stated,

> In Islam we are discouraged from leaving any directive asking not to provide every possible way to extend life. Because extending a life simply is [the] teaching of the Prophet Mohammed. He said that "If you don't seek treatment of your illness even if with hope of getting cured of 1% then you have killed yourself."

(Some Muslim physicians I interviewed disagreed with this.) A Muslim physician at a hospital in Northern Virginia explained that one Imam who would visit patients in the hospital always preached that patients and families should do everything possible rather than have comfort care, even if medical providers had explained that the patient's condition would not improve. But what struck me is that two of the Imams I interviewed were adamant that patients should return home to die so that they are surrounded by their loved ones; and furthermore, families should take care of patients, not home health services or hospice. However, a chaplain at a hospital near Washington, D.C. said that the hospital administration actually had to step in with several Muslim patients who were nearing the end-of-life because a number of family members and loved ones would come to their hospital rooms, making them extremely cramped, and thus it was difficult for the medical staff to do their jobs.

A Muslim physician in D.C. said during our interview,

> I don't know if you've heard of the statement from the Prophet or the hadith[8] ... that even if you were in the middle of an ocean, you should not waste a drop of water ... the well-being of the community takes precedence over the well-being of an individual.

What is interesting here is that there is a general consensus among Imams in my study that patients and families should request every medical intervention possible, but they do not believe that patients should die in the hospital. The hadith, as told by the Muslim doctor I interviewed, reiterates that patients should not use more resources than necessary, meaning that dying in the hospital may not benefit the community especially if treatment would not be effective. They should return home so that others can use the hospital's resources, particularly if those resources are already stretched thin. While the Imams stated that families should be the primary caregivers given the importance of family ties and progeny in Islam, the Muslim physician who recalled the hadith said that this is not always possible due to financial circumstances. For instance, people may have to work two jobs to make ends meet and would not be able to stay at home to take care of a dying loved one; in cases like this, home health services or hospice care may be absolutely necessary.

Concluding Comments: Studying End-of-Life Care as an Anthropologist

In the above examples taken from my research, I hope to have highlighted some of the contradictions that surround Islam and end-of-life care in the United States that stem from Muslims' varied religious interpretations and understandings, different readings of sacred texts, and the intimate and complicated relationship between religion and culture. My goal for this chapter was not to address my contributions to theoretical discussions and scholarly debates on Islam and end-of-life care, but rather, I wanted to emphasize that there is not a "how-to guide" or "one-size-fits-all" way to provide religiously appropriate end-of-life care. Muslim communities in the United States are extremely diverse in terms of class, ethnicity, nationality, citizenship, social status, and how they identify religiously. Abdulaziz Sachedina, a leading scholar on Islamic ethics, recognizes this when he suggests, "the solutions that are offered in the Qur'an are culture specific and not normative for a timeless application and, therefore, cannot be used as paradigmatic in delivering judicial decisions that recur throughout human history" (Sachedina 2009, 145). These "solutions" are temporally bounded, and in addition, can be applied in different ways depending on geographic location and cultural context. For example, one of the Muslim physicians that I interviewed used to practice in the Middle East. In his experience, it was much more difficult to take a Muslim patient off of life support in the Middle East than he found here in the United States. Anthropologists are trained to tease out the complexities of a situation and to uncover what is not obvious at first glance. My research on Islam and end-of-life care has led me to question how cultural competence can be truly operationalized in the US health care system and whether or not it is too abstract a concept. Because it lacks a concrete definition I ask if it is being put into practice in too narrow and excluding ways.

My interest in health care has opened up many different doors for me. I thought my career trajectory was set and it was a direct path from PhD to tenure-track position. Even though this is how I expected it to go, this did not happen. Unexpectedly my first position was at an interdisciplinary research center designing projects with a large health care organization on topics that I had not addressed in my dissertation research in Morocco and in a completely new location. Looking back on my career path, I think this was the best move that I could have made as an anthropologist. It made me aware of the vital importance of being able to speak to broad audiences and being able to move seamlessly between, and even straddle, the academic and applied worlds. I have come to enjoy explaining ethnography and anthropological theory to those who are not familiar with the discipline – a regular occurrence working in health care. With that being said, it also made me recognize that sometimes there is very little difference between these two worlds and that my work tends to be hybrid in nature – academic but inherently applied. Anthropology can make a difference in health care and policy by putting people at the center of research and putting meaning behind what might be termed by some as just anecdotal evidence.

Notes

1 I also want to point out that there are different degrees of religious practice and not all consider themselves to be practicing. There are different interpretations of Islam and in no way am I trying to use my sample and research to produce a representation of the whole.
2 A follow-up study could be on how Shiah or converts to Islam experience end-of-life care in the US health care system.
3 For more on advance directives in Virginia see: www.vda.virginia.gov/advmedir.asp.
4 This research has been supported by a Faculty Research Development Award from the College of Humanities and Social Sciences and from summer research funding for tenure-track faculty from the Office of Research and Economic Development at George Mason University. I would like to thank my student research assistants Serena Abdallah, Oliver Pelland, Elyse Bailey, and Hannah Embler for help in data collection and analysis. Thank you to Jesse Roof and Emily Harvey for helping me put together the references.
5 I have changed all names in this article and have used only vague information about the places where I have conducted research.
6 I received Institutional Review Board approval for research at the hospital in Summer 2015 and it will begin in early Fall 2015.
7 A do not resuscitate (DNR) order "is written by a licensed physician in consultation with a patient or surrogate decision maker that indicates whether or not the patient will receive cardiopulmonary resuscitation (CPR) in the setting of cardiac and/or respiratory arrest" (Braddock and Clark 1998). The DNR does not provide information about other treatments patients may receive, such as pain medication or nutrition.
8 A hadith is a narration about the statements, deeds, and acts of or related to the Prophet Mohammed that has been transmitted through a chain of translators, isnād. This is a narration of his life and not his life itself.

References

ASARB (Association of Statisticians of American Religious Bodies). 2010. *U.S. Religion Census: Religious Congregations & Membership Study*. Accessed September 20, 2014. www.rcms2010.org.

Bagby, Ishan. 2011. "Basic Characteristics of the American Mosque: Attitudes of Mosque Leaders." *The U.S. Mosque Study Report 1*. Accessed September 5, 2014. http://faith communitiestoday.org/sites/faithcommunitiestoday.org/files/The%20American% 20Mosque%202011%20web.pdf.

Baker, Kelly, and Brenda Beagan. 2014. "Making Assumptions, Making Space: An Anthropological Critique of Cultural Competency and Its Relevance to Queer Patients." *Medical Anthropology Quarterly* 28(4):578–598.

Betancourt, Joseph, Alexander R. Green, J. Emilio Carrillo, and Owusu Ananeh-Firempong. 2003. "Defining Cultural Competence: A Practical Framework for Addressing Racial/ Ethnic Disparities in Health and Health Care." *Public Health Reports* 118(4):293–302.

Braddock, Clarence, and Jonna Derbenwick Clark. 1998. "Do Not Resuscitate (DNAR) Orders." Accessed January 3, 2015, https://depts.washington.edu/bioethx/topics/dnr. html.

Brockopp, Jonathan, and Gene Outka. 2003. *Islamic Ethics of Life: Abortion, War, and Euthanasia*. Columbia: University of South Carolina Press.

Campbell, R., M. Evans, M. Tucker, B. Quilty, P. Dieppe, and J. Donovan. 2001. "Why Don't Patients Do Their Exercises? Understanding Non-Compliance with Physiotherapy in Patients with Osteoarthritis of the Knee." *Journal of Epidemiology and Community Health* 55:132–138.

Carpenter-Song, E.A., M. Nordquest Schwallie, and J. Longhofer. 2007. "Cultural Competence Reexamined: Critique and Directions for the Future." *Psychiatric Services* 58(10):1362–1365.

Catalano, Joseph. 2012. *Nursing Now!: Today's Issues, Tomorrow's Trends*. Philadelphia: Davis Company.

CDC (Centers for Disease Control and Prevention). 2014. "Minority Health." Accessed October 13, 2014. www.cdc.gov/minorityhealth.

Chapple, Helen Stanton. 2010. *No Place for Dying: Hospitals and the Ideology of Rescue*. Walnut Creek, California: Left Coast Press.

Clarke, Morgan. 2006. *Islam and New Kinship: Reproductive Technology and the Shariah in Lebanon*. New York: Berghahn Books.

CMS (Center for Medicare & Medicaid Services). 2014. "Critical Access Hospital." Accessed October 14, 2014. www.cms.gov.

Crenshaw, Kimberlé. 1991. "Mapping the Margins: Intersectionality, Identity Politics, and Violence against Women of Color." *Stanford Law Review* 43(6):1241–1299.

Gatrad, A.R., and A. Sheikh. 2001. "Medical Ethics and Islam: Principles and Practice." *Archives of Disease in Childhood* 84:72–75.

Goldsmith, Oliver. 2000. "Culturally Competent Health Care." *Permanente Journal* 4(1):53–55.

Grossman, Cathryn Lynn. 2011. "Number of U.S. Muslims to Double." *USA Today*, January 27. Accessed September 20, 2013. http://usatoday30.usatoday.com/news/religion/2011-01-27-1Amuslim27_ST_N.htm.

Hall, Stuart. 1996. "Who Needs 'Identity'?" In *Questions of Cultural Identity*. edited by Stuart Hall and Paul du Guy, 1–17. London: Sage.

Haraway, Donna. 1989. "Situated Knowledges: The Science Question in Feminism as a Site of Discourse on the Privilege of Partial Perspective." *Feminist Studies* 14(3):575–599.

Henry, Lisa. 2010. "Minorities in Canadian Media: Islam and the Case of Aqsa Parvez." *The Laurier M.A. Journal of Religion and Culture* 2:39–56.

Hughes, Cortney. 2011. "The 'Amazing' Fertility Decline: Islam, Economics, and Reproductive Decision Making among Working-Class Moroccan Women." *Medical Anthropology Quarterly* 25(4):417–435.

Hughes, Cortney. 2013. "A Place to Belong: Colonial Pasts, Modern Discourses, and Contraceptive Practices in Morocco." In *Anthropology of the Middle East and North Africa: Into the New Millennium*, edited by Sherine Hafez and Susan Slyomovics, 239–257. Bloomington: Indiana University Press.

Hughes Rinker, Cortney. 2013a. *Islam, Development, and Urban Women's Reproductive Practices*. New York: Routledge.

Hughes Rinker, Cortney. 2013b. "Responsible Mothers, Anxious Women: Contraception and Neoliberalism in Morocco." *Arab Studies Journal* 21(1):97–121.

Hughes Rinker, Cortney, and Sheena Nahm. 2013. "Stress, Survival, and Success in Academia 2.0: Lessons from Working Inside and Outside of the Academy." *Practicing Anthropology* 35(1):40–43.

Inhorn, Marcia, and Carolyn Sargent. 2006. "Medical Anthropology in the Muslim World: Ethnographic Reflections on Reproductive and Child Health." *Medical Anthropology Quarterly*. 20(2):1–11.

Inhorn, Marcia, and Gamal Serour. 2011. "Islam, Medicine, and Arab-Muslim Refugee Health in America after 9/11." *The Lancet* 378(9794):935–943.

Kaufman, Sharon. 2005. *And a Time to Die: How American Hospitals Shape the End of Life*. Chicago: University of Chicago Press.

Kleinman, Arthur, and Peter Benson. 2006. "Anthropology in the Clinic: The Problem of Cultural Competency and How to Fix It." *PLoS Medicine* 3(10):1673–1676.

Kripalani, Sunil, Jada Bussey-Jones, Marra G. Katz, and Inginia Genao. 2006. "A Prescription for Cultural Competence in Medical Education." *Journal of General Internal Medicine* 21(10):1116–1120.

Laird, Lance, Mona M. Amer, Elizabeth D. Barnett, and Linda L. Barnes. 2007. "Muslim Patients and Health Disparities in the UK and the US." *Archives of Disease in Childhood* 92(10):922–926.

Moazam, Farhat. 2006. *Bioethics and Organ Transplantation in a Muslim Society: A Study in Culture, Ethnography, and Religion.* Bloomington: Indiana University Press.

Pew Forum on Religious and Public Life. 2011. "*The Future of the Global Muslim Population.*" Accessed October 2, 2014. www.pewforum.org/2011/01/27/the-future-of-the-global-muslim-population.

Rau, Jordan. 2012. "Medicare to Penalize 2,217 Hospitals for Excess Readmissions." *Kaiser Health News*, August 13. Accessed October 15, 2014. http://kaiserhealthnews.org/news/medicare-hospitals-readmissions-penalties.

Sachedina, Abdulaziz. 2009. *Islamic Biomedical Ethics: Principles and Applications.* Oxford: Oxford University Press.

Smith-Morris, Carolyn, and Jenny Epstein. 2014. "Beyond Cultural Competency: Skill, Reflexivity, and Structure in Successful Tribal Healthcare." *American Indian Culture and Research Journal* 38(1):39–58.

Stewart, Moira, Judith Belle Brown, Allan Donner, Ian R. McWhinney, Julian Oates, W. Wayne Weston, and John Jordan. 2000. "The Impact of Patient-Centered Care on Outcomes." *The Journal of Family Practice* 49(9):796–804.

Wiener, Joshua R., and Jane Tilly. 2002. "Population Ageing in the United States of America: Implications for Public Programmes." *International Journal of Epidemiology* 31(4):776–781.

8

TIME AND THE METHOD OF THE UNEXPECTED

Sheena Nahm

Dry erase marker squeaked as I scribbled on the large white panel hung adjacent to my desk. I had created a large matrix of program deliverables and was attempting to capture the year past while plotting a plan for the year forward. I recorded both grant proposals for funding that would need to be in place in two years while also noting major milestones and achievements in this year's projects. Life as a leader within a large nonprofit organization was never dull and I felt I was thriving in this environment. I had always been engaged with nonprofit organizations, particularly those involved in education, social services, and health services among minority populations but never thought that would constitute my Monday through Friday 9 am to 5 pm schedule. I had always thought I would work in these agencies either as a committed volunteer or perhaps as a collaborative partner. In my graduate school mind, I imagined that these offices would be spaces and places where I could participate and observe in the role of an anthropologist conducting research. But in that scenario, I would always return to the university as my home base where I would then prepare syllabi and lectures in my baseline role as a tenure-track professor.

Years after walking across the stage and receiving my doctorate, I found myself dry erase marker in hand and deep in the trenches of community-based nonprofit work. This was the third major nonprofit that I worked for after graduate school. When the academic job market collapsed during the economic recession, which happened to take place just as I was preparing to graduate, I found a range of job postings in my hometown of Los Angeles. Working in research, policy, communications, and management at various agencies that had deep local or broad global reach, I found that I could integrate anthropological concepts and methods in my work. The ways in which I articulated this work had to be adjusted, of course, as I articulated and justified these methods to audiences that were not familiar with terms and techniques often taken for granted in the halls of academia. But the assumption that graduate school needed to be entirely scrapped for a new world of applied work was far from true. I found that the two worlds merged and converged, though admittedly with a great deal of work in translating and adapting theory and practice.

When interviewing for positions at various nonprofit organizations, most would-be supervisors were intrigued by my mixed background in public health, neuroscience, and cultural anthropology. They were excited to hear about my cross-cultural work and ability to balance flexibility with structure. But in the end, interest did not equate with marketability in a competitive pool of candidates. What turned interesting stories "from the field" into viability as an employee was my ability to translate my anthropological work into concrete skills. Such skills included: familiarity with specific statistical software; experience in conducting focus groups; a long record of presentations and speaking engagements ranging from community-based workshops to national and international conferences; and comfort with writing grant proposals. This is not to say that the whole of my professional identity was boiled down to tasks or skills, as many interviewers were quick to connect to me as a person and to assess whether my vision and passion for working with vulnerable populations was in line with their own mission. But on the practical level, they were interested in how my familiarity with mixed methodologies and my interdisciplinary background could best serve the needs of their own organization and how my past work as an anthropologist would be applicable to the position for which I was applying. Connecting the dots in a sense was a balance between communicating core values and assessing our alignment in these values with addressing the very practical nature of WIFM (better known as "What's in it for me?"), where the "cool" factor of cultural anthropological perspectives could be applied in ways that contributed to the organization and the clients we would serve together as a team.

This is not a unique experience, as many of the authors in this volume had similar or comparable reflections upon entering the job market. It was with this in mind that this volume was created. The collection of case studies in this volume demonstrates the many spaces in which anthropology has found a home. Anthropologists "doing" and "talking" culture outside of the academy situate their work in a variety of contexts that might not have been fully envisioned or understood during one's graduate school days. In these foreign and unexpected contexts, applied anthropologists find themselves asking the same level of critical questions that they were trained to ask while preparing for academic careers. As we have discussed in our introductory chapter, the question is less of deciphering what distinguishes applied anthropology from other forms of cultural anthropology and more of what it might mean to trace and track anthropological advancements in a variety of unexpected spaces. Across the vast expanse of places and topics explored in this volume, we find equally diverse references to theoretical frameworks. However, there is also a common reflection that begs closer examination; it centers on the role of time in our methodological approaches.

An anthropological approach takes time. After all, culture is an assemblage of ideas, symbols, and actions that are so profoundly embedded that they are hardly given a second thought. Things are the way they are. It takes a great deal of critical inquiry and deep engagement with both the data and the stakeholders participating in how data is conceived, collected, and understood to understand culture. To bring an anthropological approach to a topic, group, or place where it has not been regularly used is to unpack one's intellectual and methodological suitcase and settle in.

Engaging interlocutors means moving forward, sometimes at a crawling pace when it seems no one is willing to speak candidly with me, and sometimes at a bullet train's speed when multiple threads seem to emerge and require follow-up. With all these ebbs and flows, the project moves forward. But for the most part, classic fieldwork approaches allow enough time for the anthropologist to be fully immersed and to some extent let things unfurl. While grant funding and sometimes political or personal factors contribute to the bookends of when fieldwork may begin or end, there is a sense that one has time to wander off and to explore the unexpected. To go off script and be open to the promise of the unknown is part of the commitment to exploring assumptions and challenging norms so deep that they seem simple. The questions we propose often become reformulated in the course of fieldwork into questions about even more basic (but profound) understandings held by ourselves and our interlocutors.

In contrast, anthropologists in many applied settings are always in the field. But rather than this "always being in the field" giving more time, the constraints of everyday employment push us forward whether we would like to pause or not. Deadlines beckon and reports must be submitted. This creates a linear trajectory that seems unstoppable. There is no real pause button in sight. And yet, I would argue that any time an anthropological approach is applied there is an inherent openness to stumbling upon the unexpected. This stumbling (even in a humble office setting where we clock in and clock out daily) creates a moment to pause in a linear stream of activities that often tumble forward at a fast and furious pace because milestones and deadlines stop for no one. In the course of my own ethnographic fieldwork and in stories from the field among colleagues, I have observed that the unexpected can appear catastrophic and completely reorient one's project. But the unexpected can also be found in micro-interactions that cause me to pause and wonder why something seemed unexpected, thereby revealing assumptions and categorical definitions that I had without even knowing it. The unexpected reconfigures time, but in so doing, creates productive ruptures where new inquiries can be made and old inquiries can deepen.

The cases in this volume highlight some unexpected spaces and topics for anthropology to be applied. In examining these cases, there are insights to be gleaned for those interested in specific subfields such as medical or educational anthropology. But in looking at the common threads that tie together when the "unexpected" itself becomes a modality of inquiry, I suggest that there is a meta-methodological narrative that emerges. In this chapter, I examine how methods have developed from the classical to the multi-sited. I then turn to an exploration of alternative forms of ethnography and how they might appear in practice through a variety of methods. I ask how classic methods are enhanced when the role of time in unexpected spaces is more closely examined. I draw from my own experiences across various nonprofit organizations I have worked with and reflect on how time converges with the unexpected to create productive ways of integrating an anthropological approach.

Beyond Singular Places

When it comes to methods, anthropologists in unexpected spaces utilize the same tried and true practices of participant-observation and semi-structured interviews that have long proved critical to classic ethnographic studies. They also apply these techniques alongside other tools that have been strategically adapted to their unique settings. Classic ethnographic methods like participant-observation remain core to our work but are enhanced in unexpected spaces and topics when paired with additional strategies. These strategies may not be mind-blowingly innovative but what is critical, I argue, is understanding how time frames the workplace in such a way that these additional methods make classic methods more applicable to projects that are both shorter and longer than dissertation-style fieldwork. I say both shorter and longer because my work in the nonprofit sector has meant that reports and their associated timelines for data collection and analysis often run the span of weeks or months versus years. This contrasts with the timeline I was given when conducting ethnographic fieldwork while earning my "bread and butter" through teaching as a professor or teaching assistant within a university setting. On the other hand, the projects I conducted in my role as a research specialist, coordinator, manager, or director at various nonprofits also went on longer than my classic ethnographic study because they all built upon each other. Across funders and programmatic evolution, and even while leaving one organization for another, I continued to develop my theoretical and practical engagements when it came to the issues affecting children and families in Los Angeles County. Because my career continues to evolve across a myriad of projects and I must adapt to county-wide changes in infrastructure and funding, I find myself compressing data collection, analysis, and articulation in ways that I did not while in a university setting. But this compression is also a great expansion because I am committed to the same population and field of study across the years of my career development working in the nonprofit sector. With this juxtaposition of compression and expansion comes an understanding of time and how it affects the methods used by anthropologists in unexpected contexts.

Before tackling the new frontiers and issues being studied by applied anthropologists today, it is important to take some time to reflect on methods as they are impacted by the timeframes of unexpected spaces and topics of study. How might time be conceptualized more flexibly than traditional linear notions that follow closed sequential activity compartments of: project conceptualization, data collection, analysis, and articulation of findings? And rather than think in terms of linear flow and pausing, could we benefit from thinking about time in applied settings as a more spiral or coiled version of temporality? This coil might help us to better understand how anthropology engages with unexpected spaces and topics through micro-interactions that culminate to broader and deeper findings.

Over the past few decades, anthropological methods or perhaps the way we think about those classic methods have broadened from single-sited studies to multi-sited work. Migrant communities are followed across nation state boundaries; ideas and products are traces across global exchanges. Post-*Writing Culture* (Clifford and Marcus 1986) anthropologists have reflected on how ethnography is crafted and produced – how we write about culture and how we travel across sites to produce such work. Anthropologists increasingly followed objects, people, and ideas across cities, countries, and continents (Marcus 1995). "In response to an acute awareness that social life increasingly and more frequently, and in new ways, was being enacted in units of several sites, multi-sited ethnography became a part of the anthropological fieldwork repertory" (Wulff 2014, 198). In addition to traveling across political and socio-cultural borders, anthropologists also began to reflect on the boundaries being traversed on paper. For example, in *Tales of the Field: On Writing Ethnography*, John Van Maanen (2011) gathers together three ethnographies – or depending on how one looks at it, one ethnography written in three styles (realist, confessional, and impressionist). In anthropological circles, greater discussion around the role of the ethnographer as not only collector of data and analyzer of information but also as craftsman and author gathered steam. As reflections on writing ethnography continued, anthropologists dealt with issues of creative license and authorial voice, and, more broadly, wonderings around how to capture real life. Didier Fassin (2014) writes:

> I contend that anthropology is fundamentally an attempt to articulate the real and the true – the horizontal and the vertical – in the exploration of life. This endeavor may have been partially lost at times in the course of the history of the discipline, when imitation of the natural sciences led to somewhat rigid paradigms, whether evolutionist, functionalist, or structuralist, and when the fascination for literary studies sometimes headed in the opposite direction, with social worlds becoming less significant than their representation in words. Yet even in those formalist or textualist moments, something remained of what Maurice Merleau-Ponty (1968) calls, with a slightly different intention, the "flesh" of human life – think of Claude Levi-Strauss's story of the shaman Quesalid or Clifford Geertz's depiction of the Balinese cockfight.

Fassin frames the documenting of real lives as neither aligned with the sciences nor with the humanities. He points out that too heavy a leaning on mimicking the natural sciences will pressure cultural phenomena into rigid boxes, while too much zeal for the literary will make ethnographers more enamored with the sounds of their own voices and rhythm of their own words rather than anchoring studies into the social worlds which we purport to study. Writing that takes place after the collection of the data does not outweigh the careful collection and analysis of data. But it also should not be scrapped away as a mere iteration of some objective and obvious result of data collection. Gilles Deleuze proposed that "to write is not to impose a form (of expression) on the matter of lived experience" but rather, it is "a question of becoming, always incomplete, always in the midst of being formed, and goes beyond the matter of any livable or lived experience" (Deleuze 1997, 1). Writing ethnography does not divorce itself from the data but rather calls for a constant engagement with conversations and observations had in the field, for they are both in the process of becoming together.

Data in their raw state, in their digested analyzed state, or in their framed written narrative state are always in the process of becoming. They become meaningful relative to one another in a relational context and conjoined thus, come into being as ethnographic form. Multi-sited ethnography allows for more flexibility in how we think and do ethnography because we trace data as it comes into being across boundaries. And yet, much of our methodology when it comes to the broader framework of how ethnography is produced remains largely linear and singular when it comes to how we think about time.

I think back to my first long-term project as a doctoral student. I began by posing questions and reviewing literature while housed in the academy, most often on or near campus. I then crafted grant proposals to fund research and when all the logistics – from visas to bank accounts – were squared away, I hopped on a plane and began the process of data collection. I traveled to my two main sites of data collection in Chicago and Seoul, which led me to a series of fascinating conversations with child therapists working in metropolitan hubs in the United States and in South Korea. And so I traveled, sometimes near and sometimes far away from home. I set up camp, multiple times and in multiple places. I scheduled interviews with my interlocutors and hit record and pause, scribbling notes on proactive days and even taking the time to transcribe and translate recordings while in the field. I leafed through archives in the air-conditioned national library on a muggy Seoul day. I may even have informally begun my process of data analysis while in the field. After returning home, I began transcription and analysis with more vigor and began to code themes. I studied themes that emerged across interlocutors and over time, and was ready to produce the fruit of these labors in monograph or peer-reviewed article format. A journal article came forth and a dissertation was completed. After that, there were multiple revisions and sometimes entire chapter overhauls of that dissertation; years later, a published ethnography in the format of a book came into being (see Nahm 2014).

Even as I was finishing the final revisions to the first project's narrative, I went on to begin new projects in the role of a consultant as well as in various roles in research, policy, and management. It was in these applied settings that I began to reflect on how the production of ethnography might look and feel different.

What is unique about scholars who practice as they produce, and produce as they practice, is that this linear method of developing questions, gathering data, and articulating results is itself hybridized. The method of the unexpected therefore is not that we supplant classic strategies of data collection with a high-tech alternate but rather, that we alter the method of production from linear to spiral. In the next section, I examine the spiral nature of each of the contributions in this volume and suggest that unexpected spaces call for adapting our method of producing studies, from conception to publication.

A Sense of Urgency

Across the spaces and topics that the authors in this volume have discussed, there is a sense of urgency to produce whilst things are in progress. However, this does not mean any less thought or reflection occurs. This is sometimes the biggest misconception between applied and academic work. Let me take a moment to outline what the assumptions of each often look like and how they create a supposed divide that dichotomizes two possible career paths. These are assumptions that have been articulated over time to both editors who have "lived" in academic, applied, and hybrid worlds. Applied work is often presumed to take place under constraint; that is to say, timelines and deadlines push anthropologists to churn out results and reports so quickly that there is not enough time to let theoretical quandaries fully marinate or to reflect more deeply on the writing process. Furthermore, given the supervisory structure in applied settings where employment calls for nondisclosure agreements that limit what can be shared publicly or supervisors are protective of any reporting that does not align with public relations protocol, it is often difficult to analyze and report objectively. Ties to one's paycheck exacerbate this pressure.

Conversely, it is sometimes presumed that academics have time in abundance. This supposedly limitless time in between the occasional lecture to undergraduate or graduate students allows professors to take a sabbatical year to conduct fieldwork. Supported through university research stipends or through the additional labor of research assistants, professors have more time to pore over transcripts, readily accessible concrete and electronic archives of literature, and engage in reflective conversations with colleagues. From this abundant time and access to resources, manuscripts can be published.

While tiny kernels of truth may lie in some of these assumptions, the reality is that neither of these outlines are representative of a nuanced reality. No matter what the setting or the job title and institutional residence, there is pressure to complete tasks and record milestones. These characterizations of the academic anthropologist and the applied anthropologist are highly oversimplified and mistakenly create a more pronounced chasm between applied and academic anthropologists than that which exists in reality. An applied anthropologist may indeed have some time constraints and be under some institutional pressures as they pay their bills and maintain employment, but I would argue that the researcher at a university is also beholden to the ticking clock of tenure review, institutional pressures within the academic apparatus, a rather non-leisurely pace when taking into account the dense teaching schedules of most junior faculty, and the requirements to provide service hours via mentorship of students that includes reviewing thesis after thesis and dissertation after dissertation (and all their accompanying documents and questions). Most applied anthropologists working in agencies or institutions that hire individuals with anthropological expertise likely also have access to archives, and funds for maintaining engagement in scholarship through budget line items that include conference travel and registration. In both settings, there are examples of unsupportive networks and environments that push scholars to produce less than satisfactory work. But there are also many examples of rich supportive networks that encourage scholars to produce work that engages the public, provide applicable insights, and challenge theoretical frameworks.

Anthropologists today might be classified as academic or applied. Some are employed both by a university and a nonacademic institution. But regardless of what name appears on the paycheck, all of the scholars in this volume describe research projects where they had to rethink concepts and assumptions in order to align them to "unexpected" spaces and topics. Applied anthropology has grown expansively in the past few decades, building on what was always a publicly engaged discipline particularly when taking into account the traditions of Franz Boas, Margaret Mead, and Ruth Benedict in the United States. Over time, somehow the notion of cultural anthropology as more theory driven and rooted in the academy, or as more applied and rooted in "expected" places like international development, nonprofit organizations, or culturally responsive medical settings became engrained in our discourse. In these important "expected" spaces, anthropologists shared their methodological paradigms with others less-versed in participant-observation, though most likely well-versed in the importance of qualitative research writ large if they hired an anthropologist.

Adjusting Timeframes

When it comes to thinking about time as it impacts methodology, there are some foundational examples of a less long-term linear approach to ethnography. The first has become popular amongst anthropologists who align themselves as much with their role as teacher as researcher. Service-learning initiatives in universities, as well as being more individually implemented by professors who integrate practice into learning in their syllabi, are a good example of short-term research projects. Marc K. Hébert (2008) writes about service-learning opportunities as an experiential space in which volunteerism and learning come together. These two experiences are interwoven and, as Hébert explains, students complete field notes outside of volunteer hours while they are at the same time reflecting on their experiences in the field during class discussions.

The thing with applied anthropology in many contemporary settings, however, is that time is both extended and compressed. When I think about my own career extending across a variety of nonprofit organizations, I think about a series of grant-funded program evaluations that require a kind of compressed reporting structure that is less conducive to the wandering of my first ethnography which emerged out of five years of dissertation research – some "in the field" and some in the spaces of campus offices and computer labs, but all without too much demand on time. While there were timelines informed by advisors and committees, and by the availability of funds that sustained research activities, there was not the sense that teams and services would continue based on funding associated with the reports to which I contributed. I realize that no single report or deliverable can determine the end result of programs nor is the responsibility on a single leader, but nonetheless I did feel a greater sense of responsibility to meet deadlines in the workplace when my work so interconnected with others' work. In my academic life, I had time as if running a marathon; in comparison, in my experiences with anthropology in unexpected settings (i.e. in organizations that hired me for different skills than for my ethnographic abilities and yet where anthropological concepts and methods eventually became not only incorporated but also integral) I had to produce and articulate findings in sprints.

And yet, it is important that I do not think of applied anthropology as limited to sprinting. This does a great disservice to anthropologists who commit themselves long term either to one organization or to a consistent cause (even if they jump across various organizations). For example, since the completion of my "first project" I have had the great opportunity to work at three different nonprofit organizations, each with slightly different missions and strategies. I have had the chance to study: the impact of media on health beliefs and behaviors; the process of interdisciplinary professional development for the early childhood workforce; the development of grassroots community engagement leadership models; the impact of peer-support groups in creating employment opportunities and spaces for social connectedness for previously isolated individuals; and the implementation of private/public collaborative partnerships in addressing structural and individual issues that impact childhood obesity among low-income urban populations. The funding streams have been greatly varied, as have my own job descriptions and the supervisory structures within which I reported my progress on projects. In some roles, I had to articulate progress and findings on a weekly basis to supervisors. In other roles, I had to report verbally at meetings and formally in writing via a myriad of report templates and funding streams. Oftentimes, I had to create formal documents on a monthly basis that provided updates on major project milestones. Yearly audits were conducted by funders on occasion to ensure that both my team (and other team members I worked with) complied with contractual agreements on both financial and programmatic levels. On a daily, weekly, or monthly basis I found myself articulating findings even whilst formalizing what those findings were. It was not that any findings were articulated before they existed or made up out of thin air (as a matter of fact, I felt that they needed to be very clearly anchored in the data in a way that would satisfy reviewers interested in quantitative metrics). But there was a definite sense of urgency that I experienced. I often found myself having to overcome previous tendencies to want to sit on the data and ruminate more deeply in order to layer critical inquiry on critical inquiry, to capture nuances that contextualized those results. Because of the reporting structure to funders, supervisors, and analysts, I found myself having to articulate much more quickly in spurts, and more definitively and succinctly. In hindsight the quality of data collection and analysis were just as strong and the methodology just as rigorous, but the demands of articulation differed because of both the internal timelines of the workplace and the timelines of external stakeholders.

Public engagement to a wide variety of "publics" is always part of the process. These are the sprints that produce a kind of compressed project timeline. Such spurts of activity often comprise coils that seem nearly circular given the mundane "scene" of regular work cycles. My applied anthropological life is comprised of regular sprints of collecting data, analyzing results, and producing narratives either in report format or in proposals for additional funding based on past and current success. In my earlier years in the nonprofit sector, I worked in more entry-level research or program coordinator positions where projects had already been proposed, funded, and defined by a more senior-level person. This pre-established structure was the very thing that allowed someone like myself to be hired, so, obviously, something I was grateful for. But it was this same pre-established structure that dictated when and how I was to produce reports about the progress of projects. There was a constant stopwatch running and I sprinted hard from one project milestone to another in order to keep this structured timeline in place.

These sprints – limiting as they may seem – also allowed me to look at the role of nonprofit discourse through a long-term commitment to the field. In fact, the compilation of these experiences has led me to develop my current research project that reflects on the meta-narrative of development discourse across nonprofit organizations. This is a project that has been approved by a university affiliated institutional review board (IRB); it is also one that I am conducting apart from any specific role or job. It is one that I must work on while "off the clock" since my regular job calls for more clearly defined foci. (Incidentally, it is because I still hold an adjunct position that I was able to create a full project description in the same manner as I would have in a full academic appointment through a university IRB; independent IRB processes exist for practitioners outside of academic institutions but access to university resources prompted me to fully articulate this project and go through the same familiar channels I experienced as a doctoral student.) The purpose of the study in my second project is defined as follows:

> This study will explore the articulation of need in the nonprofit sector within the United States, focusing specifically on how need is communicated. The purpose of this study is to examine common themes in language utilized by nonprofit organizations and funding agencies that focus on serving low-income populations within the United States. Methods will include archival research, online surveys, and semi-structured interviews. Archival research will include qualitative analysis of mission statements; online surveys will collect data from individuals who identify as employees or volunteers that work in nonprofit organizations with this focus. Semi-structured interviews will be conducted in person by the principal investigator to further explore themes around the discourse of need and lack. Interviewees will also be individuals who identify as employees or volunteers that work in nonprofit organizations with this focus; all interviews will be in English and transcriptions will be

qualitatively analyzed for recurring themes. Surveys and archival research will allow data to be collected from individuals from across the United States but interviews will focus on case studies within the Southern California region. This will allow exploration of common themes on a national and local scale; national data will be quantitatively analyzed for broader patterns while local data will be qualitatively analyzed for depth of reflections by nonprofit practitioners.

I list this excerpt from my proposal because it draws from all of my applied work in the nonprofit sector while also standing apart from any specific role. While this project is independent of any past or current employment responsibilities, it was the constant articulation or "sprinting" that I participated in across various organizations that made me reflect on my own role as a producer of need discourse over the last five years. Strung together, these sprints created a need for me to more critically reflect on my own participant-observation data.

Viewed from this angle, applied anthropology is incredibly extended in that one may enter the field and never leave. If we think about an ordinary work week in the United States, for example, forty hours a week is spent deep in the beautifully extraordinary and utterly ordinary weeds of participant-observation. In a kind of Malinowskian romanticism, one could argue that classic ethnography is twenty-four hours a day and never has a clock-in or clock-out system. But the reality (for me at least and I would presume to say for many an anthropologist doing a year's worth, or however defined number of months' research funding will allow) of classic ethnographic data collection also means that there are strategic times of engagement and times spent apart "at play." This is not to say that major observations and revelations only occur whilst "at work" and never "at play." Even for the forty hours a week employee, there are observations and revelations made while off the clock. And so, given that an anthropologist housed in an organization – a great variety of which are discussed in this volume across both governmental and nongovernmental settings – spends years and perhaps an entire career's lifespan deep in the study of a consistent topic of study, applied anthropology is also quite a marathon. The difference is that this marathon is defined with structural milestones that create a staccato sense of sprinting even within the longevity of a career. These reporting and funding cadences are anchored by the internal management structure of the organizations and institutions that employ us, as well as external governing bodies that audit our work and evaluate whether such work justifies funding. Time is incredibly compressed and yet also elongated.

I submit a visual analogy to help understand the complexity of time and its role on the production of ethnography in unexpected spaces. Imagine the figure of an electromagnetic coil (or search for images if unfamiliar with this object). A wire wound into the shape of a coil or spiral allows an electric current to travel through the wire and consequently, the magnetic field generated along that coil concentrates the strength of the magnetic field in the center of the coil. One small section of a coil that is tightly wound may appear to approximate a circle if one looks at it through a limited lens but if one pans out, this section appears to just be one loop in a series of many that constitute a coil that moves incrementally forward. The presence of those circular compressed wires actually increases the strength of induced voltage precisely because of the loops that occur so close to one another and allow a concentrated field in the middle of the coil. This may sound like a great deal of borrowing from physics for a cultural anthropologist, but in thinking more deeply about the nature of time in applied anthropological settings like the nonprofit work sector, I argue that it is this almost mundane circular rhythm of forty hours a week employment, coupled with the compression of those circular coils across grant cycles and supervisor-given deadlines, that, when engaged with properly through depth of inquiry, can actually enhance the strength of our findings. It is what calls for a public engagement early on in the process of research, making public engagement part of the research formulation rather than an optional addition at the end of a project.

George Marcus (2012) has written about public engagement and anthropology. Even among anthropologists housed in academic settings, the questions of applied anthropology have converged, as public engagement requires articulation while research is still in progress. Marcus (2012, 434) writes:

> This is not just a question of what the subjects think of what the anthropologist has written about them, but how diverse responses to a project as it develops become part of its integral data sets, and then the basis for professional reception and assessment of their own products of knowledge by anthropologists themselves in a double, dialogical process by which the results in progress of anthropological inquiry are both public and authoritative knowledge. Folding receptions into anthropological research through alternative forms, such as the studio, the para-site, or the dynamic archive, responds to, and "passes" for as well, a kind of operative imperative, like that to collaborate, in neoliberal institutional arrangements and projects, to provide voice for "stakeholders."

In the dynamic archive, files are active and animated – always in the process of becoming. An example of this type of alternative form of ethnography is Mike and Kim Fortun's Asthma Files (ibid., 438). An example of the "studio" form is the para-site of the Center for Ethnography housed at the University of California, Irvine. This center is a space for first fieldwork (i.e. dissertation) projects where graduate students "in the field" can be in regular conversation with mentors and colleagues "back home." These "para-sites" are

> a resource or form in reserve, thought through as such and adapted to the conditions of doing ethnography today, especially with regard to both the imperative and impulse to collaborate, discussed previously. Para-sites are thus opportunistic, and meant to reduce the abstraction of the theoretical processing of ethnographic data, by pushing such processing into staged dialogic occasions of the ethnographic research process.

(ibid., 440)

An example of the lab form is Paul Rabinow's Anthropological Research on the Contemporary (ARC) at the University of California, Berkeley, which provides a collective space for research (ibid., 440). Finally, projects within projects are "those that are embedded within, and usually funded and given assigned 'space' by, much more powerful, often international, and cross-institutional projects"; an example of this is the Institute for Money, Technology and Financial Inclusion (IMTFI) (ibid., 440).

The conceptualization of these alternative modes of ethnographic research helps us understand how methods have been adapted to better explore contemporary issues. Public engagement and reception is included and folded into the process of data collection and analysis; this provides more flexibility than rigid linear notions that follow the order: project conceptualization, data collection, analysis, and articulation of findings. It provides a way of challenging how we think of anthropological engagements in contemporary contexts.

Folding Public Engagement into the Production Process

I realize that, for as much difficulty I encountered in the throes of a limited academic job market (perhaps a generally limited job market during an economic recession), I was fortunate to be able to leverage skills and background into multiple employment opportunities. I was able to maintain one foot inside of academia through various adjunct teaching positions and one foot outside through either full-time or part-time employment in the nonprofit sector. This provided enough financial stability to pursue side projects and continue feeding my own research curiosities and commitments. Applied anthropologists will recognize the sprints and compressed coils of projects in their own work whether employed full time or part time at a given agency. Across employers, the level of independent inquiry will vary as will some of the intricacies and details of supervisors' styles and demands. The demands placed on researchers as they articulate the value of their work and engage with various publics are strong ones. They are the same demands that often compress our work into tightly wound coils that often seem to be made for micro-interactions and micro-reflections. But when placed in a broader framework of time that is at once compressed and elongated, full-time work as an applied anthropologist allows for long-term reflection and inquiry as well.

The idea of coiled time does not throw out all notions of linearity. However, in thinking about anthropology in unexpected spaces, I ask scholars housed in academia, applied settings, or both simultaneously to reflect on the impact of time on unexpected spaces, topics, and methods. In unexpected spaces, we engage with people who perhaps do not understand what anthropology is, or who understand what it is but need it to answer a series of questions that have more structured constraints than the kind of open exploration one might normally associate with ethnographic research. In a sense, through micro-interactions that are repeated but progress forward incrementally like electromagnetic coils, our everyday lived experiences at work place us "in the field" and "at home" at the same time for extended periods of time. These micro-interactions can be mundane at times, but given the proper support for reflection and critical analysis, the compressed staccato cadence of time in the field (in our workplaces) can actually produce spaces for concentrated and focused fields of inquiry.

Acknowledgments

I would like to thank colleagues who have made me a better scholar and practitioner. You have made my experiences in the nonprofit sector just as rewarding as my experiences in academia. I want to thank my family and friends for supporting me despite my sometimes overly hurried pace of life as I run between multiple projects and jobs. I also want to thank those of you who reminded me to slow down and take care to see the bigger picture of my work rather than feeling burdened by the constantly ticking clock of deadlines. Thank you in particular to W for your support in the writing and revision of this chapter and your encouragement to embrace authenticity of voice and write with renewed vigor and joy.

References

Clifford, James, and George E. Marcus. 1986. *Writing Culture: The Poetics and Politics of Ethnography: A School of American Research Advanced Seminar.* Berkeley: University of California Press.

Deleuze, Gilles. 1997. *Essays Critical and Clinical.* 1st edition. Minneapolis: University of Minnesota Press.

Fassin, Didier. 2014. "True Life, Real Lives: Revisiting the Boundaries between Ethnography and Fiction." *American Ethnologist* 41(1):40–55. doi:10.1111/amet.12059.

Hébert, Marc K. 2008. "Teaching Research Methods through Service-Learning." *Anthropology News* 49(6):15. doi:10.1111/an.2008.49.6.15.

Marcus, George E. 1995. "Ethnography in/of the World System: The Emergence of Multi-Sited Ethnography." *Annual Review of Anthropology* 24(1):95–117. doi:10.1146/annurev.an.24.100195.000523.

Marcus, George E. 2012. "The Legacies of Writing Culture and the Near Future of the Ethnographic Form: A Sketch." *Cultural Anthropology* 27(3):427–445. doi:10.1111/j.1548-1360.2012.01152.x.

Nahm, Sheena. 2014. *The Work of Play: Child Psychotherapy in Contemporary Korea.* Lanham, MD: Lexington Books.

Van Maanen, John. 2011. *Tales of the Field: On Writing Ethnography*, 2nd edition. Chicago: University of Chicago Press.

Wulff, Helena. 2014. "Multi-Sited Ethnography: Problems and Possibilities in the Translocation of Research Methods." *American Anthropologist* 116(1):198–199. doi:10.1111/aman.12085_13.

9

ETHNOGRAPHIC EXPLORATIONS OF INTELLECTUAL PROPERTY CLAIMS TO YOGA

A Series of Unexpected Events

Allison E. Fish

Ethnography is perhaps one of the most widely used qualitative modes of inquiry into social conditions not only in the academy, but also increasingly outside of the university as well. There is no single definition or practice of ethnography, nor should there necessarily be a uniform interpretation. As Marilyn Strathern has written, ethnography, through participant-observation, interviewing, and other qualitative techniques is a "deliberate attempt to generate more data than the researcher is aware of at the time of collection" (Strathern 2003). This makes ethnographic methods eminently suited to the study of unpredictable events, complex emerging social formations, and technological and market change. Given the disposition of ethnography for documenting the unforeseen, it therefore goes without saying that this methodology often takes a researcher in unexpected directions. In doing so, this leads the ethnographer to new places, encounters, investments, and – perhaps most importantly – novel discoveries that could not have been predicted at the outset of a project.

My own entry into anthropological research proved no exception to this unspoken rule. However, despite a series of seemingly strange twists and turns, I've found the underlying research questions and political investments that draw my attention have remained consistent. Thus, while my formal graduate training has been in the fields of cultural anthropology, law, and public administration, I consider myself to be an interdisciplinary scholar using ethnographic methodologies to investigate questions of social, legal, and economic justice. In this regard I have primarily focused on how law is used by different parties to secure and regulate access to important basic resources such as agricultural commodities, jobs, health care, land, and, most recently, intellectual property. In investigating this topic I have found that anthropological ethnography is capable of providing the nuanced detail necessary to understand the complex, and often opaque, factors underpinning the lived experience of disparity.

Leaving Mexico: How a Complication in Early Fieldwork Leads Me to India

My early fieldwork focused on the use of new information technologies in the regulation of international agricultural commodity chains along the US–Mexico border. However, in the summer of 2005 unanticipated political events and violence along the border made it difficult for me to return to my research site in Arizona (US) and Sonora (Mexico) for fieldwork. Taking this as an opportunity to travel and experiment with a second project I purchased an around-the-world ticket to study the development of the global yoga industry and attempts to control this emerging market through the use of intellectual property claims. As part of this trip, I planned to spend two months in India, the "birthplace" of yoga, to study how the growing global market and the related assertion of property claims was impacting the practice in South Asia. I assumed that after my summer travels this project on yoga, organized primarily as a diversion and around my desire to travel outside of North America for the first time in my life, would fall apart and I would return to my work on a more "serious" topic. However, that was not to be the case as the next twelve weeks, most of which involved spending time with a legal research and activist team in southern India on their "Intellectual Property and the Knowledge/Culture Commons" project, opened the door to scholarly and applied research opportunities that I could not have anticipated.

It was through this series of unexpected events that I found myself, five years after first setting foot in India and at the close of my fieldwork in August of 2010, waiting for an evening flight out of the brand new international terminal at the Indira Gandhi National Airport in New Delhi. While waiting I purchased a hot chocolate from the Coffee Bean and Tea Leaf Company shop, a franchise of the southern California chain that had recently been allowed access to Indian markets, in the airport's food court and chatted on the phone with a friend. Put simply, the terminal was posh – rivaling the airports of Singapore and Hong Kong through which I had regularly transited en route from California to India – and a far cry from the slightly worn, linoleum tiled and chaotic older terminal that I had flown into earlier that summer. Taking in the difference, I contemplated not only the airport's transformation, but also how much had changed and how much I had experienced since my first arrival to India. In the intervening five years I had: traveled around the world several times; participated in meetings in Bangalore, South Africa, and Japan with Creative Commons organizations concerned with the expanding reach of intellectual property; spent time in ashrams and listening to panchyats in remote village India; and interviewed elite South Asian scholars and high-ranking members of the Indian government – all as part of a single ethnographic research project. During this process my instincts, assumptions, and initial reactions were constantly challenged as events unfolded and I learned more about the topic I had chosen to follow. This learning, I argue, was only possible because I was trained both to critically listen to and sympathetically question my informants' varied perspectives in a manner intended to bridge cultural gaps and foster understanding – an openness that the ethnographic disposition afforded to me as a researcher.

In this chapter, I draw upon my fieldwork experience in India to show the insights and new directions that sensitive ethnographic questioning and listening, keystones of the research methodology, are capable of providing. In doing so, I highlight the value in the seemingly trite anthropological refrain of making the strange appear familiar and the familiar appear strange – a process of defamiliarization that allows the researcher an opportunity to critically assess his or her own inherent biases (see Miner 1956). I also show the benefits that arise in following the classical fieldwork methodology outlined by David Schneider of "listening carefully to the natives," your informants, as "the ones engaged directly in the processes in which you are interested," while also keeping in mind that the "natives" might not always be right (Schneider 1980 as cited in Hakken 2003). I argue that it is through careful listening and questioning that an ethnographer is able to triangulate a research space and, within that framework, develop new ideas both capable of contributing to the scholarly record and that offer significant insights into the lived experience of real people in the world.

Beginning with a Question or Two

In 2005, at about the time that my research at the US–Mexico border was stalling and I was looking for a new project to occupy my summer, I read an article about a Los-Angeles-based yoga franchise engaged in a bizarre lawsuit involving intellectual property claims to a specific form of practice. What particularly drew me to this case was that it involved a popular variant of yoga, the Bikram "hot" style of yoga, which I first came across in 1999 and have, myself, practiced since, albeit irregularly. Like many others with whom I later interacted during my fieldwork, my initial visceral reaction to the story of ownership claims to yoga was a combination spanning surprise, disbelief, unease, shock, and even humor.

This mixed sentiment, sparked by the intersection of familiar, but ostensibly separate worlds colliding in strange ways, drew me to research the case, which I describe below. As my knowledge of both intellectual property and yoga expanded, a series of linked questions emerged and developed into a more concrete research agenda. The primary query, and the one that corresponded to my own initial emotional reaction, was, "How have we, as a society, come to fashion a world where it is possible to conceive of traditional cultural knowledge forms, like yoga, as property?" My legal training encouraged me, however, to look at both sides of the argument. Therefore, upon reflection, and through my growing understanding of intellectual property, I challenged my own inherent assumptions by asking, if other types of information and knowledge-making activities, such as writing or scientific invention, can become the subject of ownership, what is it about yoga and its connection to South Asia that makes so many people, including myself, think it cannot be treated in a similar manner?

In addressing these questions I found I was constantly surprised and challenged by the realization that different parties had their own unique answers and that these responses did not correspond to mine. Moreover, the response of each interested party was supported by unique logics that drew from their own situated world-views and corresponded to distinct sets of values. I also found that investigating these responses constantly led me in unexpected and new directions.

The 2005 article initially prompting my interest in intellectual property and yoga evoked in me a sense of surprise because while both topics were familiar to me, I had not thought of them as belonging to the same space or in relation to one another. In a sense what was at stake here was my own understanding of both yoga and property (more specifically, intellectual property). On the one hand, my initial assumptions about yoga were informed by taking classes at local California studios and gyms and by my own imagination regarding spirituality in South Asia, a topic about which I knew nothing at the time. From this basis I thought about yoga as either a light form of exercise practiced mostly by women in the US and Europe or an esoteric practice belonging to orange-robed spiritual ascetics living halfway around the world and adopted by local New Age communities. As I learned more about the history and supposed origins of yoga, I came to view it as a dynamic and evolving body of practical knowledge capable of accommodating and being incorporated into novel social conditions.

In contrast, I assumed that the introduction of private property rights would always lead to increased social, economic, and political disparity. In this simplistic model, I assumed that denial of private property claims to yoga would ensure its placement in the public knowledge commons, resulting in a benefit to all and a respectful treatment of the practice. However, as I explored the topic I realized that it was not the *determination* of yoga's proprietary status that was of primary importance. Instead, the key was that the question of property could be formulated and that, for many, the answer to this question clearly turned on (1) the imagined association of the practice to a specific ethnic, national, and racial community, and (2) the ability of that community to intentionally produce and create something the rest of world would find valuable and beneficial. Thus, in order to understand how inequality was produced I had to understand how the different parties reconciled their understandings of yoga as a practice that existed prior to its encounter with intellectual property, and how perceptions of both changed after their intersection.

Understanding Yoga: Both the Strange and the Familiar

Traditionally, yoga is a several thousand years old South Asian philosophy that trains the embodied mind to accept truth through a combination of physical and mental practices. The term yoga derives from the Sanskrit word *yuj*, meaning to yoke, to join together, or union. Yoga and related ascetic practices are linked to several religious traditions originating in the South Asian sub-continent including Hinduism, Jainism, Buddhism, and Sikhism. Specifically, yoga is one of six major philosophies of religious orthopraxy known as *darsanas*. Approximately 2,000 years ago, local expressions of yoga were grouped into eight separate limbs of practice by the sage Patanjali who described his classificatory scheme in *The Yoga Sutras of Patanjali*. These limbs are *yama* (abstentions), *niyama* (observances), *asana* (postures), *pranayama* (breath control), *dharana* (concentration), *dhyana* (meditation), *pratyahara* (control of the senses), and *samadhi* (enlightenment) (Flood 1996). Each school of yoga, whether contemporary or traditional, has a distinctive style of practice that consists of a unique interpretation and blending of a particular subset of these eight limbs. Thus, even in South Asia there has never been a singular style of practice, with multiple interpretations of yoga existing at any point in time.

Perceived as an esoteric Orientalized spirituality, elite European and American social circles first expressed an interest in yoga towards the end of the 19th century when Swami Vivekenanda toured the world. However, it wasn't until the last few decades of the 20th century that a noticeable and global market demand for what I term "transnational commercial yoga" emerged. A demand that was largely driven by affluent and cosmopolitan consumers located mostly in Europe, the US, Japan, and Australia. This market for transnational commercial yoga draws largely from contemporary Hatha Yoga, a derivative of the 15th century *Hathayogapradipika* text, which departs from the rigor of Patanjali in that it emphasizes the physical limbs of practice (*asanas* and *pranayamas*) over the others. The objective of contemporary Hatha Yoga is to prepare the practitioner to quiet the body so that the mind might engage in the more advanced steps of meditation and sensory withdrawal. Specifically, this transnational commercial variant focuses on the gymnastic processes of the practice, the production of a thin and flexible "yoga body," and the physical effects of weight loss, stress reduction, and muscle toning (Fish 2006; Jain 2014).

In 2012 the transnational commercial yoga market generated, in the US alone, more than $11 billion, was practiced by more than 20 million people, and was expected to grow at approximately 25% per year in the future. Recently this industry, in part because of its rising value, has seen increasing attempts by both state agencies and private parties to control this growing market. One of the most startling of the regulatory attempts was the use of intellectual property claims, primarily trademark and copyright, by private yoga corporations and individual yoga teachers to carve out and secure a niche in this valuable market. By the late 1990s more than 2,000 yoga-related intellectual property claims had been registered at either the US Copyright Office or the US Patent and Trademark Office. Despite the proliferation of these intellectual property claims in yoga, public attention to the trend to propertize the practice, and a consequent public outcry, did not erupt until around 2001 when Bikram Choudhury, the notoriously aggressive founder of the Los Angeles–based Bikram Yoga College of India (BYCI), filed suit against Kim and Mark Schreiber-Morrison (*Bikram Choudhury v. Kim Schreiber-Morrison* 2002; Fish 2006). In his suit Bikram alleged that the Schreiber-Morrisons, his former students and owners of a California yoga studio, had violated the copyright and trademarks held by Bikram over his unique twenty-six-posture "hot" yoga choreography, the "Bikram Beginning Yoga Series," and requested nearly $1,000,000 in damages.

Given the costs of litigation and the threat of such a large judgment, the Schreiber-Morrisons quietly agreed to privately settle their dispute with Bikram that was pending in the US federal courts. Under the terms of the settlement, the Schreiber-Morrisons agreed to pay Bikram substantial monetary compensation and to refrain from future infringements of the varied intellectual property rights he claimed in relation to the Bikram Beginning Yoga Series. Buoyed by this victory Bikram began to threaten other yoga studios and teachers around the world that he believed were infringing his intellectual property rights.

In response to these threats, a group of yogis from around the world joined together to form "Open Source Yoga Unity" (OSYU), a nonprofit organization that was incorporated in 2003 in San Francisco. Leading members of the organization included the owners of a yoga studio threatened by Bikram and their student who was also an intellectual property lawyer representing Silicon Valley clients. In addition, OSYU received *pro bono* legal services from leading attorneys associated with Stanford University's Center for Internet and Society. The Center is an academic unit founded by Professor Lawrence Lessig who is considered father of the Creative Commons organization and a leading figure working to curb the unchecked expansion of copyright in the age of digital media. At the time of OSYU's formation, both the Center and Creative Commons were interested in expanding their reach to assess the impact of intellectual property claims to other cultural forms. The OSYU case and the possibility of investigating the application, or misapplication, of copyright to yoga quickly caught the interest of what was primarily a local legal activist community that had previously been concerned with questions pertaining to intellectual property and the creative products of information technology.

Shortly after forming, OSYU filed a motion for declaratory judgment in the US federal district court of Northern California. This lawsuit, which named both Bikram and BYCI as co-defendants, argued that the members of OSYU had unique and urgent standing to sue because Bikram's actions were intended to and did "create the reasonable apprehension in [OSYU] members that they [would] be sued if they continue[d] the activities that Bikram claims infringe his intellectual property rights" (Amended Complaint 2003). OSYU asked that the court find, as a matter of law, that Bikram did not have the right to control through trademark and copyright who could and could not teach the Bikram series of yoga. Additionally, OSYU requested that the court, should it find that Bikram did have a viable intellectual property claim, clarify what actions would constitute a violation of his property rights (Fish 2006).

Initially the lawsuit appeared to be moving in favor of OSYU and during an April 2004 ruling the court, in the person of Judge Phyllis J. Hamilton, openly expressed skepticism that Bikram could prove a valid claim on any type of yoga series. This victory, however, was short-lived as the judge reversed this statement later the next year when she denied OSYU's motion for summary judgment. As the basis for denial Judge Hamilton suggested that copyright and trademark rights might very well exist in a series of yoga postures and that Bikram's claims were a question of fact and not law (*Open Source Yoga Unity v. Bikram Choudhury* 2005). The denial of summary judgment prompted the realization by both sides that the dispute would evolve into prolonged and complex litigation and that neither could guarantee that the outcome would be in their favor or best interest. Therefore, in mid-2005 both parties agreed to enter into a private settlement protected by a non-disclosure agreement (Fish 2006).

Because the *Open Source Yoga Unity v. Bikram* proceedings were for declaratory judgment and because the initial arguments relied on specific characterizations of the "nature" of yoga, the lawsuit had, in effect, requested the court to decide whether yoga, both generally and in specific performances, belonged to the public or private domain. Though the US courts never had the opportunity to fully answer this query the unusual case and the international attention that it has drawn over the past decade has prompted numerous unusual reactions from a diverse range of actors – including private individuals, international news venues, public officials, nation-states, private for-profit corporations, private not-for-profit organizations, and interest groups. Tracking this diverse array of reactions, as well as the implications that each had for our understanding of intellectual property rights, composed the primary focus of my ethnographic research.

As I explored the lawsuits that had been dubbed "The California Yoga Wars" in the media, and the attendant fallout, I came to realize that the cases were significant for two reasons. On the one hand, these disputes were the first to test the validity of individual intellectual property claims to yoga. On the other hand, and perhaps most importantly, these fairly low-level disputes brought international attention to the question of whether or not yoga resides in the public or private domain. This second, apparently simple question, however, appears to have confounded the American federal courts and remains in active dispute in legacy cases, almost fifteen years after the first lawsuit was filed. Reflecting on the lawsuits, I realized that the question of the proprietary status of "hot" yoga provided a provocative example of intercultural exchange between more- and less-powerful players that would allow me, through ethnographic research, to engage equally with questions of capitalism and commodification, law and social order, and knowledge management and expertise. The cases also demonstrated the utility of the classical anthropological approach of questioning socially charged assumptions by making the strange appear familiar and the familiar appear strange.

In the following sections, I highlight three situations where my ethnographic fieldwork not only challenged and surprised me, but also continued to lead me in unexpected directions as I questioned my informants – yogic and intellectual property experts (both equally my "natives") – listened to their accounts, and critically analyzed their responses. In two cases the surprises came because I realized that the assumptions I had held about the yogic "natives" were wrong. In the other case, a growing realization that the intellectual property "natives," with whom I most strongly identified both culturally and politically, might be wrong led me to also question their accounts of certain key issues.

Listening to the "Natives": Popular Confusion Regarding Intellectual Property

A major objective in undertaking fieldwork in India was to explore how, in the aftermath of the California Yoga Wars, four international yoga franchises head-quartered in India, the purported "birthplace of yoga," came to their respective conclusions that a certain type of intellectual property claim was appropriate for the management of the signature styles of practices associated with their organization. I had recruited participation from each organization because it seemingly represented the use of one of the "traditional" domains of intellectual property – copyright, trademark, patent, and a public sphere free of legal claims. Newspaper reports, preliminary fieldwork interviews, and internet research led me to the conclusion that each school had selected one of the above-mentioned traditional intellectual property claims as the tool to manage their style of practice. However, upon beginning research in India I was reminded that intellectual property is a technically complex domain and that its legally specific terms are commonly misused in everyday dis-course, often resulting in further confusion regarding the practical ramifications of claims. This highlighted the fact that many people have inaccurate understanding of the laws which govern their everyday actions and to which they are held accountable, especially those areas of law that are rapidly changing. Thus, it was difficult for many of my informants to assess the impact of intellectual property rights when they were unsure of exactly what a claim required or implied.

Two examples of this confounding situation occurred early during fieldwork when I discovered that high-ranking members of two yoga schools, the Bihar School of Yoga (BSY) and the Art of Living (AoL), had either technically misused legal terms or misunderstood their organization's proprietary claims. For example, during a conversation with me, the president of the BSY ashram in Bangalore unequivocally rejected the notion that the school made any sort of claims. In fact, the BSY organization headquartered in the northern Indian state of Bihar holds trademark and certification marks that are registered in several countries including India and the US and has attempted to enforce these claims through extra-legal channels, the use of social pressure, and appeals to morality. In the other case the president, guru, and founder of the Art of Living, Sri Sri Ravi Shankar, was quoted in multiple Indian newspapers as claiming patents to the *pranayama* technique *Sudarshan Kriya*. Initial discussions in 2006 with members of the community cast doubt upon this assertion and follow-up archival research at the patent recorder's office in Chennai showed that, while the Art of Living had trademark claims on file, there was no evidence of application for patent rights. Whether the inaccurate newspaper articles were a product of a misunderstanding by S.S. Ravi Shankar or by the journalist is unknown and, to an extent, is unimportant to the analysis here.

The differentiation between technically legally accurate and popular usages of intellectual property terms and concepts significantly altered my research frame-work. First, and most importantly, this discovery undermined the neat comparative model at the center of the original research design that juxtaposed the use of different legally defined types of intellectual property to manage valuable yogic practices. Secondly, it demonstrated the need for a more nuanced approach to the ways in which understandings of law, property, intellectual property, and knowledge management and exchange were actually articulated in the yoga schools studied.

It was particularly this latter realization that provided an important window of opportunity during the subsequent stages of research as it became increasingly apparent that most transnational commercial yoga organizations, especially those headquartered in India, did not primarily conceptualize the management of yogic knowledge in terms of market value, law, or property. Instead, in interviews with adept practitioners, I noted a deep connection to a different type of logic, one more in keeping with yoga as an embodied philosophical system. Specifically, most informants relied on notions of morality and obligation, formed through the spiritually based guru–disciple relationship, when speaking about the maintenance and management of yoga, a dangerous and esoteric knowledge to the uninitiated or unprepared.

To the extent they relied on legal claims and arguments, most members of the yoga schools that made intellectual property claims justified their use as a means to an end. For these individuals, intellectual property had the potential to ensure that obligations of care and duty between guru and disciple, or teacher and student, were fulfilled. In this sense, members of these franchised schools understood the organizations first and foremost as spiritual networks situated in specific social contexts. In some "cosmopolitan" environments, intellectual property claims were deemed to be one of several tools, techniques, or technologies that might be used to accomplish particular pedagogic objectives and reinforce social bonds predicated on the practice's underlying structures of orthopraxy and spirituality.

Listening to the "Natives": the Use of Intellectual Property Claims by Individual Yogis in India

Throughout my fieldwork I expected to find that expert yoga practitioners, especially those in India, would be opposed to the application of intellectual property claims to yoga. However, as research progressed I realized that this was an assumption based upon my own internalization of modern law and capitalist markets as universal paradigmatic structures. Initial evidence of this ethnocentric perspective became apparent when I had difficulty understanding my interlocutors' responses to questions of whether or not it was "appropriate" to treat yoga as intellectual property. In particular, two interviews with yogis in Bangalore in March 2007 highlighted my mistaken assumptions about the incommensurability of yoga and intellectual property. This realization left me struggling with the significance of what my informants were trying to tell me.

In the first of these two interviews, Swami SYS told me that she was unfamiliar with the intricacies of intellectual property, however, she was curious to know what copyright claims to yoga meant. I briefly explained the distinctions between trademarks, patents, and copyright and the types of claims that Bikram Choudhury was making (i.e. trademarks on his image and name and copyright in a yoga choreographic sequence). After asking questions to clarify a few points, Swami SYS thought for a moment and then said, "Well, I suppose I can understand that ... that might be fine." Her response triggered an uneasy feeling in me because, on the surface, it appeared that our interaction had triggered her emergent legal consciousness of intellectual property claims to yoga. On the one hand, I felt obligated to answer her questions about the subject matter of the research. On the other hand, I felt that my explanation had, in some way, provided Swami SYS with the foundation for justifying proprietary interests in yoga. In a way, I felt as if I was provoking the very process that I had set out to study, thereby, confounding both the principle of limiting my own influence and my own convictions regarding open access to knowledge.

Later that month an interview with another yoga teacher took on a similarly surreal dimension. My meeting that day was with a yoga teacher in Bangalore, Mahesh Ganapathy (a pseudonym). Ganapathy had, like Bikram Choudhury, developed a yoga sequence that would purportedly keep a practitioner in good health and published an instructional book, *The ABCD Method*, as to its performance. In addition to teaching yoga classes, Ganapathy was a practicing lawyer and our interview took place in an apartment in central Bangalore that had been converted into a yoga-studio-cum-law-office. As the interview began I explained my project and took note that, as I described the California lawsuits, Ganapathy took out a legal pad and started scribbling notes. Ganapathy then told me that he had been practicing yoga for two decades and intellectual property law for about half that time. Hearing this, I asked immediately how he felt about the Bikram lawsuits. Tapping the legal pad, Ganapathy responded that he wanted to follow up on the Bikram case because he thought the registration of the intellectual property rights, "[was] good business practice," and, similar to, "the advice [he] would give to a client" (personal contact). Moreover, he had already registered trademarks to phrases and images associated with *The ABCD Method* and had copyright in his book – a creative work through which he demonstrated the knowledge given to him by his guru. A bit stunned, I felt as if I had met, in Mr Ganapathy, the Bikram Choudhury of India! Not quite knowing how to respond, I moved forward to address the other questions I had prepared for our interview.

These two interviews highlighted for me one of my most surprising research findings, namely, that the controversy over intellectual property rights in yoga that I had set out to find and document might not actually exist. I also had to ask myself whether or not I was dramatizing the implications of the California Yoga Wars. For, if the experts themselves, the holders and teachers of yogic knowledge, were unperturbed by and even participating in this trend, then who was I to argue otherwise? It was not until I learned more about the yogic path and the primary relationship involved in the practice, the *guru–shishya* (hereafter, guru–disciple) relationship, that I understood not only the responses of my informants, but also how yogic knowledge transference was not necessarily inhibited by, but might even facilitate, the use of intellectual property rights.

Remember that the "Natives" Might Be Wrong: A2K Response to Yogis' Use of Intellectual Property

A third situation where my ethnographic research both challenged and surprised me was in my interactions with the Access to Knowledge (A2K) community. Prior to fieldwork I had assumed I would share certain commitments regarding both intellectual property and cultural rights with this group of "natives," in part because we shared a similar cultural and political background. In this instance, however, my findings emphasized that though I should listen to my informants carefully, I should realize that the "natives" might also be wrong. In this particular instance, this realization also led me to question and reconsider some of the underlying ideas about the public domain and the knowledge commons that the "natives" [A2K activists] espoused.

In the contemporary moment, dubbed by many the Information Age, the promise of rendering knowledge into a portable informational form so that it can accrue greater worth has accelerated the pace of efforts to capture the value of intangibles through the use of intellectual property (Coombe 2009; Sunder Rajan 2006). This has fostered a broad sense of crisis amongst those who suggest that the very foundations of creativity, culture, and even humanity are increasingly subject to privatization (Boyle 2008; Brown 2004; Coombe 1998; Lessig 2001; Sunder 2012; Vaidhynanathan 2001). This sentiment has prompted the organization of alternatives, largely through the assertion of the cultural commons (Krikorian and Kapczynski 2010; Liang, Iyengar, and Nitchani 2008).

How to best craft a cultural commons that is a viable alternative to intellectual property is a question of much debate within A2K. Proponents of what I term "mainstream" A2K primarily tend to focus their efforts on an active and conscious effort to turn private proprietary forms, such as copyright, back onto themselves. Creative Commons (CC), one of the A2K organizations associated with the *Open Source Yoga Unity* lawsuit described earlier, is a well-known face of this type of mainstream activism. However, A2K activists from the developing world and indigenous communities are concerned that alternative intellectual property forms, such as CC's copyleft licensing suite, and their underlying moral discourses do not fit seamlessly with their experience of the world. They argue CC practices are formed in the context of daily life in Euro-American countries and require significant revision lest they replicate imperial legacies that the regime of modern property introduced to the global world system centuries earlier. Central to these concerns are the ways in which key ideas, like openness and creativity, are defined to produce a singular, as opposed to a diverse, conceptualization of the cultural commons (Copy/South Research Group 2006; Liang et al. 2008).

These concerns were highlighted when I participated in various activities sponsored by the international CC umbrella organization from 2007 to 2008. During fieldwork I was affiliated with a south Indian organization actively engaged with the CC community and had the opportunity to meet affiliated activists from all over the world. At a conference in South Africa I spent time with two members of

CC Europe whose work is well received in the A2K community. At one point our discussion led to an interesting issue that was emerging in my research on yoga. During fieldwork I had been having trouble engaging *sanyasi* (spiritual ascetics) practicing yoga in discussing their thoughts on whether or not intellectual property claims to the practice were "appropriate." I was confident that the *sanyasi* understood the concepts, since most were highly educated, well-traveled, and socially powerful. In fact, many knew of the California lawsuits that catalyzed the core research. However, when the topic was broached, most began by describing yoga as a practice that could benefit all, but then immediately switched the conversation to other topics, usually attempting to describe yogic thought and how the guru–disciple relationship took shape.

It had taken several months for me to realize that, by changing the conversation, these *sanyasi* were indicating that my question of whether yoga naturally resided in the public domain was fundamentally flawed. The question, in fact, failed to get at the significance of the practice, as well as the social relationships that it produced. Instead, my informants stressed that the central goal of yoga is the liberation of the individual self. Furthermore, a practitioner approached this goal through a commitment to a daily practice of living explicitly structured through his or her hierarchical relationship with an expert guru who acts as a gatekeeper over spiritually powerful knowledge.

In response to my story, one CC leader scoffed at the "ridiculous" implication that yogic knowledge could be powerful, telling me it was "only information." The other suggested that this explanation was probably just "an excuse" and that some of these *sanyasi* might be authoritarian figures unwilling to relinquish the possibility of power or wealth. For these two A2K activists the idea of a stratified commons for yoga was either, at best, the product of naïve spirituality or, at worst, the product of personal greed. Reactions of both CC leaders are similar to the majority of feedback I received from mainstream A2K activists and are of concern because such perspectives fail to take the viewpoints of cultural heritage stewards seriously – an orientation that requires sincerely listening to and engaging with other stakeholders.

These surprising reactions not only led me to consider that the "natives," in this case A2K activists, might be wrong, but also led me to question and reconsider some of the ideas that the "natives" espoused. In particular it led me to reflect on the fact that in discussing intellectual property within mainstream A2K discourses there is a tendency to use the terms public domain and the commons as though they are synonymous. However, two separate histories inform these concepts with "the public" being those exceptions carved out of the private domain by law and open to all. In contrast, "the commons" references a multiplicity of systems located outside of modern property regimes where alternative social projects take shape. The CC organization seeks to reverse trends in contemporary intellectual property by re-creating the commons through such instruments as "open" and "copyleft" licenses. The thinking is that if property can enclose the commons, then property can also be used to re-create the commons. The problem with these legal techniques and their underlying logics is that they end up creating something very different – they resurrect an aspiration of the commons, but produce a space that is barren of social relationships and where informational objects are abandoned by creators. In contrast, a pre-property notion of the commons is a realm of communal caretaking and development – a space that is socially significant and quite possibly stratified.

As well as calling into question my understanding of the way that I thought about the public domain and the commons, my ethnographic research also offered some potential ways of rethinking these concepts. In particular, my experience in the way that yogis interacted with intellectual property offered a way of thinking about the commons that was not barren of social relationships. Yogic knowledge exchange is, I suggest, a way in which we can theorize a more vibrant and diverse cultural commons, as differentiated from the public domain. To do this I find the work of Lawrence Liang, Prahsant Iyengar, and Jiti Nitchani (Liang et al. 2008) helpful as they argue for a theorization of an Asian commons that isn't simply a crude cultural relativist framework with Asian-ness emerging only as "a different [and often fundamentally flawed] way of doing things." Instead, these scholars argue that both Asia and the commons should be seen as "categories in the making" that are neither stable nor singular, but diverse and always transforming (Liang et al. 2008, 30). It is with this sensibility that I suggest taking seriously the guru–disciple relationship, structured as it is around the transfer of yogic knowledge. This approach requires a refusal to discount the idea of spiritually dangerous knowledge as solely a construct of naïve or power-hungry gurus, but as indicative of a broader social project meriting consideration.

Conclusion: Bringing Us into Touch with the Lives of Strangers

A female *sanyasi* with whom I met regularly in Bangalore over several months, made an interesting comment when she described how she became a conduit through which the presence of her guru manifested during the course of instruction. Pressing her to explain, I asked Swami Saraswati where her guru, who was a disciple himself, obtained that knowledge which passed through her and she responded, "from his guru." Repeating my question again I asked Swami Saraswati's thoughts on the ultimate source of the knowledge, since this is the key figure to whom copyright is bestowed according to modern law. The swami paused and, in response to my question, said with a thoughtful chuckle, "why I think ... it is gurus all the way back."

Swami Saraswati's words recall the story in which an Englishman meets an Indian ascetic who tells him that the world rests upon a platform that rests upon an elephant that is standing on the back of two turtles. The Englishman asks the ascetic what the second turtle is standing upon and the sage responds, "Ah, Sahib, after that it is turtles all the way down." Geertz's use of this story alludes to his understanding of the incomplete nature of socio-cultural analysis and his conviction that the purpose of ethnography is to "bring us into touch with the lives of strangers" and gain access to their conceptual worlds (Geertz 1973, 28–29). My experience during fieldwork shows that gaining access to the conceptual world of a practicing yogi does not necessarily require that I "turn native" and accept the mystical, almost telepathic, connection between gurus and disciples described to me by the *sanyasis* with whom I conducted fieldwork as absolute truth. Similarly, I do not need to maintain identical political investments with those informants hailing from the A2K movement. Instead, I must subject these commitments, some of which I share, to a process of defamiliarization and sustained critical analysis. However, as an anthropologist I am invested in sympathetically listening to and critically questioning these perspectives – in short, taking these perspectives seriously. Furthermore, I do this as a supporter of both A2K and cultural rights and in the hope that an enriched understanding of the commons might emerge.

This chapter is an attempt to take seriously the social and symbolic relationships that hold the world of the practicing yogis and A2K activists together in the same space. Through doing this research I hoped to foster a conception of "openness" that was more than a technical descriptor of accessibility – though that too merits consideration. By thinking with *sanyasi* as an A2K activist, "openness" emerged as a sensibility through which engagement with other people and diverse ways of being in the world became possible. Through ethnographic research expert yogis demonstrated to me how knowledge exchange has the potential to draw people together in enduring bonds of reciprocity characterized by love, faith, and devotion strengthened by everyday practice – all in spite of yoga's exposure to modern proprietary logics that emphasize individuation and alienation. In a sense, then, fostering "openness" and "creativity" with the ultimate goal of fashioning a vibrant and diverse cultural commons may be as much a daily practice as is the goal of attaining *samadhi* (enlightenment) through the practice of yoga.

References

Amended Complaint. 2003. Amended Complaint for Declaratory Judgment and Copyright Misuse, December 3, 2003, page 9. *Open Source Yoga Unity v. Bikram Choudhury*, Case No. C 3–3182 PJH (USDC Northern District of CA, San Francisco Division).

Bikram Choudhury v. Kim Schreiber-Morrison. 2002. Case No. C 3–3182 PJH (USDC Southern District of CA, San Francisco Division).

Boyle, James. 2008. *The Public Domain: Enclosing the Commons of the Mind.* New Haven, CT: Yale University Press.

Brown, Michael. 2004. *Who Owns Native Culture?* Cambridge, MA: Harvard University Press.

Coombe, Rosemary. 1998. *The Cultural Life of Intellectual Properties: Authorship, Appropriation, and the Law.* Durham, NC: Durham University Press.

Coombe, Rosemary. 2009. "The Expanding Purview of Cultural Properties and their Politics." *Annual Review of Law and Social Sciences* 5:393–412.

Copy/South Research Group. 2006. "*The Copy/South Dossier: Issues in the Economics, Politics, and Ideology of Copyright in the Global South.*" Accessed March 25, 2015. http://kar.kent.ac.uk/6/1/CSdossier.pdf.

Fish, Allison. 2006. "The Commodification and Exchange of Knowledge in the Case of Transnational Commercial Yoga." *International Journal of Cultural Property* 13:189–206.

Flood, Gavin. 1996. *An Introduction to Hinduism.* Cambridge: Cambridge University Press.

Geertz, Clifford. 1973. *The Interpretation of Cultures.* New York: Basic Books.

Hakken, David. 2003. *The Knowledge Landscapes of Cyberspace.* New York: Routledge.

Jain, Andrea. 2014. *Selling Yoga: From Counterculture to Pop Culture.* New York: Oxford University Press.

Krikorian, Gaelle and Amy Kapczynski. 2010. *Access to Knowledge in the Age of Intellectual Property.* New York: Zone Books.

Lessig, Lawrence. 2001. *The Future of Ideas: The Fate of the Commons in a Connected World.* New York: Random House.

Liang, Lawrence, Prahsant Iyengar, and Jiti Nitchani. 2008. "*How Does a South Asian Commons Mean.*" Bangalore: Alternative Law Forum. Accessed July 11, 2008. www.altlawforum. org/intellectual-property/publications/How%20does%20an%20Asian%20Commons%20 mean.pdf.

Miner, Horace. 1956. "Body Ritual among the Nacirema." *American Anthropologist* 58(3):503–507.

Open Source Yoga Unity v. Bikram Choudhury. 2005. 74 U.S.P.Q. 2d 1434.

Strathern, Marilyn. 2003. *Commons and Borderlands: Working Papers on Interdisciplinarity, Accountability, and the Flow of Knowledge.* Herefordshire, UK: Sean Kingston Publishing.

Sunder, Madhavi. 2012. *From Goods to a Good Life: Intellectual Property and Global Justice.* New Haven, CT: Yale University Press.

Sunder Rajan, Kaushik. 2006. *Biocapital: The Constitution of Postgenomic Life.* Durham, NC: Duke University Press.

Vaidhynanathan, Siva. 2001. *Copyrights and Copywrongs: The Rise of Intellectual Property and How It Threatens Creativity.* New York: New York University Press.

10

SURVIVING ACADEMIA 2.0

Lessons Learned from Practicing Hybrid Anthropology[1]

Sheena Nahm and Cortney Hughes Rinker

As graduate students writing our dissertations between 2009 and 2010 at the University of California, Irvine, we began to feel the first ripples of a shrinking job market for tenure-track academic positions in anthropology. There were questions, in hushed whispers as well as anxious and frantic outbursts, about how long the recession would last, whether we should "wait and see" before graduating, or apply now and just cast a wider net in terms of schools and searches. The 2009 Anthropology Faculty Job Market Report opened up with, "AAA has been increasingly concerned with the academic job market. Anecdotal evidence suggests that faculty lines are being lost and searches cancelled" (Terry-Sharp 2009). Given uncertainty, we both chose the latter option and had the good fortune to find employment in academic institutions – Cortney Hughes Rinker at the Arlington Innovation Center for Health Research (Virginia Tech) and Sheena Nahm at the Norman Lear Center (University of Southern California). Interestingly enough, neither of us entered these institutions through the traditional route of the tenure-track position. Although our jobs were quite unique and different from each other, they both were in research centers focused on contracts and grants and were not solely situated in the realm of cultural anthropology, the field in which we are trained. Nahm worked for the University of Southern California as a research specialist where she evaluated the impact of entertainment education interventions. She conducted quantitative and qualitative analysis on surveys assessing viewers' changes in knowledge, attitudes, and behaviors after watching television shows and films containing health information. In this role, she regularly reflected on how results could be communicated in a way that resonated with a wide variety of stakeholders, including professionals situated in the medicine and/or entertainment sectors. She presented her work at academic conferences and contributed to reports that were released to nonacademic audiences. Hughes Rinker's position was primarily in health services research, which is a multidisciplinary field that focuses on the quality of and access to health care, health care costs, and patient outcomes. Even after completing our time in each of the positions, we continued to publish, teach, and work in applied fields. Nahm went on to a career in the nonprofit sector while also teaching for various colleges including The New School, while Hughes Rinker took a tenure-track position at George Mason University in the Department of Sociology and Anthropology where she continues to teach, mentor, and conduct research.

Because of the lessons learned through our initial experiences after graduate school, we began to reflect on what it means to be a cultural anthropologist contributing to dialogues in a changing world that often has been referred to as "Academia 2.0" amongst our colleagues.[2] In this chapter, we address two questions: What skills do we have from doing academic fieldwork that can be applied to the nonacademic world? What is it from our work in applied research that helped us transition back to academia? In particular, we examine the impact of living both inside and outside of academia in the current climate, and offer strategies and skills for a cultural anthropologist negotiating the current job market. These questions are what ultimately led us to put together this volume. We wanted other "hybrid" anthropologists who straddle the academic and applied worlds to have a space to share their own experiences and work, since sometimes we feel we have to choose one side or the other when conducting research or publishing.

Working in a Liminal State: Being Inside and Outside of Academia Today

While it is more present in our daily conversations and in our anxiety-ridden cover letters, Academia 2.0 calls into question whether there was ever an inside or outside of academia. When we use the term, we ask how we can think of academics as publicly engaged in applied fields and how we can think of anthropologists who choose careers beyond the boundaries of tenure-track positions as academic in their applied worlds. Philip D. Young writes,

> Is it possible to combine a career as an academic anthropologist with that of a practitioner? The short answer is yes, but some types of anthropology are easier to combine than others, and you need to carefully consider this in making your choices.
>
> (Young 2008, 56)

While the statement helps to create an opening where the applied and academic terms of anthropology might be thought of as more hybrid in character, it still primes us to think about convergences in limited and expected terms. What are the ways in which academia can be thought of in updated terms through the notion of the "2.0"? What are the ways in which applied anthropology, itself often limited to certain subfields, can be seen in unexpected spaces and topics? And if the opportunities for anthropological application are far broader than we once suspected, what are some ways in which we can mentor young professionals to prepare for these diverse possibilities?

The topic of preparation (or lack thereof) of graduate students for viability in a job market not limited to academia has gained momentum, as seen by the multitude of columns and career-advice-related questions posted on higher education media. Over a decade ago, Peter Fiske wrote, "On average, scientists write more professional documents and speak in public more often than other professionals. So it is natural that we consider communication one of our discipline's strong suits." But he also added that

> academia also favors careful and deliberative communication over communication that may be quicker but is less accurate. As a result, young scientists learn to be careful and conservative in what they say and to speak up ONLY when they can speak as a true expert on a subject.
>
> *(Fiske 1999, original emphasis)*

Although Fiske was speaking to scholars primarily situated in the biological sciences, he was calling for academics in general to consider informal communication strategies, or what bosses outside of academia have called "your elevator pitch," the time it takes for you to describe your work in the limited time you have with someone on the go. How is this possible when dissertations written on hundreds of pages seem like not nearly enough space to capture the complexities of a topic? And yet, the world outside of academia has pressed both of us to develop our "informal" communication skills as well as to understand the impact of "good-enough" explanations. Fiske also asks how we might think of the many tools developed by graduate students on their initial path to tenure-track goals in practical terms that translate well to any sector, even to those less familiar with anthropology. Part of this requires looking back at many of the things that are taken for granted in the milestones of a graduate career and breaking them down to basic skills rather than content language. For example, rather than spending lengthy paragraphs in a cover letter developing your theoretical knowledge of post-structuralism or Continental philosophy, it may be more effective to think about your experience speaking in public at large national or international conferences, your ability to write, and your attention to detail in project management (if ever there was an opportunity to attend to detail, we would submit the applications to some Internal Review Boards and the required formatting of various grant applications for your review).

These are some practical transitions that a graduate student with preparation for tenure-track positions (but perhaps not for applied positions) may have to consider. But more essential than this basic skill reframing is the shrugging-off of the kind of rigid hold to only one manifestation of success – the production of solid ethnographic work. If we open ourselves up to the possibilities of hybrid positions and of a world where we can have deep reflective conversations with peers who can critique systems of power in between two cubicles at an office nowhere near an R1 (research-intensive) university campus and imagine also the level of public engagement that a well-respected academic could have, then we might see these hybrid positions not for what they lack but rather, for what they allow.

The "good-enough" was a horrific thought for idealistic graduate students dedicating our lives to the pursuit of knowledge. A document is never perfect and oftentimes, the type of person who gravitates toward a life of research, questioning, and learning is also the type of person who believes a document can also reflect deeper thinking or more-fine-grained analysis. As graduate students, the only thing that prompted making a document final was perhaps a deadline for submission, with the dissertation writing process barely the ultimate example of flexibility in deciding when a document was ready for final submission. Our professors told us in graduate school to "enjoy it while it lasts" because they warned us that the day would come when we would not have dedicated courses about a particular subject or the time to read and think once we finished our doctorates. Indeed, we have both come to learn that time is of the essence in both applied work and in the academy. In fact, it was living outside of academia or in hybrids better classified within notions of Academia 2.0 that gave us a deeper appreciation for what many of our interlocutors face: the understanding that the work is not done and yet still must be articulated and submitted for scrutiny. Funders requested reports more regularly than we ever had to produce for graduate school and internally supervisors or project collaborators asked for progress updates. Ethnographic data had to be packaged into real-time results that could justify funding not only from their original grant date and final report but throughout the process. Furthermore, the limited amounts of time also pushed us to be able to code-switch, staying faithful to the core of our messages but understanding the power of using certain "languages" strategically. Our writing appeared in email correspondence as well as in drafts for peer-reviewed articles. It allowed us to engage with diverse audiences and across many disciplines.

What is striking is that the lessons learned while traveling "outside" of academia were and are the same lessons that translated into better scholarship "inside" of academia. For instance, while at Virginia Tech, Hughes Rinker worked on a project that examined how to better integrate end-of-life care into family medicine in a rural Appalachian town. While applicable and understandable to health care professionals, her work was theoretically informed by the Trajectory Model by Corbin and Strauss (1992). She drew heavily on medical anthropology and sociology as she conducted needs assessments and gathered preliminary data for the project, and in the process, enjoyed getting to educate medical providers and other health care administrators who were unclear as to what these fields really are. While working with a national nonprofit organization, Nahm also found herself revisiting major theoretical contributions of anthropologists – specifically the concept of "situated learning" and "community of practice" as described by Lave and Wenger (1991). As she led a local group of leading county, state, and national experts interested in developing more interdisciplinary approaches to enhance services for children, she also integrated literature reviews and critical analysis of program implementation methods based on the work of Lave and Wenger. The concepts of "situated learning" and "community of practice" were familiar to her because they had also been part of her dissertation work studying local and global networks of therapists who co-developed theory and practice and nurtured each other's personal and professional development.

Both of us published articles based on research projects we worked on the year after graduating with our PhDs and prior to our re-entering academic institutions as professors. Nahm eventually went to work for a nonprofit organization, in addition to teaching and researching, and discovered a knack for managing budgets, facilitating interdisciplinary task forces, conducting community outreach, and presenting to diverse audiences. In fact, these skills were merely outgrowths of seeds germinated in the experiences of participant-observation during fieldwork; they were simply nurtured and brought to the forefront out of necessity. In our return to academia, we discovered that multi-tasking and quick timelines were feasible, and completing required service work, such as sitting on committees and advising students, was easier to manage on top of our teaching and research. In addition, interdisciplinary collaborations necessary for grants and publications came more easily – not simply in theory, but in practice.

Making the Transition from CV to Resume

When new anthropology PhDs read a nonacademic job ad that states, "Please send a one page resume and cover letter," their blood pressure rises and their heart beats a little faster, at least that is what happened to us. Is it even possible to cut down a multi-page curriculum vitae (CV) to a one-page document that is comprehensible? Will future employers really know what we are all about and what we have done? Our fear came from the fact that we felt the interviewers would not get a sense of our accomplishments and what we can bring as anthropologists to their organization. Kim Thompson and Terren Ilana Wein write of the CV,

> It is an all-encompassing portrait of who you are intellectually and should include everything you've been involved with academically since starting graduate school. But send a document like that to an employer outside of academe and it will most likely end up in the "toss" pile.
>
> (Thompson and Wein 2004)

Initially trained as academics in the traditional 1.0 sense, our CV, in a way, defined us. It packaged our work into the intelligible terms of search committees looking for professors to fill positions in the university setting. So when faced with the call to transform it into a brief snapshot of our education, experience, and skills in terms other than those we had been so familiar with, there was a certain degree of emotional consternation. Others may experience something similar. Moreover, coming from the Ivory Tower, we may believe that we do not have enough "real-world" experience or the proper skill sets to even compete in the nonacademic job market, but, "the important thing at this stage is not to let your past experiences actually get in the way of your future ones" (Thompson and Wein 2004).

While Hughes Rinker was writing her dissertation, she faced a tight job market and personal dilemma. As she mentioned in her chapter, her partner, who is a nonacademic, was based in Washington, D.C. After two years of a long-distance relationship while she was finishing her fieldwork on reproductive health care among working-class women in Morocco and writing at UC Irvine, they decided it was time to settle in the same zip code. We recognize that being separated is a major issue faced by many academic couples today, and in addition by many couples where one is an academic and the other is not. Part of this is due to the fact that tenure-track jobs are not as plentiful in certain fields as they once may have been and therefore, being able to relocate together may be difficult. This limited Hughes Rinker's job opportunities and she decided it was best to apply for research and nonacademic positions in the Washington, D.C. area even though she intended to also apply for tenure-track positions. Through a job search engine, she found a position of "Postdoctoral Associate in Health Services Research" at Virginia Tech – National Capital Region. The posting read, "The successful candidate must have a doctorate degree in a field suitable for interdisciplinary health systems research … Interested applicants are requested to send a resume and a letter of application." As a medical anthropologist, she believed that she could be a fit for what the center wanted, but the problem was, how does she get this across in a resume? She remembered some advice from her undergraduate English professor: tailor. Write for the audience at hand. She had to prioritize what would be important from a CV for this particular position: Is her teaching assistantship or conference presentations more important? Should she list publications or special skills instead? How does she include the ethnographic research she conducted in Morocco?

She began by making a mental map of the requirements for the position and then fit her experiences during graduate school into each category. Making the most of these experiences was important, given that she would most likely be competing with individuals who had worked in applied fields after receiving their PhDs. For instance, as briefly mentioned in her chapter, the advertisement mentioned, "experience working in a clinical environment is desired," and she clearly had that from conducting research in reproductive health clinics in Rabat, Morocco for almost two years. This is where she thought she could really compete with others since she had the on-the-ground experience of conducting qualitative research within a health care setting. She decided the best way to emphasize her experiences relevant to the position was to divide the resume into two main parts, "Research and Experience" and "Public Health Experience." The first included main points from her dissertation fieldwork, thus demonstrating she had worked in a clinical environment, and as a graduate research assistant at UC Irvine, while the second included the internship at an NGO in Rabat as part of her fieldwork and a certificate in Global Population and Reproduction she earned from the University of Michigan over a summer, which showed she had knowledge of the field. Given the space constraints of a resume, it was imperative that she highlighted the theoretical and methodological training and experience, as well as the interdisciplinarity of her work that would make her stand out from other candidates. Later on Hughes

Rinker discovered that the Center interviewed two engineers in addition to her for the position. The Center's coordinator later stated that they were impressed with her cover letter and resume and with the fact that she could conduct research in a health care setting. What was interesting was that the Center's Director – who is a physicist by training – actually employed a medical anthropologist on his research team at his previous institution. He understood what value we can bring to health research and the insights we can provide about impacts on people's daily lives and bodies; thus he was intrigued by Hughes Rinker's materials and possible contributions to their projects.

Similarly, Nahm found herself reconfiguring elements of her academic cover letters and CV in order to apply to positions at nonprofit organizations. She, too, felt it was important to stay in Los Angeles where she had personal and professional roots; in looking forward to a return and reinvestment in her hometown after many years of living outside of California, she first turned to academic job posts but soon realized that employment had to be thought of in broader terms than tenure-track positions. In addition to the strategic mapping, packaging, and re-articulation of skills used by Hughes Rinker, Nahm also found that anthropological analyses had trained her to see connections between seemingly disparate ideas and skills. This sensibility was especially useful during interviews whenever a potential employer would question how anthropology fit with their own work. Instead of narrowing down to a country or group that she had experience studying, Nahm emphasized key lessons about social dynamics. For example, at the first nonprofit organization where she worked, she emphasized how her dissertation on child play therapy in Korea and the United States showed the impact of media on social stigma surrounding pediatric mental health issues. This was crucial, because this organization was situated firmly at the nexus of media and medicine, entertainment and education. At her second job with another nonprofit organization, she emphasized the experience child therapists and families had depending on which services were and were not covered by insurance. This helped her receive an offer to become a policy coordinator and later a policy and communication specialist at a regional office for a national nonprofit organization. Through this lesson, Nahm emphasized her ability to analyze media impact and policy, respectively. As she grew in these roles, she continued to teach at various colleges and it was this initial translation and launch pad that set the foundation for her current ability to thrive as a hybrid practitioner who serves as a program director for a major Los Angeles-based nonprofit organization while also continuing to develop and implement courses in anthropology and sociology for a university. These strategies helped to illustrate how ethnographic experience in graduate school could be seen as equivalent to work experience with regards to topics and skills that were most relevant to potential employers.

Back Translating

Linda Bennett and Sunil K. Khanna write, "Anthropology in the United States manifests a history of being a multifaceted discipline with regard to training, career opportunities, and practice" (Bennett and Khanna 2010, 648). Upon graduation, students can take their careers in several different directions both inside and outside of the academy. While the previous section dealt with how to make anthropological training in graduate school relevant to nonacademic positions, here we think through what working in applied fields has given us for our professional pursuits in the university. Young (2008, 56–57) reminds us that combining an academic and applied career can be challenging because it depends upon how your department "[defines] 'research' and where you publish your work," and doing this could be detrimental to a junior faculty member's career. But, working in applied fields before entering academia provided us with the ability to explain our work in terms that the public can understand and appreciate, to make our ethnographic work relevant across academic disciplines, and to collaborate with scholars from different fields.

When Hughes Rinker was a postdoc at Virginia Tech and working with a large health care organization, she worked on developing two projects that would ultimately result in providers in a rural area offering patients higher quality care (one project on end-of-life care that she briefly discusses in her chapter and a second project on psychiatry and telehealth). She was tasked with communicating the purpose and methods of the projects to medical providers and various members of the organization's administration. When one administrator called her ethnographic project "softer" than medical research, she knew she had to convey anthropology's importance in a language that could be easily understood by nonacademics and non-anthropologists. Rather than discount the administrator (which would have been difficult given the collaborative structure of the project), she thought carefully about how to articulate her work and the impact of anthropological approaches. She re-engaged with the administrator by emphasizing that as an anthropologist, she could help the organization see what was not obvious to providers and staff, as anthropologists like to look for connections and discrepancies that are not always visible to the naked eye. She would be able to provide them with the "why" in addition to the "how." Why do patients make particular choices when it comes to their health? Why do they do one thing and not another? However, she had to learn how to remove the academic jargon from her speech and to talk about "practical" solutions to the critical problems the organization was facing.

So when she was asked to give a job talk about her current position in 2011 in a way that could be understood by a mixed audience (faculty from inside and outside the department, graduate and undergraduate students, and some staff), she was not particularly panicked because of the experience she had working with the health care organization where it was common for her to sit with doctors, nurses, economists, and statisticians around the same table talking about the theories, methods, and the significance of the projects. She learned how to discuss her work in an interesting way that is understandable and yet retains the complexity and theoretical importance of the research. One way she did this was by learning the vocabulary of those she was working with on the projects, which meant adopting acronyms the medical providers used and reading articles on relevant topics by scholars from disciplines represented in the projects on which she was working. More recently she began a collaborative project with a physician in the Washington, D.C. area (who is also an active researcher) in which he will conduct a survey and quantitative analysis and she will conduct ethnographic research. As they sat in his office discussing the details she explained the premise of ethnographic research and its objectives, but had to remember that the physician said he has not done any type of qualitative research. He is used to clinical research where there is an aim, hypothesis, and primary and secondary outcomes; there is a clear line when to stop the study and write up the results. (Ethnographic research can also have these elements, but they are usually articulated in a different form.) She had to remove the jargon and figure out how to make it known that ethnography is rigorous and can provide complex details about people's lives that may be missed by surveys and quantitative methods. It is much more than just "exploring" a particular topic; it is a way to understand the world through the participants' eyes. We suggest the communication skills that we refined in our work "outside" of academia helped us to gain confidence in sharing insights from our projects with diverse audiences and writing grant applications that would be read by those from different backgrounds.

More recently, Nahm presented at a national conference for scholars interested in the anthropology of childhood. Although most attendees were graduate students or professors coming from a university setting, she was thrilled to meet a long-time human rights activist. This activist had spent decades in the field in this "applied" role but was recently courted back to serve as part of the leadership team steering an interdisciplinary university-based research center. This transition back to the university was possible not only because academic administrators acknowledged her work in human rights advocacy but also because they honored and respected it. When Nahm commented how exciting this was to find an academic home after years happily engaged in applied work, the activist stated that she truly believed that this rare opportunity was becoming less and less so as academics and practitioners alike articulate their work simultaneously in clear applicable terms while also engaging critically with theoretical paradigms.

Conversely, our experience teaching college students, researching, and writing articles and book manuscripts allows us to feel confident when conducting outreach and facilitating meetings with community leaders, funders, and policy makers. In her various roles at nonprofit organizations, Nahm has facilitated meetings and given presentations alongside professionals who represent the tops of their fields. Although public speaking was not something she gravitated to earlier in her career, she now finds herself comfortable in leadership and communication roles. When colleagues ask whether she took special training classes for communication and public speaking, she often reminds them that expensive workshops or private lessons could never compare with teaching college students who demand engagement at all times and will make it evident when articulation falls short of clear command of the content. Teaching and presenting regularly at academic conferences prepares academics for success in nonacademic worlds by forcing us to be articulate and concise; these activities benefit us just as much as navigating interdisciplinary documents and discussions in nonacademic words enhance our scholarly capacity as academics.

Conclusion

Between graduating from doctoral programs and our present employment, we have lived with one foot "inside" academia and one foot "outside" of it, but as we hope this chapter has shown, we were always-already dual citizens. Living in the borderlands has helped us think outside the box theoretically and methodologically, and given us skills to promote a public anthropology that can speak to the relevance of the discipline in the United States and abroad. As academics, our future research projects may not be labeled as "applied" per se, but this does not mean they cannot be used to address critical social and political issues. Our endeavors as more applied researchers and as academics have converged at more than just a few points in time, and skills we gained from each trajectory have translated nicely between them. It is our hope that anthropologists in the future, particularly freshly minted PhDs will not be so scared of the academic/applied divide and will see that it is possible to successfully exist in a liminal state between the two.

Acknowledgments

We would like to thank our colleagues and students at Virginia Tech, George Mason University, the University of Southern California, and The New School for challenging and supporting us and for helping us grow professionally as anthropologists. The American Institute for Maghrib Studies and the American Philosophical Society funded Hughes Rinker's fieldwork in Morocco. She received a seed grant from the Institute for Society, Culture, and Environment at Virginia Tech for her work in Appalachia. The Korea Foundation supported Nahm's fieldwork in South Korea and numerous funders supported her work in the nonprofit sector.

Notes

1 This chapter is reprinted by permission of *Practicing Anthropology*, volume 35, issue 1. New material has been added to the original article.
2 See "Considering Academia 2.0, Writing, & the Community College" at www.cayuga-cc.edu/blogs/bower/?p=72 and "Research as a Second Language: Writing, Representation, and the Crisis of Organization Science" at http://secondlanguage.blogspot.com/2010/03/academia-20.html.

References

Bennett, Linda, and Sunil Khanna. 2010. "A Review of Tenure and Promotion Guidelines in Higher Education: Optimistic Signs for Applied, Practicing, and Public Interest Anthropology." *American Anthropologist* 112(4):648–650.
Corbin, Juliet, and Anselm Strauss. 1992. "A Nursing Model for Chronic Illness Management Based Upon the Trajectory Framework." In *The Chronic Illness Trajectory Framework: The Corbin and Strauss Nursing Model.* Edited by Pierre Woog, 9–28. New York: Springer.
Fiske, Peter. 1999. "Strategic Communication Inside and Outside of Academia," *Science*, August 27, http://sciencecareers.sciencemag.org/career_magazine/previous_issues/articles/1999_08_27/noDOI.5184557921375989263.

Lave, Jean, and Etienne Wenger. 1991. *Situated Learning: Legitimate Peripheral Participation.* Cambridge: Cambridge University Press.

Terry-Sharp, Kathleen. 2009. *Anthropology Faculty Job Market Report*, American Anthropological Association, last accessed May 31, 2012, www.aaanet.org/resources/departments/upload/job-survey-_for-web.pdf.

Thompson, Kim, and Terren Ilana Wein. 2004. "From CV to Resume," last accessed May 31, 2012, http://chronicle.com/article/From-CV-to-R-sum-/44712.

Young, Philip. 2008. "Practicing Anthropology from Within the Academy: Combining Careers." *Napa Bulletin* 29(1):56–69.

CONCLUSION

The Unexpected and the Future of Anthropology

Susan Trencher

I began my anthropological training as an undergraduate in 1965. The text in use at the time was *An Introduction to Anthropology* by Ralph L. Beals and Harry Hoijer. Beals and Hoijer (1965: 741) wrote,

> Although some anthropologists look with disfavor upon attempts to discover practical uses for their knowledge, few scientists, however devoted to 'pure' and apparently impractical research, do not at bottom hope that at some time their findings may contribute to a better life for their fellow men.

Aside from the now arcane reference to humankind as "fellow men," Beals and Hoijer assert the sense among anthropologists that their work is important and relevant, in short, they hope it matters. But at the time, applied work was out of fashion and out of favor, as interventions by social scientists, most of them not anthropologists despite working abroad in Latin America and Southeast Asia, were the subject of negative attention. As an undergraduate I was trained in four-fields anthropology, went to a terminal MA program, also four-fields, in which I specialized in cultural anthropology but also took comprehensives that covered the four fields. I worked in several positions, one of them at the National Zoo, related to anthropology, and in several jobs, and started a family. I include these facts as a means of pointing out that I was in the applied world prior to returning to university for my PhD. I returned for my PhD because I love anthropology's promise and prospects as an intellectual effort that matters, and think it should matter more than it does, both in academia and out. I consider myself a generalist with a specialty in cultural anthropology.

My "regional focus" is American culture writ large. I have used American anthropology as a heuristic device to understand American culture and vice versa, in an on-going reflexive project that I see as a route to grasping the American culture and its impact both at home and abroad. As part of this interest I also study the history of American anthropology, which I construe as the anthropology of anthropology. That is, I study this history using anthropological methods (see Hallowell 1962, who argued that the history of anthropology should be done as an anthropological effort). This is also consistent with George Stocking's (1965), criticism of "presentism" in history – seen as producing history through the current theoretical position of the writer. My effort then is to seek an understanding of American anthropology and activities within it, including research, methods, and events, as a way to understand what things mean in the context, including the time frame, in which they occur. I understand anthropology as the best means through which an understanding of most things in the human world can be constructed. In addition to my earlier experience in the usual world of work unrelated to academia, while in academia I have worked as a consultant for the Census Bureau. While there I worked along with other anthropologists and social scientists, some of whom began careers in the applied world, and others who left academia to go there. My own applied work has been more sporadic than continuous which may in part account for my sense, to which I briefly return at the end of this piece, that it is more comfortable to walk back and forth across a bridge, than to "straddle," research and practice, a position that, as set out below, I see as fostered in part by intransigence in academia.

Based on the "Precedings"

Editors Sheena Nahm and Cortney Hughes Rinker, have brought together an eclectic mix of essays that demonstrate both the flexibility of anthropologists, many of whom have always struck me (and colleagues of mine outside the field of anthropology) as interested in many things and willing to expand the range of things they find interesting – thus the choice of anthropology in the first instance. I see this as central to what I see as the "project of anthropology" as part of a disciplinary study that will never be complete as it seeks to understand the nature of the human animal and what it means to be human in comparative and holistic ways. The interdisciplinary nature of the discipline itself (a point made regularly in the preceding chapters) is unique in the social sciences and means that intradisciplinary work in anthropology is often played out as multidisciplinary elsewhere.

Fieldwork is the common method in all areas of anthropology, albeit variously performed in the major sub-disciplines (cultural, linguistic, archaeological, and biological) that sit under "anthropology" as the umbrella. In cultural anthropology, the sub-disciplinary setting in which the work described here was undertaken, fieldwork is often set out as the use of the ethnographic method, including observation, participation, participant-observation, and semi-structured interviews, all undertaken with an outsider's perspective to gain access to the insider's ("actor's") point of view, that creates the possibility of seeing the world through the sense that others make of it (Geertz, 1973). Fieldwork has often held anthropology together, and the nature of ethnographic work, as taken for granted in the works of this collection, makes clear the ways in which despite diverse and unexpected settings, the anthropological approach binds anthropological work together.

Unexpected Sites

The effort and intention in this volume as set out by Nahm and Hughes Rinker highlights new territory for anthropological exploration and application, and new strategies for locating them. As Zilberg points out, finding oneself in these places can be unexpected in ways that he sees as serendipitous. I use "sees" because from an outsider's perspective there is evidence in the work as presented for Zilberg's own agency in movement across and within these projects. Yet his view serves as a reminder that getting the "actor's point of view" is now foundational practice in anthropology, as exemplified in the works in the present collection. An interesting aspect of this work as a whole is the ways in which training in the anthropological method, and its application in different venues ties the chapters together in ways that define practice. In other cases, "unexpected" refers less to serendipitous connections than to unmet expectations (desire is probably more apt here) tied to career aspirations and goals. For example, in the search for academic positions in a tight job market (as discussed below, this has been more common than not since 1969), where the search for an assistant professor's position can lead to applying anthropologically based skills in and to unexpected work settings. As noted in several of the contributions here, anthropologists are hired in various positions in part because they are seen as bringing different perspectives and creativity to their work. From the standpoint of the anthropologist, this is part of seeing any and every venue as a place to do fieldwork.

From the point of view of the traditional subject matter of cultural anthropology, an "unexpected" aspect of the chapters in this book is that they apply anthropology as research tied to practice, in settings where the subject is not Culture writ large or even cultures as discrete or globalized entities. Here in arenas in which culture is not set out as *the*, or even *an* explicit subject of research and application, anthropologists use familiar methods to research and cogitate.

While the traditional spaces in which cultural anthropologists worked were often investigated as discrete entities, contemporary venues included here, e.g. nonprofits in the US and Australia, museums in Indonesia, a faculty support center in a university, the practice of payday lending, are constructed as various spaces in which actions and meanings are already culturally situated, but delineating aspects of that culture is not a focus of the work. From a certain perspective, cultural underpinnings in which behaviors are grounded and through which they make sense, are less accessible in such settings. This makes it more difficult to sustain the outsider (sometimes marginalized) perspective that anthropologists have used to identify taken-for-granted assumptions that flow through the spaces and people in which they do their work. In venues with different populations, with variant comprehensions of what is easily mistaken for common ground, interaction, ideas, and meanings must be interpreted and disentangled as they come together as praxis. For example,

Hughes Rinker's work with Muslim patients and end-of-life care in American health care settings, and Murphy's work as an applied linguistic anthropologist attending to conversations and comments in which patients at Walter Reed define and understand themselves through and/or in spite of disabilities and differential benefit allocation. Both take apart and piece together observations and conversations, thus identifying differences in ways that enlighten. Aiken's chapter based on her work for NASA makes the point that new spaces in which anthropologists find work provide venues to create and use knowledge beyond all kinds of boundaries, and in the process challenge us to redefine the boundaries of even the *pro forma* definition in introductory textbooks in anthropology. As a field that studies "what it means to be human in all of time and space" Aiken's work forces us to reflect on our notion of "space" as familiarly referring to geographic locations on Earth. Focused on humans in space, defined as both an infinite entity and a location, her effort encompasses crafting an understanding of how humans understand cultural (as personal) space, and the culturally defined need for privacy in relation to universal traits of the species. Outer space as a place in which understanding what it means to be human in everyday activities and life, brings with it the reminder of humans as a single species. Clear in its applications, the notion of where we find anthropological research and practice must be extended, and inclusive.

Where Do We Expect to Find Anthropologists in the United States?

Aware of the ways in which anthropology (and psychology, sociology, and a raft of other disciplines) have used ideas of difference to define and refine diverse notions of identity, applied anthropology has most commonly been defined by what it is not, that is, academic anthropology. This has always been an ideational differentiation, and now perhaps more than ever, potentially destructive. Part of the initial argument, in theoretical terms, comes in anthropology as it does in other disciplines (including the natural sciences), from an effort to defend or assert "pure" knowledge as a product of activity and investigation in the empirical without losing the ethical high ground (as variously argued) when the work was considered relevant to interests outside of academia.

Social work stands as an interesting example of a field or application originally connected to academic sociology, which over the years has been disconnected from it, literally in practice and in theory. The sciences, whether natural or social, have not successfully resolved the conundrum of who finds what, who uses the findings, and how, but the effort reveals dilemmas of research and practice as sometimes separate, but always potentially connected, activities. For instance, in Miller Griffith's work she describes having done work as directed by the head of the unit (with the Dean's involvement) focused on supporting faculty in pedagogical work, when she was faced with a request/demand for material about a particular professor. From the standpoint of Miller Griffith and her co-worker, sharing of material about those whom the center assisted, was unethical, and detrimental to the role of the center as a place where faculty could seek assistance with impunity, and entered into personnel issues that would be damaging to those the center served. While Miller Griffith reported this as initially problematic, the center administrator accepted their view. The question of course is, what happens when the ability to demand research results is given precedence?

Taking a Road Less Traveled

As Nahm and Hughes Rinker note, the history of applied anthropology is different in the US from in Canada and the UK, to which other countries are easily added (e.g. in Scandinavia and Brazil). In part this is arguably as a by-product of aspects consistent with long-identified aspects of the American cultural self, including distrust of authority and the familiar assumption (set in place following the Vietnam War and across the intervening years among many American academic anthropologists) that anthropologists working for the government in any capacity in the US were engaged in questionable, likely unethical, work. Exceptions of course exist, but in general, applied anthropological work, especially since the late 1960s, has been denied by the generation of anthropologists who came of age after World War II, as acceptable work. Yet here is Scroggins, volunteering to participate in what is essentially a project in applied anthropology, defined as consistent with Sol Tax's action anthropology. Here, applied work is done on behalf of a community, not imposed on it.

What can be seen as the element of distrust in anthropology is exemplified by accusations in the absence of findings (e.g. against all anthropologists working in Southeast Asia during the Vietnam War; or the anthropologists working or contemplating work for the Human Terrain System). (The famous censuring of Franz Boas in 1919, when he accused other anthropologists of spying, differs, given that he accused them of something of which he knew them to be guilty: being in the field under false pretenses – charges which three out of the four of them later admitted.) This view has been something of an albatross in American anthropological work as it was applied, inconsistently and anecdotally in many cases, to anthropologists who created the Society for Applied Anthropology (founded in 1941 by some of the anthropologists employed by the Bureau of Indian Affairs for $1 a year and room and board on a reservation during the New Deal). Later during World War II, most American anthropologists participated in different ways useful to the war effort. Probably best known was work for the Office of Naval Research, as part of the Department of Defense, where Margaret Mead, Ruth Benedict, Geoffrey Gorer, Gregory Bateson, and Rhoda Metraux used the methods of culture at a distance to aid the war effort, in its most successful instance in Benedict's (1946) *Chrysanthemum and the Sword*. In 1947, Mead was among those who argued with the Executive Board of the AAA about the necessity to bring the Society for Applied Anthropology as a partner under its aegis, at a time when Julian Steward as President of the Society for Applied Anthropology threatened to start a completely separate and competing organization. The Executive Board acceded to the demand and Ruth Benedict was elected as President. She served half a term before becoming ill, and Julian Steward served the remainder of the term, thus cementing the position of the applied group at that time – a position that it has never regained in the politics and practice of the AAA in the years that followed.

In the heat of the Vietnam War twenty years later, anthropologists doing work in Southeast Asia were considered guilty of violating ethical boundaries that resulted in the formulation of the AAA's first AAA statement on ethics. Anthropologists in the AAA were split by generation, and experience in practice. Anthropologists of the generation following those who had fought for or worked on behalf of the World War II war effort were decried as violating anthropological ethics (see Trencher 2000 for a detailed account of these events). In later years those writing from a presentist point of view (e.g. Price 2004) were seen as telling the truth about anthropology. Dyer refers to the "hostile undertone" she picked up from applied, engaged or practicing anthropologists toward academia. The hostility from the academic toward the applied side has been returned in kind with only some variation in degree.

Only in the last few years, as the second decade of the 21st century began, did the pendulum begin to swing, given that the academic future for anthropologists has been dim since the 1970s (see D'Andrade et al. 1975, who while looking at then current trends cited the wrong factors, but nonetheless correctly predicted a downturn in available positions for those who wanted to go into academia lasting at least into the 1990s).

It is worth noting in relation to the above, that while Nahm and Hughes Rinker in their chapter encapsulate the concerns raised by their cohort as "Academia 2.0," the picture for academic employment has undergone no large-scale shift since the end of the 1960s. As Nahm and Hughes Rinker note, they and others were caught in a recession in 2009, something that has occurred on several occasions in academia and many of its disciplines, including anthropology. The new economic pressures exacerbated an on-going slide in the number of academic positions. While the reasons for the loss of existing positions and the dearth of new ones is beyond the immediate purview here, there are several relevant points that can be used to construct a brief context that continues to influence the one in which anthropologists find themselves navigating.

The Yellow Brick Road

What is now sometimes called the "golden era" of American life was comprised of the two decades between the end of World War II and the late 1960s (1967 as a visible turning point). This scant score of years was a period of enormous expansion and optimism in the US and clearly visible in anthropology, newly discovered as of use by the government, especially in the war years. For the first sixty years of its existence the new discipline of anthropology grew, but remained small enough to meet in single sessions. The late 1960s were an exception only to the extent that the expansion in the discipline and interest in it was especially pronounced. Between 1947 and 1962 the number of professional anthropologists tripled, and jobs for anthropologists were so plentiful that the AAA considered recommending the MA as a teaching degree in universities, while the PhD would be primarily for those trained to do research. The idea for the teaching degree never made it into practice, and instead many anthropologists were hired at universities immediately on their return from the field, as "ABDs" (All But Dissertations) and frequently given up to ten years to finish their degrees while working as faculty. But by the end of the 1960s, decline in government support for many disciplines was clear and anthropology among others was hit particularly hard (see Trencher 2000). By 1970 in a general atmosphere of "belt-tightening" the mood at the AAA meetings was described as "somber" and attendance fell by 800 members from the previous year (*AAA Newsletter* 1970). This is not to say that no new positions opened in the intervening years, but to note that the number of anthropologists with PhDs produced since that time has always exceeded the demand for them in academia.

This is compounded by the explicit view among agencies and groups outside of academia, that support and connect universities to their institutions (including the Atlantic charities, the Pew Charitable Trust, the Carnegie Foundation for the Advancement of Teaching, the Woodrow Wilson National Fellowship), that argue that training for PhD students in most disciplines has not kept up with societal and cultural changes. This sense is more often related to PhD programs than MA programs, especially terminal MA programs which in the academy have traditionally been seen as "second class," but in the world outside the academy make employment much more likely. As Dyer notes in her chapter, quoting Nolan (2013), the nonacademic job market for MA anthropologists is expanding and that trend is projected to continue. Since the 1970s there have been more anthropologists doing work outside grant funding programs to encourage change in the academy, e.g. "Re-Envisioning the PhD" and "The Responsive PhD Initiative" in the 1990s through the early 2000s. The aim of these programs was to encourage universities to prepare students for positions outside academia based on projections of limited growth in academic positions but projected growth in both the public sector and private industry. These initiatives failed in part due to what supporting agencies saw as institutional intransigence, the pronounced tendency for PhD programs and faculty to replicate themselves, thus failing to prepare students for work in nonacademic settings.

The Unexpected and the Future of Anthropology

I noted earlier that "straddling," while one way to describe having one foot in research as part of academic work and another foot in unexpected sites as part of practice, whether starting in academia or the applied side, is a distance that anthropologists can bridge. Anthropology, despite its professional and political fractures, still has a methodological core that frames and underpins its conceptual possibilities. This method is common to all these works. At base and at its best, anthropology as an effort, exhibits curiosity and yields respect for other ways (and forms) of life. Anthropologists seek to understand and where possible explain the nature of the human world. None of the elements that define anthropology in its American incarnation confine it, although its practitioners are responsible for careful formulation of the questions we ask, and responsible for ethical and responsible action in all the settings in which we work. Despite and because of its four-fields grounding, the discipline has much room for picking and choosing.

All of the anthropologists here take for granted their use of anthropological methods and in so doing, exemplify praxis in a powerful way that models a path for the future of anthropology and the important work that will continue. An important and hopeful observation made by Nahm and Rinker in this book is that, while there are difficulties in the discipline, including concerns about the job market, despite the "decrying" that may connect to the disunity of the discipline, they find signs of greater unity in conversations and activities. Certainly in recent university life where the so-called ivory towers have been carved into the shape of businesses in which student scholarships are described as "discounts" and faculty are measured against "ROI" (return on investment), it behooves anthropologists concerned about the future of anthropological work in all its venues to be ready for the next chapter, literally and figuratively. In work and explorations of the kind set out here, the creative expansion and meaning to be found in the work of anthropology, matters.

References

AAA Newsletter. 1970. 11(1).

Beals, Ralph L., and Harry Hoijer. 1965. *An Introduction to Anthropology.* New York: Macmillan.

Benedict, Ruth. 1946. *The Chrysanthemum and the Sword: Patterns of Japanese Culture.* Boston: Houghton Mifflin.

D'Andrade, Roy. G., Eugene A. Hammel, Douglas L. Adkins, and Chad K. McDaniel. 1975. "Academic Opportunity in Anthropology, 1975–1990." *American Anthropologist* 77(4):753–773.

Geertz, Clifford. 1973. *The Interpretation of Cultures.* New York: Basic Books.

Hallowell, Irving. 1962. "The History of Anthropology as an Anthropological Problem." *Journal of the History of the Behavioral Sciences* 1(1):24–38.

Nolan, Riall. 2013. "Introduction." In *A Handbook of Practicing Anthropology*, edited by Riall Nolan. Oxford: John Wiley.

Price, David. 2004. *Threatening Anthropology: McCarthyism and the FBI's Surveillance of Activist Anthropologists.* Durham: Duke University Press.

Stocking, George S. 1965. "On the Limits of 'Presentism' and 'Historicism' in the Historiography of the Behavioral Sciences." *Journal of the History of the Behavioral Sciences* 1(3):211–218.

Trencher, Susan R. 2000. *Mirrored Images: American Anthropology and American Culture.* New York: Praeger Pub Text.

INDEX